CLAREMONT READING
CONFERENCE
63RD YEARBOOK
1999

STRATEGIES FOR HOPE

Claremont
GRADUATE UNIVERSITY

STRATEGIES FOR HOPE

SIXTY-THIRD YEARBOOK

OF THE

CLAREMONT READING CONFERENCE

Sponsored
by
Claremont Graduate University

Edited By

PHILIP H. DREYER

Continuing Conference Theme:

READING, THE PROCESS OF CREATING
MEANING FOR SENSED STIMULI

Price $25.00

Back issues of the Claremont Reading Conference are available from two
sources. Volumes still in print may be ordered from the following
address: Claremont Reading Conference Yearbook, Harper 200,
Claremont Graduate University, Claremont, California 91711-6160.
Write for information concerning books in print and special price list.
All past Yearbooks are available through University Microfilms, 300
Zeeb Road, Ann Arbor, Michigan 48103.

ISBN #0-941742-20-2

Published by
The Claremont Reading Conference
Institute for Developmental Studies
Claremont Graduate University
Claremont, California 91711-6160

ii

TABLE OF CONTENTS

ACKNOWLEDGMENTS

The 1999 Reading Conference was organized by a committee consisting of Abbie Prentice, Sue Abel, Faith Bade, Nancy Brashear, Jane Carrigan, Thomas Caughron, Doty Hale, Sally Thomas, Carolyn Angus, Kay Grable, Carol Jago, June Hetzel, Bruce Matsui, Carole Anne Weeks, DianaVanderWall, and Gordon Williamson. This group met regularly throughout the year and chose the conference theme as well as the keynote speakers. Each gave unselfishly of his or her experience and each deserves particular thanks. The entire conference was coordinated by Jane Carrigan who organized meetings, managed the mailing lists, corresponded with speakers, made the room arrangements, oversaw the publicity and the printing of programs, and solved the hundreds of problems that go with a conference of this size with good cheer and efficiency.

The preparation of this Yearbook was done by Teresa Wilborn and Ethel Rogers of Claremont Graduate University's Center for Educational Studies, while the cover design, layout, and printing were coordinated by Martha Estus of Claremont Graduate University's Public Affairs Office. Jane Carrigan organized the mailing and distribution of yearbooks.

Special thanks also go to the faculty in The Center for Educational Studies of Claremont Graduate University, especially Sally Thomas, Bruce Matsui, and David Drew whose creativity and support are essential to the continued success of the Conference.

Philip H. Dreyer
Reading Conference Director
Yearbook Editor

INTRODUCTION TO THE
62^(ND) YEARBOOK

Each year the planning committee for the Claremont Reading
Conference begins its deliberations with an energetic discussion of what
the theme for the next Reading Conference should be. The discussion
which led to this year's theme, "Strategies for Hope," was born out of the
members' overall sense of despair about the current state of reading
instruction and the highly charged political climate in which teachers
must work. When the committee first met, its mood could best be
described as gloomy. Classroom teachers seem to have less autonomy
than ever; political groups at the state and district level have dictated
what curricula teachers must use; and all teachers have been ordered to
emphasize phonics based reading approaches and to reduce or eliminate
literature based approaches, self-authored materials, and other so-called
"whole language" methods. The debate over the reading curriculum,
which has now been raging for over five years, seems destructive of both
the teachers' and the students' best interests, and the committee at first
had difficulty finding a theme which inspired positive options.

As the discussion proceeded, the gloom began to abate when the
committee realized that it was faced with a marvelous opportunity—the
chance to offer positive ideas about teaching in this difficult situation,
how to inspire children, how to bring new creativity to the classroom,
and how to promote literacy in new and exciting ways that transcended
the stagnant rhetoric of the "reading wars." Brainstorming then began in
earnest, and it was not long before someone suggested the theme
"Strategies for Hope." The conference could provide teachers with new
ideas about literacy instruction, including how to enhance both reading
and writing, how to provide a constructive approach to phonics within
the context of stories and poems, and how to motivate students to read
enthusiastically. From there we identified potential keynote speakers—
individuals who not only had marvelous ideas about literacy instruction
but also could reach teachers with an effective speaking style. Speakers
such as Patrick Dias, Janet Kierstead, Mary Poplin, and Lil Thompson
were recruited, and their ideas are represented in this volume. Each is a
brilliant teacher with a passion for the process of reading in the broadest
sense and how to promote literacy among people of all ages. From that

point on the design of the workshops that made up the rest of the conference came together easily and with remarkable coherence, as you will read in this volume.

The purpose of the Claremont Reading Conference has not changed since its inception 65 years ago. It has always advocated a constructivist view of reading—that reading is a process of making meaning from the experiences we have with our environment. Reading in this view is an active process of engaging the environment and working to understand it. It includes the perception of not just printed text, such as alphabet letters and words, but also other visual images, as well as sounds and textures. In short, we "read" our environment continually as we struggle to understand what various sounds and symbols represent and come to "mean" for us. This view is the basis for our "hope." All humans read their environments continually, so how can we as teachers of children in traditional schools help students apply their skills and wisdom to the task of reading visual text—words, sentences, and paragraphs. What strategies can we suggest for helping them connect the words they speak, the words they write, and the words they see before them in printed form? What are the secrets of poetry? Of stories? Of dramatic play-acting? And how do we change ourselves in order to change our work and make it more useful to our students?

One of the exciting aspects of this view of reading is that it is free from technology. We want children to be able to read books only because books have been the common medium of ideas for several thousand years, but the theory can just as easily be applied to computers, films, musical concerts, or trips to museums. Each of these stimulates active engagement with the environment, a need to make sense out of what is going on, and the desire to communicate one's understanding to others by speaking and writing. School is critical in the literacy process because it is at school that children learn the basics of how to survive and thrive in a particular society, and thus reading books, writing stories, and practicing good communication skills are the basics of the schools' academic purpose, and it is where children are held formally accountable for these competencies. The school also represents an environment to be sensed and understood and a technology to be mastered, so schools are to be taken very seriously in this view.

Another way to express this idea is to say that we are free to make the best use of any technology or experience which we as professional teachers and concerned parents feel will promote the mastery of the reading process by children. Legitimate competency then lies not within a particular technology but within a particular individual, and we must devise better ways of measuring these individual skills. Our current means of measuring these skills, through what we call "standardized" tests, are profoundly inadequate, and it is imperative that we improve our measurement practices before we condemn yet another generation of students and teachers as "failures" and "incompetents". However, the measurement problems must be the subject of another, different conference.

The richness of these ideas inspired the variety of presentations at the Conference and the papers written from them, which are printed here. The 66th Claremont Reading Conference itself was held on the campus of Claremont Graduate University in Claremont, California, on March 19 and 20, 1999. Lil Thompson, who has spoken at this meeting every year for more than two decades, appeared at the Conference from her home in the United Kingdom by means of a live, satellite transmitted videoconference, the first in the history of the Conference.

Philip H. Dreyer, Ph. D.
Professor of Education

CONTEXTS FOR ENABLING POWERFUL READINGS

Patrick Dias

Margaret Donaldson, in her groundbreaking book *Children's Minds,* speaks about the awesome responsibility we assume collectively "when we make laws which compel our children to go to school." We believe it is for their good, she says, but she urges that we consider seriously this enforced period of conscription and ask "whether the school experience" *is* really good for our children—"as good as we can make it"—and, it follows, is it good for the society they will form when they grow up? I sometimes imagine teachers of older, disaffected students looking at the eager, bright faces of young children in their early years of schooling, and wondering, in the words of the title of last year's popular film, "Is this is *as good as it gets*?" It is therefore with a deep sense of gratitude that I embrace the theme of this conference, "Strategies for Hope." Oscar Wilde is reported to have said, "A map of the world that does not include Utopia is not even worth glancing at." And during the Paris Revolution of 1968 (a great year for revolutions), one of several graffiti that appeared read, "Be idealistic! Demand the impossible!" What I hope to outline in my talk is neither impossible nor utopian; rather, in the spirit of the graffiti that appeared much earlier, during the Paris Commune revolt in the late nineteenth century, a graffiti that read, "Be realistic; have ideals!" I hope to remain idealistic and yet propose something that is very real.

This upbeat theme, "Strategies for Hope," encourages me to launch an argument and propose a set of strategies that can make school as good as we can make it, and by that I mean a place where students of all ages and abilities can be fully engaged as learners; for if we believe there is no learning without engagement, then we are deluding ourselves as teachers if we proceed with our teaching without laying the ground for ensuring engagement. And such ground is precisely what I wish to set out this morning, using the reading of difficult and challenging texts as illustrative material. How can we create in our classrooms the kinds of situations that enable students of all ages and particularly the reluctant and uncertain to realize their full potential as readers?

Ground for Engagement

Several years ago, as someone involved in the preparation of teachers of English, I often used poems as a way of getting into how we might teach literature. Poetry is a convenient genre, short and immediately present to readers. But as soon as I presented a poem and asked for comments, I was greeted by silence. Clearly, my students, all of whom had majored in English Literature as undergraduates, were reluctant to speak because they were all afraid of being shown up publicly as poor readers. I was aware also that such uncertainty about poetry extended to teachers in school as well. Invariably, when my students began their internships, they would be asked to teach the poetry unit. More often than not, they would be greeted by a collective sigh of disappointment as soon as they announced to their students that the class was going to study poetry. Why was there such insecurity about teaching poetry and why such antipathy to poetry among students? I decided to find out.

I hypothesized that the source of antipathy among students arose from a strong conviction that they could not understand a poem on their own without the mediation of the teacher. I was also convinced that such a belief was widely shared by teachers as well. I wondered then if I could somehow shake that conviction. What would happen if I inquired into the real capabilities of students as readers of poetry, told teachers that this and this is what students could be left to do on their own, and that they should then decide what their task was as teachers of poetry? After all, teachers did assign stories and sections of textbooks for students to read on their own without expecting to direct that process.

I began my inquiry by spending two weeks with a group of middle of the range sixteen-year-olds who confessed that they had a profound dislike for poetry. I asked them if they would discuss poems I had chosen each day in small groups with the goal of reporting their understandings to the large group in a plenary session. Since I had announced that I wished to know what they could do on their own, they did not feel that they had to perform to my expectations. Strategically speaking, I had placed myself in a position of being informed by whatever they said, which, as it turns out, is a context that allows students to articulate and elaborate on their own responses rather than look to an authoritative source for constant affirmation and approval. I taped their discussions so I could keep track of the processes by which they arrived at the understandings they were about to report to the large group.

I had prescribed a certain ritual, one that made sure that all students in their groups had their say, and that the process was truly collaborative. Briefly, I read the poem, clarified unfamiliar vocabulary when asked, encouraging them to draw on contextual cues, asked another student to read the poem aloud to the large group, and finally had one student in each group read the poem within the group. So the poem was heard at least three times before discussion began.

I say this knowing from a survey of about 80 teachers, that they usually read the poem once or at most twice before they asked the first question. There is a lesson here for all that teach. How can teachers who have read a poem several times, become familiar with the text and read commentaries on it, probably taught it several times, how can they expect that one or, in rare cases, two readings will allow students to respond with any conviction to their questions? It is not surprising that most such questions are greeted with silence or guesswork but seldom with the responses teachers expect; and it follows therefore that they begin to guide and redirect their students toward the preferred response. Any student who has been attentive to his or her own response is soon persuaded that the wiser path is to wait and discover what it is the teacher is really looking for. I am using poetry as an example, but my contention is that such expectations operate across genres and in other subject areas as well. In our haste to teach something, we short-circuit the process by which they might learn something.

Following those three readings, the next step is to ask students within their groups to share their initial responses *in turn, without any interruption from other members of the group.* My concern is that such initial and often telling responses soon dissipate when an articulate member of the group announces a more or less finished account. Two things happen. Every student, reader and non-reader, gets an opportunity to speak. This is an important step for releasing language: it is not easy for uncertain readers to speak out, and saying even a few words ensures a stake in the conversation and often, as it turned out, provides a telling cue that illuminates the poem. The other thing that happens is that in the face of these varied tentative responses and puzzlements, the usually dominating self-assured readers have cause to hesitate and wait.

After that round of initial responses, which I insist they do in turn, I suggest they read the poem stanza by stanza or a few lines at a time and take turns paraphrasing those lines. My intention is to get them back into the text and try to place those initial responses, and then develop an account they will report to the other groups—all of whom are engaged in the same task. I allow about 20–25 minutes for this phase.

Towards the last five minutes I announce that they ought to start preparing an account they will report to the large group. They appoint a reporter (all take turns through the two weeks). The reporter, by the way, is not allowed to take notes during the discussion but must report her sense of the discussion—not the minutes of the discussion, but where they have arrived rather than where they have been. That not taking notes turns out to have been a good decision. In reporting back, they are not therefore bound by what they have written; they are necessarily attentive to what other reporters are saying. Thus when it is their turn to speak, their reports have altered in the light of such new information. Something they had ignored in their discussion as irrelevant suddenly became relevant and reportable. Often the group is surprised by what their reporter is saying because they do not recall such realizations emerging during their discussion.

The reporters were encouraged to build on the reports of other groups. The order of reporting changed from one day to the other so that no group consistently reported first or last. Their having to report back both justified and focused their discussion and kept them engaged. They were accountable not only to one another but to the other groups as well. I was trading as well on their natural curiosity about how other groups had read the poem. Those accounts often confirmed the observations of some uncertain readers and found them new respect within their groups. "Did you hear what he said? Didn't I say the same thing?"

During the first few days, after all groups had reported, the class turned naturally to me as teacher and asked if I would now tell them what the poem really meant. My response was to suggest that I had heard so much that was new and revealing to me, that *I* had questions they might help me with. Having had little to do during the discussion but just eavesdrop and encourage them to keep on talking, I was able to recall several puzzling moments in the discussions and ask the students involved to raise those questions with the large group. Over a number of days, they seemed to have lost interest in hearing my account of the poems, so that on the eight day in the sequence, I dared to ask whether they would like to know what I thought and received an emphatic though embarrassed "no!" I now knew that they trusted themselves as readers, that they would rather come to terms with their own understandings before the voice of authority imposed a certain reading. As they had been asked to reread the poem that evening in the light of what they had heard and to write their response in a journal entry, *they* also needed time to reflect and revise (see Dias, 1996 for a fuller account of the procedure and the larger study).

So what did I find? Over a number of days, students trusted to read and discuss poems on their own in small groups came up with more attentive and richer readings than I could expect by teaching them directly. I could now tell those teachers who were so distrustful of their students' capabilities as readers of poetry, that they could do no better than I had done and wait to be surprised. In looking for an answer to a question about the real capabilities of students as readers of poetry, I had arrived at a process by which I could allow students to exercise and cultivate those abilities. I had videotaped one such class towards the end of two weeks, and got much use out of this recording when I wished to argue for the real abilities of students as readers of difficult texts.

I realized soon, that if I wished to generalize from this experience, I must repeat the experiment with a wide variety of groups of students. I returned to the school I had begun the experiment in, this time to work with a teacher in Grade 8, who volunteered in the interests of establishing some validity for my research to implement the approach in three of her classrooms, which in those days had been streamed into an advanced, average, and below average group. She would teach over two weeks a set of fourteen poems to the advanced group in the way she would normally have taught them; she would use the small group approach with the average group using the same set of poems in the same order; and I would use the same approach with the below average group. We administered a written pre-test to all three classes and planned a post-test to discover the effects of the two approaches; what I labeled full-frontal teaching versus non-directive teaching. I expected that if the below-average group performed as well or came close to the performance of the advanced teacher-led group, I would be more than satisfied. Nothing would have been lost and a lot would have been gained.

Four days into the experiment, the teacher approached me and asked if she could make a slight change in the design of the study. She asked if she could abandon the teacher-directed approach with the advanced group and use the small group procedure instead. In the first place, she was aware now how much the mid-level class that was working in groups was gaining from the process and that her own teaching was selling the advanced group considerably short. Moreover, she was aware that the advanced group were extremely bored by the process and having got wind of what the other groups were doing, were clamoring to be taught in the same way. I had no choice but to accede to her request and abandon the research as originally conceived; but I had converted at least one teacher.

Since those many years, I have tried the approach with students from Grades 2 to twelve and in my university courses, including graduate courses, in the latter classes dealing of course with non-literary and very difficult discourse. I should say something about two of these classes because they will help make the points I am building towards.

Working with Grade 2

I was conducting a series of workshops with teachers in Juneau, Alaska and had volunteered to visit classrooms in the district during the day. In one school, I was dismayed to find that the class I was to work with was a Grade 2. I wasn't making any claims for the process at that level, but I was grateful that the teacher believed that the process would work with these seven-year-olds. I was even more dismayed when I saw the poem, which the teacher had chosen from a graded reader; it had the appearances of a poem but the sentiment was trite. Moreover, the material did not justify the effort I was about to ask of the class. We hurried to the library and after much scrambling found a Robert Frost poem, "A dust of snow," a very short poem which I hoped to use as a warm-up to demonstrate the procedure to the class; the second hasty choice and main course was Langston Hughes' "Mother to Son."

When I entered the classroom, I saw not only thirty-two children at their desks, but also several adults lining the walls. Moreover, the group had been supplemented by an intake of eight children from the "resource teacher's" group—forty pupils in all. I had already made clear that such demonstrations were more likely to fail than succeed; the kind of climate I advocate could only happen over time with growing familiarization. While I would not recommend "A dust of snow" as easily accessible to seven-year-olds, I chose it because it was short but challenging, and would serve to demonstrate the process for the whole group before they went into their small groups to work with "Mother to Son." We went through the different stages of the procedure with "A dust of snow." After ten minutes or so, I felt assured that the children understood what they were supposed to do in their small groups, though they might not feel very much enlightened about this rather cryptic poem. At least they understood that they need not feel inhibited about speaking out or about the rightness or wrongness of their contributions, but speak they must.

After I had read "Mother to Son" aloud and cleared up difficulties with unfamiliar words, I asked for volunteers to read to the class. A host of eager hands responded, but as I chose a reader, I was told in loud whispers, "He can't read!" and looks of concern on the faces of the teachers along the wall confirmed I had picked a member of the "resource teacher's" group. But the child did read a few lines with stops and starts, thus encouraging other guests from his special class to volunteer as well. What is heartening here is that members of that group volunteered to read probably suspecting I did not know how they had been labeled. Throughout that session they were eager participants.

As the children read the poem within their own groups, shared their first impressions in turn, and then reread and talked about specific lines and sections of the poem, it was cheering to see the groups so engaged by their task and to hear their attempts to make sense of the poem. I recall bright-eyed Jennifer explaining to her group [my approximation of what she said]:

> You know Jim, this stair where it says the wood is
> splintered, that is like when your parents were divorced;

and Greg when you were ill and away for weeks, that's
like this step where the carpet's all worn; and this bit
where the step is missing is like when my father lost his
job...

I had not realized that seven-year-olds could make such profound
connections with their own lives to work out metaphorical implications;
and from the faces along the wall of those who had eavesdropped
(Jennifer's voice had risen with the excitement of discovery), I could tell
neither had the teachers. The children were eager to report on their
understandings when I called the groups together. Again, some of the
"resource teacher's group" were eager to contribute at all times. Because
they were "integrated" with the larger group, I was not privy to their
labeled identities, and they were recognized much to the consternation,
and edification I might add, of some of their peers.

When it came time to report, the effort each group had put into their
inquiring translated into an attentiveness to the account of each reporter.
Two of those reports were particularly moving: Jennifer reported for her
group expanding on what she had already said earlier within her group.
Her account obviously registered with the other groups, because almost
all the reporters who followed grounded their remarks in her account.
Angela's report, however, took another tack. This, as I recall, is in part
what she said:

> This poem talks about the homes of the white people and
> the homes of the Indians. The white people's houses
> have crystal stairs and fridges with lots of food in them
> and nice furniture. The houses of the Indian people have
> broken stairs, no fridges, and little food. This person is
> saying don't give up...

From the Indian reservation just outside Juneau, Angela could not have
been more than eight years old, but she spoke with a spirit that belied her
age. She had made the poem her own story, what she encountered daily
in a contrast of wealth and deprivation. I had not expected this class to
take to this process and poetry in such powerful ways. At its heart, this
simple strategy enables children to speak to others like themselves on
their understandings of difficult but powerful texts. There are no
constraints; simply the obligation to attend to the text, to one another,

and to report to other groups who will want to know what they make of their common text, the poem.

At the Other Extreme: Small Group Work with Non-literary Text in a Graduate Course

The procedure I have outlined for engaging and empowering groups of readers (and speakers and writers, as I shall argue below) is not limited to the reading of poetry. I have used it as well, with modifications, for other genres of literature such as short fiction and novels, and for the study of non-literary texts. I have written elsewhere at some length about how I have used the same approach in graduate courses in Education (Dias, 1994). Briefly, I assign four or five core readings on the week's specific topic and ask students to identify five (or three, depending on the length of the class session) key points in each reading, such that if colleagues who hadn't read the text inquired what they might take away from that text as important and relevant, those would be the five points or passages in the text one could point to. Having done so with all the assigned readings, they then must find a quiet moment and write for about half an hour about what remains uppermost in their minds about those selections. These writings are handed in to me when they arrive for the next weekly class. In that class they assemble in their groups (five to six members) to report their choices about what are key notions in each of those texts. The discussion follows one text at a time, and their task is to agree on the five points they will report in a plenary session as the group's idea of what matters in that text.

It is not consensus that matters or whether they have focused on the points that are really central to the reading. The task of negotiating agreement on those points has them ranging across that text, clarifying, explaining, justifying, so that as each speaker is heard the text takes on meaning and life, connecting with their experiences and previous readings, and as a by-product making those notions and concepts familiar and a part of their working vocabulary. There is never enough time to negotiate the five points for each of those texts, and it remains for the reporter to obtain a quick consensus or briefing as to what he or she might report to the large group. The mood is intense and exciting, so that when I call a break after an hour and a half in a three-hour class, I have to physically force some of them out, as they continue their discussion in their walk toward the cafeteria. It is the imperative to report responsibly to the other groups that drives them, and of course they expect no less from those groups in turn.

When they report (reporters take turns from week to week, and groups change each week with one member moving out to the group on the right and another joining them in turn from a group on the left—assuming that the groups are arranged in a circle) their five points for each reading in turn, each member of the class confirms and renews her sense of the reading. Some of the same points are mentioned in each report, and their differences reflect some of the differences that emerged within the groups. So much intense reflection and talk about what matters in each text, the confirmations and disconfirmations, make each text a familiar object; so much so that weeks later in the course, they are able to refer to relevant passages and expect that everyone else will know what they are talking about. It is I of course who have been left out of these conversations who am the least familiar with what they are talking about.

I refer again to the fuller account for the considerable advantages this approach affords; but I shall mention two of them as instances. One of the students in summing up how the course had worked for her mentioned how invigorating the whole process was, especially when we consider that most of these students had already spent a full working day as teachers in their own classrooms. Moreover, she said, she could not come to a session unprepared, knowing full well she was implicitly committed to reading carefully and well all of the assigned texts. I know that where I have lectured "up-front," I can be sure that a large percentage of the students have not read the assigned texts and are depending on me to have done the reading for them. My second point arises from the increasingly articulate and longer reflections on the readings I received each week from the students. It was clear they were responding as active participants in an exchange with those writers, rather than as passive recipients expecting that the text would show its meaning and relevance when it was decoded in the classroom. The formal papers I received from them reflected their confidence as readers and as writers, and their easy familiarity with the varieties of disciplinary discourse they had met in those readings. Much of this fluency had of course developed in their weekly exchanges within the groups. Thus one formerly blocked and reluctant writer volunteered triumphantly with the first or two formal papers she handed in (a fairly challenging assignment), "This paper virtually wrote itself!" This student's record over the previous two semesters listed five "incompletes," all awaiting the final papers she was unable to conclude. Increased articulateness, both in speech and in writing, is a natural by-product of this procedure throughout the grade levels. Intense conversations about challenging texts with the goal of settling on agreed understandings and the high level of participation cannot but have some impact on fluency and confidence in using one's language. But what I really want to discuss here is the notion of community of readers that is implicit here and which enables the kinds of reading I describe as "powerful" in my title.

Becoming a Community of Readers

The first and essential criterion is the interdependence that exists among readers in each group and among the groups. The atmosphere is collaborative; each group has a stake in the reports of the other groups— it matters to each group that other groups provide full accounts of their reading. Within the group itself, dominant members realize quite early that there is value in listening, and because of the change in reporters, no one member has a monopoly on meaning. Differences within and among the groups are reported; it is good to consider alternate readings. As one 14-year-old reported, "I hate it when they [reporters for each group] agree; then I have nothing to write in my journal." Differences allowed her to reconsider her reading and in trying to accommodate those disparate understandings, enlarge on her own readings.

Over time and with other such collaborative work (I change groups from one project to the next), students begin to value the contributions of others. Such collaboration also contributes to a sense of self-worth, a knowing that others rely on them for their own individual contributions, that the morale of the group requires that they be there to keep a good thing going. Parents often report how much children resent having to be absent during such collaborative projects.

Students also learn that not everything has to be resolved immediately; that interpretations change in time and with rereading; they learn to live with and value ambiguity. And they are not so dogmatic about their own readings. I hope it is becoming clearer now what I mean by powerful readings—this is exactly the way we read as confident readers, unafraid to say we are not sure and open to newer understandings. Because they trust each other and in the privacy of their own groups, they are now more willing to share personal experiences that relate to their readings and help clarify them. "I had an aunt who was just like this." "When my grandfather died...." If we do not come to value reading for the ways in which it helps us understand our own experiences and the experiences of others; if we are not moved to moments of sympathy and empathy, assent and dissent, then we are unlikely to become readers. In such trusting communities, they learn quickly that they are not always alone in feeling the ways they do or in the ways they have read something. At the same time, uncertain readers do not shelve so easily their own understandings or hesitancies to adopt the readings of more confident readers.

Because they are responsible to other readers for the meanings they make, members of such groups read with greater attention and with questions: the ones they will raise when they meet in groups. These are the very questions that spur us to look for other people who have read the same book or seen the same movie. Did you see this or did you notice that or weren't you surprised when this happened? This is why I believe we are so eager to lend books so that we may confirm and disconfirm our readings, and where disagreement can only be seen as expanding our own reading.

In arguing for community of reading and readers, I am arguing for a strong justification for bringing people together as readers. Where else and when, except in classrooms, will we ever find a group of thirty or so people who have read the same text? And should we not therefore exploit that situation, the diversity and richness of readings it promises? I have provided just a short rationale and description for making such communities happen. But their happening depends on a delicate balancing act, which brings me to the crucial role of the teacher.

The Role of the Teacher

I had said earlier that the antipathy to poetry among students could be directly attributed to the role of the teacher as mediator and final arbiter of meaning. I suggested that this need to control meaning was directly related to the teacher's mistrust of students' abilities as readers of poetry. I am not putting teachers down; we have all grown up with the notion of the one right meaning mediated by informed readers and critics. So the first task for the teacher is to shed this role as final interpreter; to allow readers to make meaning for themselves. We ought to acknowledge that our students will not grow as readers if we cultivate a dependence on expert readers to confirm and form their own readings. In our own lives, an informed critic is not the first person we want to converse with soon after reading a novel. We look for others like ourselves.

This role of authorized readers is unfortunately bolstered by a mistaken notion of responsibility. Should I let them go home with the wrong interpretation? Should I at least not offer them a clue that would guide them to the right meaning? This belief in a stable, unchanging set of meanings has been fatal to the development of confident student readers. Teachers need to accept that meanings are not fixed in the black and white marks on the page but are made by readers; the text exists only as it is read, as Louise Rosenblatt (1978) has often said; and each reading is a recreation of meaning by a unique reader. To shed ourselves of this onerous responsibility for the one right meaning, we need to remind ourselves how when we reread a book that is an old favorite, we are not merely recreating the earlier experience. Too much has happened between the two readings for us to be able to replicate that earlier reading.

We have lived longer and have read a great deal in between; but the text has not changed. It is the same with old films we watch again on television; we may feel nostalgic about them but we view them very differently the second or third time around, and are often disappointed that the film has somehow lost its old magic. Of course, the experience can also be rewarding and enhancing; but it is never the same.

We need also to remind ourselves how so much in schooling and classroom practices assumes that our sixteen-year-olds are reading the same *Macbeth* or *To Kill a Mockingbird* that we read whenever; again the words are the same, but we bring a different sensibility to these words—informed by shocking events of the past several decades, by the tell-it-all cinema, by maybe a growing awareness of civil rights and past injustices. How then do we justify twenty or fifty-year-old readings of these classics as they are enshrined in our textbook commentaries, or what is worse, in the teacher's guides that trade so much on our own insecurities as readers.

Rosenblatt's admonition that no one can do our reading for us is pertinent here; as she puts it, it would be like asking someone to do our eating and digesting for us. And we need to remind ourselves constantly that we cannot recover the experience of reading *Charlotte's Web* or the *Diary of Ann Frank* as we read them for the first time; so we ought not to suggest that our reading these books as twenty-five or fifty-year-olds can and ought to displace our students' first time encounters. Our regret should be that we shall never again see these books through our eight or thirteen-year-old eyes, and that as teachers we ought to relish the opportunity to eavesdrop and recover them through our students' readings. To put matters in perspective: those of us who are parents would be most reluctant to tell our children, however young, that we have a much better, more informed version of the television program or movie they have just seen, and that they ought to defer to our account— they will justly rebel at any such notion or if we persist, give up watching television or going to the movies. Secondly, while they are not accountable to us or to anybody for that matter for how they understand and respond to what they see, they will seek out their peers to see how their understandings correspond.

And to return to the teacher who is concerned about letting her students go home without having put them right as to the preferred reading: we can assuage any sense of guilt by reminding ourselves that we cannot be everywhere looking over the shoulders of our students and ensuring that they get their magazine reading, and their newspaper and fiction reading right. Their very ability to read critically and responsibly will be cultivated in the kind of collaborative classroom I have described. And I can point to instances of powerful readings in such groups that would put to rest any doubts about the value of teachers getting out of the way as informed and expert readers.

Finally, a crucial warning about where things go wrong. At no time must a teacher intimate that she holds in reserve a better reading but is for several good reasons not willing to share it: this stance that I know something but cannot tell you can be devastating to the kind of context I am suggesting we set up. If students know that there is a preferred reading out there in the head of the teacher, it becomes the students' task to ferret it out. And of course they have had long training in finding out what it is the teacher wants.

I have thus far outlined a notion of teaching that removes the teacher from the center of the process and focuses on learners; I have argued that we should consider the situation of thirty or so separate individuals gathered in one room to exploit the social exchange that is so central a part of learning and language development; and I have discussed the role of the teacher in making the classroom a hospitable place for such learning. I would like now to expand on how the social context is so vital to language production and the development of confident and responsible readers.

Contexts that Enable

Over thirty years ago, the sociolinguist William Labov gave a series of lectures at McGill University. One of his lectures was entitled "Teachers and testers as creators of verbal disability." What stands out in my mind is the conditions he said that must prevail to enable the maximum flow of language. The situation must be informal and non-judgmental, there must be equal power relationships between speaker and audience, and thirdly, there must be a maximum degree of shared knowledge between speaker and audience. Clearly such a situation does not prevail in the typical classroom; however, the type of small group work I have described does meet all three criteria largely because all significant exchange is among peers and not mediated by a teacher, who whether she likes it or not is defined institutionally as judgmental and all-knowing. A later study done in Detroit also casts some light on why the small group situation is essential to the flow of talk (Steffenson & Guthrie, 1984). The study involved 31 children between 3 years, 5 months and 5 years, 5 months. Where the experimenter/interviewer was in a position of "needing to know," the children verbalised more and their responses were more syntactically complex than those of children who were in a situation where the experimenter clearly knew what the children were being asked to tell. Being in the situation of *needing to know* is something we must build into all our work. This is not difficult when we consider that as teachers we do not really know how readers have responded to a story, or how they perceive a certain situation, and that we really want and need to know. Putting the child in the position of powerful informant does release a flow of talk and is the trigger for the development of both reading and writing skills. As researcher, I was inevitably in the position of needing to know and depended on the students as informants—a reversal of the typical classroom situation that can be most productive for teachers who adopt a consistent stance as researcher.

In all this my prime concern is to create optimum conditions for children and adolescents to realize their full potential as speakers, readers, and writers. At the heart of such an effort is the recognition that our students must be able to use language freely in order to articulate their thinking. I am arguing for an active role for students, not a passive receptive role, for opportunities to use language in a variety of ways to get a variety of things done. I am thinking of language as not out there as a resource one has to draw on, but as a resource within oneself that has to be drawn out and exercised, and it is from that sort of platform that the child will reach out to others around her to incorporate dialogically the language of others, including other texts. But first the child must need to want to do this.

Recently I worked with a class of 11-year-olds in order to set up the kind of classroom that applied the principles I am arguing for. We worked in groups, I got out of the way as mediator between them and the texts they read and produced, and because I was a researcher, they assumed I was genuinely curious about what they thought. In all the work I devised for them, I chose texts and designed tasks that were far more challenging than the fare they were used to. The challenges posed by the reading or the assignment justified their coming together in groups and turning to other groups for further elaboration. A criterion and a justification for all such group work ought to be that tasks must be beyond the capability of any single individual—no challenge means no interdependence and, it follows, no collaboration.

British educator Douglas Barnes (1971) once described the outcome of most classroom lessons as arriving without having travelled. The assumption in such classrooms is that through a process of question and answer, students are gently led to their destination. When a question is asked and an answer is given, the assumption is that every individual in the classroom has arrived at the same plane of understanding as the person who answered the question. There is no firm basis for such an assumption, and soon enough a large number are left behind on the journey and told where they ought to have got to and what they ought to have found. Truly, in Barnes' words, they have arrived without having travelled. As travellers, we all know the journeying is worth far more than the arriving. What I have tried to describe is a way of teaching and organising our classrooms so that all our students can participate in that journey and all know *for themselves* the country when they arrive.

References

Barnes, D., Britton, J., and Rosen, H. (1971). *Language, the learner, and the school.* Harmondsworth, England: Penguin.

Dias, P. (1996). *Reading and responding to poetry: Patterns in the process.* Portsmouth, NH: Heinemann-Boynton/Cook.

Dias, P. (1994). Initiating students into the genres of discipline-based reading and writing. In A. Freedman and P. Medway (Eds.), *Learning and teaching genres* (pp. 193-206). Portsmouth, NH: Heinemann-Boynton/Cook.

Donaldson, M. (1978). *Children's minds.* London: Fontana.

Rosenblatt, L. (1978). *The reader, the text, the poem: The transactional theory of the literary work.* Carbondale, IL: Southern Illinois University Press.

Steffenson, M.S. & Guthrie, L. F. (1984). The effect of situation in verbalization: A study of black inner-city children. *Discourse Processes, 7,* p. 1.

YES, A BALANCED APPROACH
BUT LET'S GET IT RIGHT!

Janet Kierstead

I began making the annual pilgrimage to the Claremont Reading Conference as a primary teacher in the mid 1970's. Change was in the air then – as now. The highly structured, direct instructional practices of the "back-to-basics" era were giving way to talk of personalized, child-centered methods which would allow students to learn by doing – to acquire skills by using them for real-life purposes. Concerned about lagging achievement levels, especially among the increasing population of non-English speaking students, the California Department of Education (CDE) had just launched the Early Childhood Education Program. It was designed to encourage teachers to leave the skill-drill, teach-test methods behind and adopt a more "natural" approach, based on children's own language and interests.

Encouraged by CDE reform efforts, many of us had cast aside the Janet and Mark basal readers so popular at the time. Instead, we were experimenting with ways to move students into reading by first showing them their "talk written down" and then helping them write it for themselves—while at the same time exposing them to good children's literature and using trade books as their reading material. We called it the language experience approach to literacy, and the Claremont Reading Conference was our home.

Since its establishment by Peter Lincoln Spencer in 1938, the conference had been the center for such ideas. Spencer had the idea that reading was a generic form of behavior, namely that, as in our normal use of language, we can say that we read many things. He saw print reading as one item in that panoply. But he did not get into methodology; instead, he left it to the teacher to figure out what his ideas might look like in the classroom. Presumably, the conference was his vehicle for facilitating that work. By the time I began attending, it was a highly regarded gathering place for some of the best-known and respected leaders of reading theory and practice within the nation and abroad. The Claremont Reading Conference was where classroom teachers struggling to translate the new ideas into practice could rub shoulders with those conducting the research and formulating the theories to lead the way.[1]

It was an exciting time. "The law" was on our side, but most educators were resisting the latest educational reform that we so enthusiastically embraced. So we had a mission. Back at our individual schools, most of us were working alone to develop the practical strategies needed for success with this complex approach. At best, our fellow teachers at school viewed us as suspect and at worst, as a threat to the status quo. So we needed the Claremont conference both as a place to exchange ideas and a way to maintain the courage to continue the struggle.

In the ensuing years, many educators did move away from back-to-basics — but as so often happens, many went too far, adopting a laissez-faire approach that left far too much to chance. Little or no phonics instruction began to replace meaningless drill of letters and sounds in isolation. New crops of beginning readers began to falter — this time due to too little structure, rather than too much — too little help with spelling/phonics, the writing conventions, and too little guidance for moving into books. Many teachers apparently began to believe that merely exposing children to good literature would be sufficient to ensure their success, that anything more than occasionally pointing out the sound-symbol relationship in passing would hinder what they saw as a natural, but fragile, process of learning to read.

Shortly after devising what I considered to be a balanced approach in my own classroom, I left the classroom to enter the doctoral program at The Claremont Graduate School. At the same time, with the Early Childhood Education program well underway, CDE asked me to help move their reform efforts into the middle school and the high school levels. So, for several years, as a consultant to CDE, my focused shifted from beginning reading/language arts to helping upper elementary and secondary teachers design interdisciplinary, project-based curriculum.

While still busy in this other arena, in the mid 1980's I began to notice that something was amiss in the field of reading/language arts. Phonics was becoming such a taboo subject that I soon learned not to mention it in my occasional meetings with specialists within CDE or with their counterparts in the field. During my reunions with colleagues from my Claremont days, I began to hear echoes of my own concerns: things were going too far. The laissez-faire approach was not providing enough structure to allow children to bridge the gap between oral and written language. Too many were "failing" to make the leap across the divide. It was only a matter of time until another violent reaction would set in.

And here it is. From the highest levels the call has gone out again for change, and this time the reform is mandated and very specific. Recent state and national legislation[2] establishes strict new guidelines for reading instruction, requiring the direct instruction of phonics, isolated from context. A change that was introduced as a balanced approach in California in 1996 now, as spelled out in Assembly Bill 1086, requires systematic, explicit phonics instruction that is not embedded in context, and specifies that decodable text be used for reading instruction. School districts wishing to use state funds to support reading programs must use only staff development programs that have been state approved according to guidelines which includes the following definitions:

> "Systematic explicit phonics instruction" means an organized, sequential program in which letter-sound correspondence for letters and letter clusters are directly taught and blended, practiced in words, word lists, and word families, and practiced in "decodable text," (sic) "Decodable text" means reading material in which a high percentage of words are linked to phonics lessons. Systematic explicit phonics instruction builds from basic elements to complex patterns and teachers provide prompt and explicit feedback. Systematic explicit phonics instruction does not mean "embedded phonics instruction" which is ad hoc instruction in phonics based on a random selection of sound and word elements.[3]

This latest reform is well intentioned. But it is an over-reaction, and the inherent dangers are obvious to those who have been through this before. No distinction is being made between child-centered, natural approaches and laissez-faire. So, current reformers reject natural approaches without making a careful analysis of what they involve. Such approaches teach sound-symbol relationships, *as children need them* to sound out and spell the words they are using *to communicate their ideas*. Without taking a close look, it can appear that helping children to learn phonics in context and in the sequence needed for their daily writing is haphazard and unpredictable. But this simply need not be the case, as I will explain later in detail.

For now, I will make just one more comment about the guidelines. Writing is not recognized in the guidelines as playing a significant role in learning to read, when quite the opposite is true. Without seeing writing as the means of developing a firm foundation in phonics, that leaves memorizing phonics in isolation and hoping for transfer to reading.

But that practice did not work for so many children before. So, why would we think — especially given our increasingly diverse student population — that it would serve them well now? The choice need not be *either* phonics out of context *or* laissez-faire. Either extreme makes learning to read much more difficult for children than it need be – one putting up barriers, the other leaving gaps too difficult for many children to overcome. Neither capitalizes on the child's inherent drive to communicate in increasingly complex ways. There is an alternative.

What's needed is an appropriate balance between the two — what can be thought of as a "child-friendly" approach. Such an approach incorporates phonics instruction into structured daily writing activities that allow children to build upon what's familiar to them — their own thoughts, feeling and speech. It provides enough guidance to systematically develop spelling/phonics and other prerequisite skills, setting high standards for quality at each step along the way. Yet, it is personalized so that children are writing about what is of special interest to them, and thus it does not interfere with their natural enthusiasm for communicating their ideas. It follows a logical sequence and is individualized to allow for comfortable pacing, so that it is virtually fail-safe. With the appropriate balance between structure and freedom, children build a foundation from which they launch effortlessly into reading. Let's look at both why and how this happens.

Why and How a Balanced, "Child-Friendly" Approach Works

With today's over-emphasis on phonics and direct instruction – and the corresponding pressure on teachers to show test results – we can easily lose sight of our purpose. So first, let's clarify our task. Are we teaching children phonics? Are we teaching children to read? Or, should we be viewing our challenge as something different from either of those?

I sometimes walk into classrooms where most of the children have mastered "phonics." They get high marks on phonics tests. They can, in the words of Veatch, "hiss, spit and bark" accurately at print. But they can do little or nothing with the new set of associations. They can neither read (make meaning from print), nor write down their thoughts in a way that others can readily interpret. Acquired out of context, the sound-symbol relationship is useless to them. Our purpose, then, is not simply to teach phonics in isolation, and test scores that show that we have are meaningless. But neither are we teaching reading. For helping children learn to read is not something we do *to them,* any more than we teach them to walk and talk. Fortunately, our job is much easier and more doable than that. For in reality, *we are helping children continue a process they have already begun.*

How Far Can Children Go On Their Own?

Once we give up the notion that reading is an alien task — something new we must present in bits and pieces — and take a closer look, we see that actually all we need do is support children as they continue an effort they began at birth. For in infancy, they began a dual process: communication (transmitting information) and reading (interpreting facial expression, gesture, touch, etc.). By the time they present themselves to us in the primary grades, they have come quite a long way, made a great deal of progress along this path on their own for several years.

First, consider communication. Children move through what can be viewed as a series of spheres of communication as they learn to transmit their thoughts and feelings. (See Figure 1.) From birth, the infant uses body language (lunging, smiling, etc.) and the crying sounds with which we are all too familiar. Over time, the toddler begins to develop speech, which is then followed by scribbling (this *says* "cat") and drawing (this *is* a cat). The final sphere is writing. Here, we must intervene. Children need help in unlocking the secret of communication through print — help in knowing that adults use certain symbols (letter sequences, punctuation, types of lettering/fonts, etc.) to represent the sounds, cadence and emphasis of meaning heretofore transmitted through words, body language, and inflection.

Now, consider reading. Children's reading ability grows naturally from birth as well. Very early on, infants learn to read the face, tone of voice, and body language of those around them. Preschoolers "read," or more accurately at this stage, they "recognize" the McDonald's arches, traffic signs, and the Nordstrom and Macy's signs at the mall. Up to this point, the child's increased awareness comes naturally, just from incidentally associating the symbols or written names with those places and things. From there forward, however, someone must directly intervene.

What Do Children Need From Us?

First, they need to know that talk can be written down. If they have not watched someone write notes, make grocery lists, compose letters from them to Grandma and the like, they must experience such things in school. So in the beginning stages, both within the total group and individually, the teacher will need to write down their self-selected words and sentences for them and help them "read" them back. This quickly gives them the idea of what print is all about.

Next they need to discover that certain letters represent the sounds in their own speech and that the clumps of sounds they make are represented by groups of letters (words), with spaces (the infamous "two fingers") in-between. Eventually, they will notice that the same word looks and is spelled the same from place to place, whether it appears in their own writing or that of their friends.

Writing, Reading and the
Natural Progression of Communication

— Figure 1 —

As children develop, their attempts to communicate
"grow" naturally from the inside out:

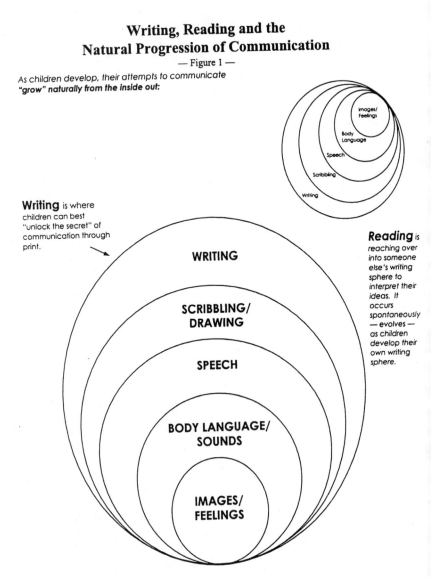

Writing is where children can best "unlock the secret" of communication through print.

Reading is reaching over into someone else's writing sphere to interpret their ideas. It occurs spontaneously — evolves — as children develop their own writing sphere.

WRITING

SCRIBBLING/
DRAWING

SPEECH

BODY LANGUAGE/
SOUNDS

IMAGES/
FEELINGS

No controlled, "decodable readers" need be contrived, for children are writing their own decodable readers, since they use a fairly controlled vocabulary when they speak. Even before they begin to write their own simple sentences, and just from "reading back" their own dictation, they will have learned to recognize the verbs, pronouns, and simple connecting words that appear repeatedly in their speech. Later, if someone helps them figure out which letters are needed to spell unfamiliar words each time they write, they will also learn to "sound out" words for their writing—the foundation skill needed to sound out unfamiliar words in their reading. By this stage they still are not yet reading in the way we commonly refer to it. But they are getting close. Eventually they will not only notice that when their classmates write about the same subject, they use the same printed words, but that the same is true of children's books. Slowly but surely, in this fail-safe and apparently effortless way, *reading evolves from a structured writing process.*

Teachers have devised a variety of ways to structure a child-friendly approach so that children can make these discoveries without dampening their natural enthusiasm and creativity. What follows is an example from my own classroom.

An Example of a Child-Friendly Writing Process: "The Steps"

I worked for several years in my own K - 2 classroom in a small rural school in Southern California, where forty percent of my children were from the families of the migrant farm workers and came to me speaking only Spanish. Usually their parents were illiterate, and so they had no experience with print. The rest of the class came from the shopkeepers, landowners, or professionals who had moved out to enjoy the country life. They often had a rich foundation in reading skills, and they spoke only English. So it was not unusual for the reading levels in the class to range from virtually zero (one year, a child came speaking no language at all) to reading at the sixth grade level. So I had to develop an individualized program which supported each child at the appropriate developmental level and provided for very different backgrounds in language and life experience.

Developmentally Sequenced "Steps" Toward Writing/Reading*

— Figure 2 —

The "Steps" activities accompany "Key Words" and incorporate
SYSTEMATIC, EXPLICIT PHONICS INSTRUCTION from Step 2 forward:

Step 1 (Phonemic awareness begins here.)
Child dictates "key word."
Child glues copy.

Step 2 (Phonics begins here.)
Child dictates word and sentence.
Child glues copy.

Step 3
Child dictates, cuts up, reassembles and glues.

Step 4
Child dictates and copies into book.

Tadpole
My tadpole can swim.

Step 5
Child dictates word only and "builds" a sentence.

kitty

My kitty can catch a

butterfly.

Step 6
Child writes alone, with no key word.
Child applies and extends writing and reading to the content areas.

Mini Projects

Action-Based Projects

*Developed in the classroom of Janet Kierstead.

I devised an approach which incorporated phonics into an individualized writing program that moved emergent readers into trade books. For the writing program, I developed a sequence of six increasingly complex activities based on Ashton-Warner's Key Vocabulary. I came to refer to those activities as "The Steps." They are described below. (See Figure 2.)

Key Vocabulary

Each of the Steps activities begins by eliciting a "special," or "Key" word from the child. The teacher sits with each child individually talking about something of interest to that child until a special word comes forth (in the child's home language): *I want fish today because yesterday my mom let me pick out a gold fish at the pet shop. They put it in a plastic bag, and we took it home, and I get to keep it in a bowl in my room, and I have to feed it every day, etc.* The child watches as the adult writes the word on a "word card" made of heavy card stock. The child traces over the word with the index finger of the writing hand as the teacher watches for correct letter formation. The child punches a hole in the card and places it on a metal "word ring." The next day, if he/she can remember it, it stays on the ring. If not, the teacher says something like, *That wasn't a very good word for you, let's get a better one today,* and removes the card from the ring. The follow-up activity the child carries out for that word depends on which "Step" he/she has reached. Follow-up activities are described below.

Step 1: The adult makes a duplicate of the special word and the child glues the copy into his/her "writing" book. The child draws a picture about the word and returns to the teacher to have the work checked. The child then receives a clothespin to pin on his/her shirt or blouse, signifying that work is complete. These are the "tickets" to recess. That gives them a sense of responsibility and completion, and it allows the teacher to make sure that each child has done what was expected during the writing period. This signal, along with carefully taught routines and procedures for carrying out the work and an extensive collection of self-teaching activities for children to engage in when finished early, frees up the teacher to work intensively with individuals.

At Step 1, then, the child is first learning —

- That written words are a means of communication
- Correct letter formation
- Use of the glue, pens, paper punch
- Responsibility for completing work and having it checked
- Responsibility for not disturbing others

Most children will remain at Step 1 for about one to three weeks (but longer at each subsequent Step), depending upon how long it takes for them to become comfortable with the procedure. Each day they "read" all the words from previous sessions and get a new word. Recall that the teacher will remove any that are not special enough to be remembered, but this seldom happens, as the word is the caption for a mind-picture of special importance to that child. This same basic procedure for getting a word is followed at each Step, with variations in the follow-up activity, as described below.

Step 2: While writing the word for the child, the adult now teaches the spelling for ONE of the sounds that will be needed. (More than one a day can be confusing.) The child then dictates a sentence about that word, and the teacher writes the sentence on the BACK of the word card: *I want "bird" today, 'cause we put up a bird feeder in our back yard and now lots of birds come around and eat the seeds, and its really fun to watch 'em 'cause sometimes they fight over 'em, and my daddy says, etc.* Again, the child watches as the teacher writes "bird" on the front of the card. Then the teacher helps the child trim down that long sentence to something easier to remember well enough to "read" back. This might be, *We put up a bird feeder in our back yard.* Again, the child watches at the adult writes.

At Step 2 the child is first learning —

- The spelling for simple sounds (usually just the consonants)
- That clumps of sounds are written as separate words
- The meaning of "sentence"
- That sentences begin with a capital letter and end with a period
- A few simple punctuation marks (,?)

Again the teacher makes a duplicate, the child glues it in, makes a picture, has it checked by the teacher, and receives a clothespin.

Step 3: Same procedure as in Step 2, but this time while the adult writes, the child helps supply the letters he/she knows, as well as learning one new spelling. Also, this time the duplicate is written by the teacher on a narrow strip of paper and the child cuts it up. Each word falls on the table out of order, the child scrambles them up and then reassembles and glues them to recreate the sentence.

At Step 3 the child is first learning —
- More complex spelling for sounds (the remaining consonants, some short vowels and perhaps a few digraphs, depending on what the child has already learned)
- Use of sound-symbol relationship and configuration as clues for identifying words
- Use of scissors

Step 4: Same procedure as before except that the child copies the sentence directly into the writing book.

At Step 4 the child is first learning —
- More complex spelling for sounds (remaining short vowels and digraphs, and perhaps long vowels by now, depending on what the child has already learned)
- To correctly form letters independently
- Use of lined paper (not always, but perhaps, depending on the child's motor skills)

Step 5: Same procedure as before, except now the adult only writes the word, and shows the child how to "build" a sentence from all the supporting materials on the classroom walls: charts of frequently used words; lists of special words for holidays, favorite foods, pets, and the like, brainstormed by the total group; charts of any songs or poems learned by the class; and a class "wall strip" dictionary hanging within easy reach and used for recording needed words (a set of 4" wide strips—one strip for each sound—cut lengthwise from chart paper of card stock, so they can be removed by the child, taken to an adult, and then replaced).

At Step 5 the child is first learning —

- More complex spelling for sounds (whatever spellings remain unfamiliar to the child by now)
- How to spell words by "sounding out"
- How to locate spelling for words when unable to sound them out
- Use of more sophisticated spellings as clue for identifying words

The first time, building a sentence will take the child as long as twenty minutes. But in a few days, he/she can write several sentences with ease, and moves on to Step 6.

Step 6: The child no longer gets a "special" word, and instead, writes long and complex stories and carries out projects related to math, science, or social studies. Children engage in two types of projects. One is a "Mini Project": Making a map of the classroom to scale, writing about it, and putting it on display; creating a three-dimensional model of an animal's habitat, writing about it and putting it on display; etc. Mini Projects are valuable as a way to apply and extend learning, but are simply demonstrations/exhibitions of what students know and can do.

The other type is an Action-Based Project: Making a map of the classroom to scale that shows how it might be rearranged to make room for a new interest area, writing a persuasive essay about the idea, presenting both to classmates and the teacher in an attempt to enlist their agreement for making the change; creating a model of an pet's habitat, writing a brochure describing the health, nutritional, grooming and exercise needs of the pet, and using both as part of a "Pet Fair" to teach other children how to better care for various animals. Action-Based Projects go beyond Mini Projects to persuade an *authentic audience* — here, the child is trying to make a positive difference in some aspect of the surrounding world. (See Figures 3 and 4 for examples of projects for older students.)

Action-Based Projects For Older Students
--Figure 3--

Students have carried out such projects as those designed to—

- improve their diet—prepare for career goals
- keep younger students out of gangs
- keep drugs off campus—convince younger students to stay away from drugs
- reduce the serving and clean up time in the cafeteria
- make better use of the school parking lot—reduce time it takes to exit after school
- provide nutritious snacks at school—improve school lunches
- set up and run an accounting system to manage the high school academy's budget
- create a useful invention—design and market a new product
- establish and un a successful small business on campus (snack bar, a "special events" video service, help with research on the Internet, etc.)
- provide a community service for preschoolers—the elderly
- get others to better prepare for a disaster at school—at home
- reduce the waste generated on campus—graffiti on campus/in community

In an Action-Based Project, students select a problem, challenge, or task of particular interest to them related to a teacher-selected topic—and—try to "make a positive difference" through their own action and/or by enlisting the help of others.

Project Example for Earth Science
— Figure 4 —
"How can we get our family to conserve water at home?"

GATHER DATA (FACTS, OPINIONS IDEAS):
- Interview Family: "How do you think we could save water?"
- Read and Analyze: water bills — compute last 3 months
- Observe: how family brushes teeth, rinses dishes, washes car
- Interview Water and Power: Common ways people waste water and what might
- be done about it.
- Phone for pamphlets on water conservation strategies and order water saving devices

FORMULATE TENTATIVE PLAN AND GENERATE PRODUCTS:
- Pool ideas from others' research
- Develop action-plan
- Prepare "sales pitch" for family, including background info and facts
- Make graphs and charts to show family: "Water usage observed in our home— compared with other homes."
- Make checklist to gather commitment from family for who will do what (install/change behaviors)
- Make matrix chart to keep track of target behaviors

REVISE PLAN AND TAKE PERSONAL ACTION:
- Present plan and "sales pitch" to teacher, classmates and outside expert for feedback — revise as needed
- Present information and ideas to family — plan for installation of devices and gain commitment for change of target behaviors
- Routinely chart target behaviors
- Periodically pool findings with class and create updated charts showing comparison of how different families are doing.
- After 2 months: recheck water bills

MEANWHILE, DOCUMENT PROCEDURE: Keep a record of activities in a log book
(including charts as they are created) and use them to create a factual report of what was done. Possibilities include:
- sequential cartoons with captions (hand- or computer-drawn and written)
- narrated video tape
- a pamphlet of "How You Can Help Your Family Save Water," and so forth

EVALUATE ENTIRE ENTERPRISE AND DECIDE WHAT TO DO NEXT:
- Present in class and get feedback on process and products
- Could use products already created -
  - to teach other classes how to do a similar project
  - to kick off a school water conservation project
  - to interest the community in water conservation

At Step 6 the child is first learning —

- How to transmit information of a more academic nature to others (to teach or persuade)
- The use of more complex punctuation ("___" !)
- Responsibility for sustaining interest in and commitment to work lasting several days or weeks
- How to self-edit, present materials for peer and teacher review, and prepare written material for publication

State Guidelines and Characteristics of This Program: Recall that state guidelines call for systematic, explicit phonics instruction, requiring that phonics be "directly taught" and practiced in "decodable text." Also, phonics is not to be embedded in context — not to be random, or ad hoc. Ad hoc is defined in Webster's as being "for the particular end or case at hand, ***without consideration of wider application.***" (Emphasis mine.)

How, then, does the Steps example of a natural approach measure up against the guidelines? Taking each requirement in turn, we find a close match to virtually all of them. For phonics instruction within the Steps is—

- *direct instruction.* This may be a bit clouded, as there is often some confusion over direct instruction and *group presentation,* with some thinking that children must come together in a group to receive direct instruction. Actually direct instruction given individually to the child for some purpose in his/her work (in this case to communicate) is vastly more effective than that given in a group. For not only can the teaching be closely tailored to that child's skill level, but it also is tied to the need to know something of importance to him/her. So, interest is high, and the child watches and listens carefully. The Steps therefore, provide a powerful version of direction instruction.

- *systematic.* Not only does the teacher keep track of what the child has learned, but introduces new sound-symbol relationships in a framework beginning with consonants and ending with digraphs and long vowels. It is only the *specific sequence of letters within the framework* that cannot be predetermined, because that depends on what words the child needs to spell.

- practiced in *decodable texts.* As explained earlier, each child is writing his/her own decodable text, which is first a means of applying and later practicing the new learning by reading it back.

- *not ad hoc.* The learning will be *applied/used immediately and daily thereafter.* For children reread all their words daily, and since they tend to use similar language as they repeatedly talk about the things that interest them most, they will continue to apply the new learning as they create each day's new decodable text.

There is, however one glaring -- and quite intentional -- mismatch with the guidelines. *Phonics instruction within the Steps is embedded in context.* But is this really against what reformers are trying to accomplish? Reformers do not want instruction to be *ad hoc,* which we can only believe is because they do not want the teaching to be "without consideration for wider application." Introducing and practicing phonics *out of context* as called for in the guidelines, however, denies students the chance for immediate application. For, by definition, application can only occur embedded in context. Practice can take place out of context, but application – no. So, it appears that reformers were forced into this position because they did not recognize the alternative available to them: the opportunity to use writing to develop the foundation skills children need for reading.

Let's think about this in another set of circumstances. Say you had a new set of several phone numbers of business associates, family and friends that you would like eventually to know from memory. Would you choose to spend several weeks memorizing them ahead of time– waiting that long before you used them to make calls to anyone? Or, would you rather rely on the list to make your daily calls, while at the same time focusing on learning maybe one or two new numbers each day—committing them to memory *while you made those calls among all the others?* Which way would be the most effective use of your time? Which appeals to you more? In which case would your learning be more

apt to "stick"—be available to you later for "wider application"?
Further, think about all the other information you would miss learning if
you delayed your actually calling for several weeks. While it is not an
exact analogy, as I have attempted to illustrate here, children can learn a
lot more than phonics from a carefully structured daily writing program.

Now consider an instance with children. We have all seen children,
having practiced their spelling list diligently, get every word right on
Friday's spelling test—only to turn right around and misspell some of the
same words in their writing. But as so many of us who work with
children within a strong writing program have experienced, when
children learn to spell new words *as they use them repeatedly in their
writing,* they do not suddenly forget them later.

Again, memorizing phonics in isolation and hoping for transfer to
reading did not work for so many children before. So, why would we
think—especially given our increasingly diverse student population—
that it would serve them well now? Our choice need not be *either*
phonics out of context *or* laissez-faire. Either extreme makes learning to
read much more difficult for children than it need be—one putting up
barriers, the other leaving gaps too difficult for many children to
overcome. Neither capitalizes on the child's inherent drive to
communicate in increasingly complex ways. Can we really afford to risk
another generation of children while we discover this once again?

Two Other Ingredients in a Natural Approach: Total Group "Play" with Sounds and Letters—and Individual Reading Conferences

While it is outside the scope of this paper to describe every aspect of
a child-friendly, or natural, approach—of which mine is just one
example—I do not wish to leave the reader with the impression that the
daily writing activities and projects stand alone. At least three other
ingredients deserve mention here. First is the total group activities
devoted to what is currently begin referred to as "phonemic awareness"
(songs, chants, rhythms, phoneme substitution, etc.). Next is the *very
light-handed treatment of occasional* group phonics activities designed to
associate sounds with different combinations of letters (experimenting
with letter substitution, building word families, and so forth). Finally,
regularly scheduled individual reading conferences are essential. Here,

children who are reading independently (at about Step 5 and beyond) are shown how to select a trade book appropriate for their reading level and then required to keep a reading folder to document their work. (These including thoughts about the book, what they "got" out of it, difficult vocabulary encountered, dates they read independently or with a tutor, any project work that pertains to the book, etc.). These children meet individually with the teacher for a "reading conference" often enough to keep them practicing, enjoying and/or applying their reading to their project work. (The reader will find a more extensive description of these and other aspects of this approach in Kierstead, 1984 and 1990.)

Maintaining and Strengthening the Middle Ground

One day, we will have gone beyond this latest swing of the pendulum as we have so many others, and advocates of the middle ground must be ready for that. Education has passed through several such swings in this century (Kierstead, 1987). Each time advocates of "child-centered/ progressive/ natural/ open-classroom" approaches— whatever the current terminology—have had their chance again, but somehow have been unable to get the message across. It is important for us to realize that it is now our responsibility to keep our eye on the ultimate goal. It falls to us now to maintain and strengthen the middle ground. We must see to it that we are ready when our chance comes again.

We cannot afford to throw up our hands in disgust and despair. Neither can we fight head-on the forces against us. It is simply a waste of our energy. But we can stand firm in our beliefs and practices. We can come together here at the annual conference, much as we did in the 1970's, to exchange ideas and maintain our resolve. We can help one another refine practices that work and clarify how we might explain them to others. In so doing, we will not only have protected the children for whom we are responsible now, but we will be ready to share our work when the time comes. And never doubt that our chance will come again. It's only a matter of time.

This, too, shall pass.

Notes

1. Information about Spencer's ideas is from conversation with Malcolm Douglass. The Claremont Reading Conference journals are rich with the names of these leading educators, but the one who facilitated my understanding of these issues the most is Malcolm Douglass, Professor of Education, Claremont Graduate School, then Chairman of the conference.

2. Ken Goodman examines the development, contents, and implications of the national Reading Excellence Act (HR 2614, Senate-passed version) in Comments on the Reading Excellence Act (U.S.). (Reading on Line, International Reading Organization. Critical Issues: http://www.readingonline.org/home.html)

3. A summary of AB 1086 appears in Reading Instructional Development Program, Elementary Education. (California Department of Education, Reading/Language Arts. Application Materials for Providers of Professional Development in Reading: http://www.cde.ca.gov/cilbranch/eltdiv/rdg99summary.htm)

Suggested Reading
(T=Theoretical; A-R/P=Action-Research/Practical)

Adams, M. (1990). *Beginning to Read,* The MIT Press. (T)

Adams, M. (1992). *Modeling the Reading System: Four Processors, Theoretical Models, and Processes of Reading,* ed. Ruddell, et. al. Newark, DE: International Reading Assn., pp. 842-863. (T)

Adams, M. (1991). "Why Not Phonics and Whole Language?" *All Language and the Creation of Literacy*, ed., William Ellis. Baltimore, MD: The Orton Dyslexia Society. (T)

Adams, M. and Bruck, M. (Summer, 1995). "Resolving the Great Debate," *American Educator*, vol. 19, no. 2. (T)

Allington, R. and Cunningham, P. (1995). "Visiting in the Primary Classroom," *Schools That Work: Where All Children Read and Write.* NY: HarperCollins College Pub., pp. 225-231. (A-R/P)

Ashton-Warner, S. (1971). *Teacher.* NY: Bantom Books

Calfee, R. (1992). "Authentic Assessment of Reading and Writing in the Elementary Classroom," *Elementary School Literacy: Critical Issues.* Norwood, MA: Christopher-Gordon Pub., Inc., pp. 211-226. (A-R/P)

Kierstead, J. (1991). "A Day in the Life of an Integrated Language Arts Classroom," *Claremont Reading Conference Fifty-Fifth Yearbook,* ed. Philip Dreyer. Claremont, CA: Center for Developmental Studies. (A-R/P)

Kierstead, J. (1987). "Is This Just Another Swing of the Pendulum? That Depends....," *Claremont Reading Conference Fifty-First Yearbook,* ed. Malcolm Douglass. Claremont, CA: Center for Developmental Studies, 1987. (A-R/P)

Kierstead, J. (1984). "Outstanding Effective Classrooms," *Claremont Reading Conference Forty-Eighth Yearbook,* ed. Malcolm Douglass. Claremont, CA: Center for Developmental Studies. (A-R/P)

Pearson, D. P. (December 1995). *Reclaiming the Center,* paper presented at the Michigan State University Winter Reading Symposium and reprinted in *Early Reading: A Powerful Tool for Learning,* California School Leadership Academy, California Dept. of Education. (A-R/P)

Stanovich, K. E. (1991). "Changing Models of Reading and Reading Acquisition," *Learning to Read: Basic Research and Its Implication,* ed. Riegen and Perfetti. Hillsdale, N.J.: Lawrence Erlbaum Assoc, pp. 19-31. (T)

Veatch, J., et. al. (1973). *Key Words to Reading.* Columbus, OH: Charles E. Merrill Publishing Co. (A-R/P)

OUT OF THE HEART: CHANGING OURSELVES IN ORDER TO CHANGE OUR WORK

Mary Poplin

I would like to begin today with a quotation from the book of Matthew that frames what I want to say today about the heart and change. In chapter 15, Jesus is talking with his disciples about the conversation he has just had with the Pharisees. They had accused him because his disciples did not wash their hands properly when they ate their bread. You'll remember most of the disciples were fishermen, tax collectors and the like. The religious leaders of the day believed a person became defiled if they did not wash appropriately. Peter asks for an explanation of what Jesus said to the Pharisees:

> Do you not yet understand that whatever enters the mouth goes into the stomach and is eliminated? But those things which proceed out of the mouth come from the heart and they defile a man. For out of the heart proceeds evil.... These are the things which defile a man....[1]

I'd like to speak today from diverse bodies of literature and experiences and weave them together into what will hopefully be a unified thesis. My thesis is that significant change will come about in the schools when those inside schools change their hearts, not their methods, daily routines, curriculum, career ladders, or assessment systems. I'm not denying the viability of such systemic experiments and changes, but I am challenging the degree of confidence we place in these things to *significantly* improve academic and social experiences and achievement in schools for all children. I will be sharing with you from some relatively recent reports on the latest reform efforts, results from the ongoing study of *Voices from Inside the Classroom*, and lessons I am

---

[1] Matthew 15:17-20

learning in my own spiritual journey, some of which come from my experience working with Mother Teresa and the Missionaries of Charity in 1996.

Recent Reform Efforts

All through the 1980s, reports emerged on the state of schooling in America. Most of these reports documented the decline of achievement test scores of students in this country; some compared this decline to similar scores of other countries. While achievement scores were the primary data, different reports recommended different strategies for improving school achievement. These strategies included increasing the length of the school day or year, creating new structures such as schools within schools, reducing the curriculum "less is more," using new constructivist methods such as hands-on science, math with manipulatives, and whole language instruction, as well as initiating more interdisciplinary efforts. We also attempted to reform the teaching profession by increasing standards and testing of new teachers, developing career ladders, involving teachers in school decision-making, and instituting a new National Board Certification. Schools also sought more parental input and recruited parents to sit on school site committees alongside teachers. Increased standards and more rigorous testing of students has been instituted as well. Most schools in the country have attempted one or more of these and the costs in human effort and money have been great.

And now, in the late 1990s the data is beginning to emerge.[2] In general, research does not find these reforms to have significantly increased student achievement or even affected whole school change. Researchers find that many of the teachers who were voluntarily a part of the reforms gained personally and grew professionally. The key unit of change was the individual classrooms of some of the teachers. Many

---

[2] Muncey and McQuillan. (1996). *Reform and Resistance in Schools and Classrooms*. New Haven: Yale University Press. Brouillette, L. (1996). *A Geology of School Reform*. New York: SUNY. Lipman, P. (1998). *Race, Class and Power in School Restructuring*. New York: SUNY. Lindsey, D. (1999). *Evidence of Engagement*. Dissertation: Claremont Graduate University.

teachers report profound changes in the way they view their students, classrooms and in the ways they teach. They often report it was the most professionally renewing experience they have had as teachers. The teachers increased student responsibility in learning; frequently this made more work for students. Some students resisted these changes. In addition, these changed classrooms employed more group work and cooperative learning strategies. They employed new assessments including student portfolios and exhibitions alongside traditional ones.

These teachers' enthusiasm, however, was often met with jealousies and conflicts from other colleagues. Power in schools shifted to those involved in the reform efforts, and there became in-groups and out-groups. Structural changes such as schools within schools were implemented without the whole school staff reaching consensus. Teacher unions frequently challenged efforts of individuals and groups to make desired changes. Those most involved in the changes report experiencing a great deal of stress, many have simply given up and gone back to working alone behind closed classroom doors. Some have returned to old methods easier for the teacher and students, some have maintained the instructional innovations. Structural changes have disappeared as involved faculty and administrators have taken new positions.

The situation for poor students and students of color in particular did not change, equity issues were not addressed in the reforms. Teachers of color report that their input was still marginalized in these efforts and racial dialog stifled. In fact, some have suggested that many of the classroom reforms such as the more constructivist activities have been unwisely applied with students of color who also need explicit instruction in the very skills that these methods assume develop naturally. These same Black educators suggest that teachers of color are unlikely to receive the coveted national credentials given a bias in teacher styles imbedded in the national assessment itself.[3]

---

[3] Delpit, L. (1995). *Other People's Children*. New York: The New Press. Foster, M. (1997). *Black Teachers on Teaching*. New York: The New Press.

Research on the Inside

Another study in the early 1990s here at Claremont in which I was involved and subsequent related work seeks to listen to what those inside schools say regarding the challenges inside schools.[4] Since most of the national reports and strategies were determined by those on the outside, e.g., business and political leaders, looking at achievement data we wanted to look from within. In listening to parents, teachers, students, administrators and other school staff such as janitors, secretaries, aides and cafeteria and security employees—different pictures emerge. Our findings suggest achievement is not the root problem, but the consequence of more fundamental problems. Today I will be addressing only the first three of these problems found in the original study—relationships, racism and values.

Relationships

We find in every school in which we have worked the most frequently raised issue is relationships. Many relationships are mentioned in one way or another, students with students, teachers with administrators, teachers and teachers, and teachers and students' parents. But the relationship that most dominates discussions inside schools is between teachers and students. Parents' greatest fear is that their child's teacher will not like their child and will not treat them with respect. Students speak poignantly of teachers who do or don't treat them with respect. Teachers complain of students who are disrespectful. Staff members describe teachers'and students' respect or disrespect for one another. Since the primary relationships around which the schools revolve are between students and teachers, students rarely even mention any other adults inside schools. Words that are used by the various people to describe this issue include care, respect, relationship, and attitudes.

---

[4] Poplin, M., and Weeres, J. (1992). *Voices from the Inside: A Report on Schooling in America from Inside the Classroom.* Claremont, CA: The Institute for Education in Transformation at Claremont Graduate School.
Poplin, M., and Rivera, J. (In process). Voices from Inside Schools and Classrooms in America.

Now one of the problems I see with much of the care and relationship literature in the social sciences is that it fails to acknowledge the difficulty of caring, respecting, and developing good relationships with people with whom we have not chosen to develop a relationship. Such is the task of teaching. This literature frequently assumes a kind of sweetness that is not necessarily respectful or caring. When people know I have worked with Mother Teresa they often approach me discussing her as though she were some sweet little old lady. Well..., Mother Teresa was not sweet: she was strong and sacrificial. Healthy and healing relationships are just that, strong and sacrificial.

Mother Teresa took her definition of care for others from her faith. It was neither sweet nor tough. In Matthew 25 is found the Scripture that forms the foundation of the Missionaries constitution. Here Jesus says: *"I was hungry and you fed Me, I was thirsty and you gave Me drink, I was naked and you clothed Me, sick and you tended Me, lonely and you comforted Me, in prison and you visited Me."*[5] To which the people replied, "When did we see you hungry or thirsty, naked or sick, lonely or in prison and help you?" He answers, "When you did these things for the least among you." Because of this, the Missionaries see every person they encounter as a hungry, hurting, thirsty Christ. This insures a level of respect in every thing they do, not just in relationships but in physical labor. If they are washing diapers, they are washing Christ's diaper. If they touch a body, it is Christ's. If they are cooking, it is for him. The attitude in which they approach every task and each person is a sacred one.

We are teachers and it is not always easy to love, to care, or to show respect, but it is our calling just as it was hers, indeed it is everyone's calling. And the degree we can do this will be the degree to which our students can also. But in addition to our expansive knowledge of content and methodology, we also bring enormous attitude problems such as anger, bitterness, and depression into our classrooms because they are in our hearts. Sometimes these things have been with us since childhood. It is these attitudes that inhibit our being able to respond in healthy ways even to the students we know best—those most like us. But we also are called to teach other people's children and sometimes we don't

---

[5] Matthew 25: 35-36

understand them or even like them, but we are called to have a right attitude and to teach them as though they were our own.

Racism

The second issue we find commonly discussed especially by students in the schools is racism. Students describe racism in the curriculum, in their parents, each other, their teachers, and society. I am convinced from my own experience that most, if not all, of us who are white are largely unconscious of our own racism and of the racism that exists in the institution that makes it more difficult from the outset for some people's children to succeed than for others. Things in schools that I never noticed, that look natural or normal to me are stumbling blocks for other people's children. In our dialogs with teachers in the schools over things students say about racism in schools (students usually call it prejudice) we find several ways educators attempt to soften the conversation or avoid it altogether. I can say this because I have been a part of these strategies myself, and I'm sure I still have more that I cannot even yet see.

A common mistake is for white educators to over emphasize our similarities and to gloss over our differences. Others make the opposite mistake sometimes of overemphasizing differences. A second strategy used to soften the conversation about racism by making it more abstract (thus less convicting) is to suggest that before we talk we should first define our terms, such as race, ethnicity, culture, etc.

A third strategy frequently used to avoid conversations about what students say about race is to change the conversation by suggesting that the issue is not race really, it is economics. While I would never suggest that economics are not extremely important and inextricably bound up with race for all kinds of social, political, economic and historical reasons, it is race, not class, which students describe. Another strategy is for white adults to describe instances in which they were either oppressed for being white or different in some way or to vociferously describe times when they have acted in defense or solidarity with people of color (friends, colleagues, etc.).

The most deadly of all the strategies however is the strategy that I call "grandfather stories." This is when white people say something like, "well, I'm not a racist, but my grandfather sure was…." The reason this strategy is particularly dangerous to dialog is that it doesn't just distort, abstract or change the conversation, it denies and stops it. We have just said racism was once a problem but no longer is. There is no where to go from there.

I have come to the conclusion that the best thing a white person can do is to say and believe (or at least be open to the possibility) that "Given the circumstances of my birth and my life, I do have racist assumptions and attitudes within me, but I do not want to. Help me learn what I need to know." Then we need to be quiet and listen so that we can evaluate where what is being said is actually also true of us. We can silently apply any instances of oppression in our lives as a place from which we can begin to understand the pain that is being expressed. Parker Palmer[6] in his book, *The Courage to Teach*, says we must be quiet enough to hear what we are thinking and saying—what is really inside us as teachers.

We must also know that it is highly unlikely that we have suffered as much oppression due to our race as those who are not white. Before we speak we need to ask ourselves if what we are going to say is said out of defensiveness or whether it will add to a solution? The Missionaries of Charity have a rule that would change the atmosphere of teachers' lounges – they are not allowed to speak during work time unless it is necessary in order to get the work done. And we also should speak only when it adds to the solution.

I am not saying that there is never an instance of discrimination on the basis of being white. Certainly after all these centuries the sins of our forefathers must have had some result. However, our challenges because of our race are still much fewer and much more recent than the hundreds of years of racism that has taken its toll and still takes its toll on Native Americans, African Americans, Latino Americans and others. Discrimination faced by people like myself so pales in comparison to my colleagues of color that they are rarely worth mentioning.

---

[6]   Palmer, P. (1998). *The Courage to Teach*. San Francisco, CA: Jossey-Bass.

What helps us most is to listen carefully to our colleagues of color, seek out their advice for our teaching, and study books and journals that address issues of racism. Books by Lisa Delpit[7], Michele Foster[8], Janet Hale-Benson[9], Gloria Ladson-Billings[10] help us do that. The work of Maria Montano-Harmon[11] on discourse styles of various cultural groups and Native American evangelist, Craig Smith[12] are all sources that help us see ourselves, our blind spots, and the many ways institutions have embedded racist assumptions in their day-to-day existence, whether they be schools or churches. Mother Teresa sought to see all those with whom she worked from God's perspective and so whether she was confused by differences or not, she believed God had sent each person to her and it was her responsibility, not to judge, but to love and to help. Since it was God's will, she need only to remain close to God who would give her all the necessary resources and wisdom to do the task well (divine providence). She had a clear-cut value system that allowed her to turn challenges into opportunities.

Values—Parents and Educators

There are two issues that get raised in conversations about schools that come under the general rubric of values – one is raised by adults and another by students. First, we find that many adults working in the schools, particularly professionals, believe that parents have different (lower) values than they do. There are often instances where school professionals grossly underestimate the values present in students' homes and overestimate their own. For example, we found that teachers at one school felt that the students' problems came from their being from "broken homes," but when we examined the situation closer we found the same percentage of "broken homes" existed in the teaching staff as in the students' homes. Teachers in this same school felt that the Latino

---

[7]   Delpit, L. (1995). *Other People's Children*. NY: The New Press.

[8]   Foster, M. (1997). *Black Teachers on Teaching*. NY: The New Press.

[9]   Hale-Benson, J. (1982). *Black Children*. Baltimore, MD: Johns Hopkins.

[10] Ladson-Billings, G. (199). *Dreamkeepers: Successful Teachers of African American Students*. San Francisco, CA: Jossey-Bass.

[11] Montano Harmon, M. (1988). Discourse features in the compositions of Mexican, ESL, MexicanAmerican/Chicano, and Anglo high school students. Dissertation, University of Southern California.

[12] Smith, C. (1997). *Whiteman's Gospel*. SD: Indian Life Books.

parents didn't care as much about school as EuroAmerican parents, but when we held a parent night in Spanish, five times the number of Latino parents attended as had EuroAmerican parents at the English parent night, though both groups share approximately 30 percent of the school population.

Exacerbating these misunderstandings, many teachers and administrators do not live in the communities in which they teach. Indeed some are afraid of the neighborhoods and their fear often makes them unable to see the community and parents' strengths and dreams and visions for their own students. They are unaware of the real life of the community, never shopping in the stores or attending the churches, or community events.

I came to appreciate the fact that Mother Teresa and the Missionaries live within the poorest communities in which they work. They walk through the neighborhood in pairs, they buy their food and supplies at local stands and shops: they know the people. They know what it takes just to get a meal on the table when you are cooking over coals, what it takes to bathe on the street from a public water spigot, and what it takes to wash the only other garment you have while you wear the second one. Because they live like the poor you do not find them blaming poor parents for the plight of poor children. Like Palmer suggests, the Missionaries sought to spend time in self-reflection (for them, recollection and confession). They were sensitive and flexible; they could bend with the circumstance in a neighborhood. For example, we often had children in the center where I worked which was for sick and handicapped children, who were not sick. The Missionaries were keeping them because their parents were ill and they simultaneously were serving the parents with medicines and food. But schools maintain a distance from which we often accuse rather than seek to serve parents.

Values—Students' Concerns over Goodness and Evil

But the issue for students and values was a different one. Students were concerned about "*goodness and evil*." They are concerned about the evil they see in their neighborhoods and in the world. They are concerned about their own "badness" when they find they are not who they want to be. One young child said, "I don't like my knees, the color of my skin or when I'm bad." Other children report they have no one to talk to when they are "bad" except gang members.

Before we commit ourselves to the now worn phrase "it takes a village to raise a child" we need to look at the village. We found in one school in a poor neighborhood that most of the fourth graders did not believe they would live long enough to choose to go to college. Villages here are a far cry from the villages in Africa from whence this saying was derived. In part, the problem in Columbine was that the village did raise those children, the Internet raised them, their peer group raised them, and the school raised them.

We have a society that is addicted to watching evil. We prefer to watch it live as the news coverage of wars and tragedies, but we will take it pre-recorded, simulated or even fictionalized. We have no idea how this affects our children or ourselves as teachers. Try not watching any television, not even the news, for a week and see how your mind, emotions and work are affected. In the absence of serious discussions of good and evil, you will find students seeking their own explanations on television, videos, Internet, books and magazines. They develop activities with one another where they can work out their place in all this, which range from joining prayer groups, cliques, gangs, or hate groups obtaining and storing weapons. Add to this the fact that the discussion of values in schools is held up by petty arguments of "educated" adults over whether teachers can use the Ten Commandments. So we end up teaching vague values such as self-esteem, pride, courage, and independence, all of which were values of Timothy McVeigh and the Unibomber. None of which are values in any world religion.

Parents and teachers are afraid of disciplining their children; soon they become afraid of their children. We have a strange notion in the white middle class America (where most of the most gruesome murders are) that discipline stifles creativity and that challenging authority is more important than living in obedience. Parents find it easier to give in and let their children be entertained by the media and the neighborhood than to challenge them. Teachers make dangerous truces that exchange real work in schools for good behavior or at least for non-violence. There are children in gifted classes who say things to their teachers and classmates for which a poor child in a remedial program would be punished. Even teachers not so infrequently can be heard to make the most disrespectful comments to students, colleagues and superiors. It is common to see vicious arguments between parents and children or even adults in public. Television portrays the best and brightest using their intellect to make the most cutting and rude comments and actions. Contemplate for a moment what it means that the name of the Columbine yearbook was "Rebelations." These things have serious consequences and the schools and the society are experiencing them.

Children in our culture face challenges few of us even thought about as children. Yet no one is teaching students how to overcome adversity, trials, or what to do with suffering. To Mother Teresa suffering was a necessary part of life and when done well would develop character qualities such as patience, kindness, self-control. She always said the U.S. was the most difficult place they had to work because everyone was so comfortable that they didn't think they needed God. She said we are materially rich and spiritually poor. To her and her sisters even the publication of a vile book about her was "a call to become more holy." This is a far cry from the response to social slights the two Columbine boys enacted. Why are we not teaching our children that their identities, their destinies are not bound up with how much money they make or what others think of them. In Judeo-Christian terms, one finds one's identity in getting close enough to God to be able to discern and do His will for our lives. In any terms, one must find for oneself what is their purpose in life and keep their eyes on something larger than the slights of other students or colleagues. We must find the way to help students (and ourselves) struggle effectively with their own hurts, disappointments, angers, fears, and bitterness – what they call their own "badness."

Small Things with Great Love

Many people complained that given her fame Mother Teresa should have gotten more politically involved in the economics of poverty. Others complained that she should have not simply fed the people but "taught them to fish." But Mother Teresa was not moved by these criticisms. She simply replied that God called others to do these things, he only called her to feed and care for the poorest of the poor. One of the most difficult things for a secular world to understand about her is that Mother Teresa did not do her work for man, she did not simply feel sorry for the poor. She was called by God to do what she did. The poor, the rich, admirers, or critics could not dissuade her from her calling. She often used a phrase attributed to her namesake Therese of Lisieux, "small things with great love." She said too many of us wanted to do great things, but we are really called to do small things with great love.

I had two lessons on this as I worked with the sisters. The first was with a fragile infant named Babloo. When I met him he weighed seven pounds and was three months old. He had been born prematurely and contracted a vicious intestinal virus shortly thereafter. His mother had brought him to Mother Teresa's because she felt she would not be able to keep him alive. We were keeping him alive until his body could fight off the virus for which there were no medicines. Then he could go home (and he did at about five months old). His mother came to see him several times a week. But when I met Babloo he was only drinking one ounce of fluid at a time. One of the sisters and I were determined to increase his intake. She shared with me the most powerful prayer she knew (she herself had recovered miraculously from tuberculosis of the brain). We prayed it every day together. We found a bottle nipple that seemed to work better than others did, and set out to expand his capacity. At first it took us 2½ hours to feed this tiny infant a four-ounce bottle. For days we labored at each feeding to keep him awake long enough to take four ounces. But soon the time it took diminished, his stomach was stretched, and his muscles strengthened and he could consume the entire bottle in about twenty minutes.

But I was not always so pure of heart. There was another baby boy there, seriously deformed who I avoided. He never seemed happy no matter what you would do, he always looked as though he were miserable. And most of us did not gravitate to him. But one sister, rather stern in her countenance to us, always picked him up and fed him. When she held him, she looked at him with so much love that you would have thought it was being returned. She paid no attention at all to the fact that this child did not give her the usual rewarding baby glances. She spoke to him and held him as though he was her own special treasured child. She had the sacrificial attitude toward caring that is perhaps even more accurately depicted in Luke 6, here Christ says to His disciples, *"What good is it if you love those who love you, do not even sinners love those who love them?"*[13]

One day when she was not there, I noticed as I returned Babloo to his bassinet that this young baby had thrown up his entire bottle all over himself, the bassinet and the floor. He was sobbing quietly. Looking around quickly to see who else could help, I found no one. I went to him through my resistance and began the task of cleaning him and his surroundings. I stopped and thought of how Sister Joachim would be doing it and realized I was cleaning but I was not even trying to comfort this child. At that moment, I saw inside my real heart—and I knew it was a sin, it was evil. I began to imitate Sister Joachim and for a few moments I felt what she must have felt with him, but it was not easy, nor long lasting. And I dislike sharing that with you because I know it is wrong, but I know it is the truth.

And that is the way it is for us in schools. The students with whom we are least successful need small things done for them with great love. They need time; time with adults who are determined, who will not let their feelings of tiredness or dislike impede them. And it takes a great deal of time at first but not always. But it does always take a heart that is right, one that knows, like Mother Teresa, that love is strong and sacrificial and it has very little to do with how we feel or what we think.

In the Hebrew text of the prophet Ezekiel there is a lovely passage about receiving a new heart. God is speaking to the Jews, his people whom he loves, he is telling them how he longs for them to turn back to him and when they do, he promises:

Then I will sprinkle clean water on you, and you shall be clean; I will cleanse
you from all your filthiness and from your idols. I will give you a new heart
and put a new spirit within you. I will take the heart of stone out of your flesh
and give you a heart of flesh.[14]

---

[13] Luke 6:32
[14] Ezekiel 36: 25-27

STRATEGIES FOR HOPE

Lil Thompson

Each year I look forward to receiving the theme for the Claremont Reading Conference and this was no less true this year, my 26th as a presenter. Strategies for hope made me consider the meaning of "strategy" and I came to the conclusion it was a "plan" or a "device." So perhaps this year I should look in detail at all the ways I have used to help children read. I realized, many years ago as a young teacher, and have been told by many researchers since, that reading is a social activity. I had never looked upon it as a "problem" and I expected my children to read. It was only when I visited schools in California that I realized that great emphasis was placed on getting children to read. Professor Peter Spencer had told the Claremont Conference in 1932 that children "read" from birth onwards and that they "see" from experiences, read what they see; their mother's face, etc. "As soon as the child is born," he said, "there are new things to observe which are experienced, learned, and stored for future use." I knew this to be true.

Looking back to when I started teaching almost sixty years ago, I realize that there are many changes. The young teacher of today has more problems than I had, but the "material" they work with, the children, are the same. They may have their videos and computers, but learning still goes on from birth. It does not start when they enter school. They already have learned so much. They are unique, and if we are to be successful teachers, we should observe them closely. We should discover where they come from, where they are, and where we hope to take them. The woodcarver or sculptor examines the material he works with so that he knows where to put in the chisel; teachers must do the same, for no two children are alike. Some will learn quickly, some will be much slower. In England we have a National Curriculum. I think we need a separate curriculum for each child.

One of my strategies was surely the creation of an environment where learning could take place naturally. I hoped it was exciting, full of activity where children could enjoy new experiences; beautiful things to look at, things to touch and smell, and often to taste. There was a balance always between the creative activities of art, music and the basic activities of literacy, reading, writing, and mathematics. I am reminded by A.A. Milne of Christopher Robin talking to Pooh Bear. "What I like doing best, is nothing. It is when people call out to you just as you are going to do it. 'What are you going to do Christopher Robin?' And you say, 'Oh nothing,' and then you go out and do it." At the very end of *The House at Pooh Corner*, Christopher Robin has begun to learn about the letter "A," about factors, about Kings. He has to leave this forest for school and the business of knowing and growing up. "Pooh" he calls to his bear, "I am not going to do nothing anymore." "Never again?" asks Pooh. "Well, not so much, they won't let you." I would think many of the children we teach could echo Christopher Robin.

Another most important strategy for me was language! Children were expected to 'sit up" and "shut up." But not in my school. I knew they loved to talk and I encouraged them. Our prestigious newspaper, *The Times*, had stated, "Learning to talk is the most difficult intellectual task a human being has to cope with and on a child's verbal facility gained early in life, depends much of its future development." My children talked about the things they were doing, they asked questions of their peer group as well as their teachers. Research has taught us about neuron basic circuitry. I knew nothing of this but I practiced it. My children were primed to put "sounds" into "words." I realized that the more a child heard the faster it learned the language. This was very important. Looking at language learning I could not always decide which came first, listening, talking, reading, or writing. Observing young children, I knew they loved to scribble, long before they were shown letter formation, and they could "read" their scribble to me. Young John, who had scribbled over a newly decorated wall, was asked why he did it. "It says, I love you Auntie Lil, I love you." I believed him! I knew that children loved to talk and if there was a willing listener they had tales to tell. A child needs to communicate with other human beings in order to establish and develop personal relationships, to order and control thinking and to interpret and express ideas, relationships and impressions. I marvel how the child learns to talk without a "teacher." A child can, in those first years, acquire twenty new words a day! It is not taught how to make the plural of a noun but we know that by age three it will follow the rule of adding an "s" and will say "sheeps." It is not taught how to make the past tense of a verb but it will say "A bird flied over," "my Daddy builded a garage," and "my Daddy digged up the garden." Children listen to themselves talking and I have a tape of Alison, aged three, telling me a story. "They dug up them," she said, and then corrected it to "They dug them up."

One of my most important strategies in getting children to read was the journal writing which began when the child was in the reception class at age five and coming together with the teacher to share news. As the children sat around their teacher they would tell their news. The most interesting would be chosen to go into the daily news book. The teacher would write each letter carefully, talking about the letter as she wrote. Having finished the sentence she would read it to the children. As they already "knew" what it said, they too could read it. She would play all sorts of games with the words. Some children could choose to wear one of the words especially if it had been their news. Other children could wear words, too, and they could stand in a line to make a sentence. On one wall there would be an enlarged sheet of card divided alphabetically into sections. Suppose the news chosen was "John's mother has had a baby girl. She is a sister." The words would be added to those on the alphabet wall card, for future reference. The teacher's copy would be made into a weekly news book. By Friday there would be five pages in the book. Each morning the children would read the preceding day's news before they did "today's news."

After a few weeks, some children wanted their own news book and they would copy the teacher's sheet and illustrate it. Soon they would want to write their own news in their book using words from the wall card. At the next stage they would have their own "word book" or "spelling book." They would be encouraged to develop their own vocabulary in these books. News or journal writing would be a daily activity throughout the school. It usually began with "Today is Monday. It is a fine day. The temperature is 60°. The wind is in the West." The child's personal news would follow. As the child progressed there would be further weather details, personal and national news of interest. The children would read the news to the teacher, linking reading and writing. They could read it because they knew what it said because they had written it. The teacher would use this journal to discuss spelling and punctuation, "eyeball to eyeball." This was far more effective than a class lesson and far more meaningful to the individual child. These news books were very precious and my parents were always very keen to see what had been written. Often with my nine-year-olds, I would write a whole page of news to discuss with the children. I would make about ten mistakes in grammar, spelling and punctuation and they had to find them. They loved to correct the teacher!

The talking, listening, reading, and writing would go on against a background of stories and rhymes. The reading together in story time was a very valuable means of getting young children to see what reading "says." Reading to children builds vocabulary and background knowledge. It establishes a reading/writing connection. It exposes children to a wealth of experiences outside their own. It stimulates imagination. It stretches the attention span. It nourishes emotional development. It encourages compassion and reshapes negative attitudes. When I read from *The Enormous Crocodile* by Roald Dahl, "In the biggest, brownest, muddiest river in Africa, two crocodiles lay with their heads just above the water. One of the crocodiles was enormous. The other was not so big." I know from experience they would repeat the word ENORMOUS. Listening comprehension comes before reading. It is usually two or three years ahead, and it is a child's listening vocabulary that feeds its reading vocabulary.

I did not use basals; my book corners were full of wonderful books for children to read and enjoy. A favorite book would be chosen from the book corner and the children were encouraged to browse whenever they wished to do so. As a young teacher I asked myself whether I wanted to be concerned about the development of a skill or to get children excited by books. Should reading be a skill or a pleasure? I quote Professor Malcolm Douglass, "There are other ways of inferring whether reading has occurred - if we need such. I suspect however, that we are spending far too much time in these activities. It would be better to give children more time to read, rather than asking them so often to prove that they have read something. In more simple words, reading is a very private behavior and must necessarily and thankfully remain so."

My children were never tested. I was once interviewed by the educational correspondent of the *Los Angeles Times*. She had heard me lecture at Claremont. "You don't believe in testing?!!" she asked. "No," I said, "Children are unique and there are many areas of education which cannot be tested." "What do you do?" she asked. "Let me put it like this," I said, "I think when you test you pull up the plants to see if the roots are growing. Instead I look at the leaves to see if they are green and if there is a flower growing in the middle." I could have added that I make sure the soil is fertile in which the plants have to grow. The more experiences a child has the more it will grow.

There was a lot of reading material in the classroom which did not come from books. There would be labels on the Nature Table and in the science corner. When I worked in a summer school in Tulare, I had five-year-olds who had never been in school before. I had made a Home Corner which the children changed on their first day into a McDonald's. They demanded a menu and from their instructions and suggestions I wrote one for them. By the end of the first week I needed two menus and those five-year-olds surprised the visiting Superintendent of Tulare by asking him what he wanted. They read the menus to him. He could not credit that these children could read in so short a time. I thought of some of my early experiences in teaching. I had sixty-five children in my class and a headmistress who said I had to hear every child read every day. We had one set of basal readers called *The Pixie Readers*...pure phonics; with sentences like "Meg is bad," and "I must go up to an ox." They were hard work to excite children to read. *The Pixie Readers* were followed by *Janet and John*. No excitement from the material in these either.

> "Come, come, come
> Come and look.
> Look up, look down
> Come, come, come."

So much for a good story line!

Therefore, one of my strategies to get children to read was to make sure that they had books they could enjoy. I quote Roald Dahl again, "The prime function of the children's book writer is to write a book that is so absorbing, exciting, fast, funny, and beautiful that the child will fall in love with it. And that first love affair between the young child and the young book will hopefully lead to other loves for other books and when that happens the battle is probably won. The child will have found a crock of gold. He will also have gained something that will carry him most miraculously through the tangles of his later years."

There are many such books for children to read these days, and I wonder why we still find schools that use basals. How many of us would visit a library if we had to accept and read the book handed out to us by the library. Part of the joy comes from being able to wander amongst the bookshelves to choose our own book to read. We should credit our children with having such a need. Jeanette Veitch, who used to present at Claremont, believed that children should be able to choose. Her critics said that they would choose unwisely, books that were too easy or too hard. She devised a rule of thumb that if a child had a number of unknown words on a page, the book was too hard. As teachers, too, we assume that the subject matter in the books we choose for our children will suit them all. This is a wrong assumption and I remember David who was not at all interested in books. I discovered he had a favorite football team and I introduced him to my husband's sports newspaper which had an excellent article about his team. "Read it to me," he said. "No," I said, "It is a pity you can't read it yourself." He gave it much thought and at playtime brought the paper to me and said "If you read the words you know and I read the words I know we can read it together." We did just that and when the class came in David said, "If anybody wants to know about my team, I can read it to them." He never chose another book but avidly read the sporting paper I took to school each week.

Dan Fader, writing in *Hooked on Books,* tells the story of a thirteen-year-old non-reader who chose *Jaws* to read. "Isn't that hard for you?" asked Dan. "Sure, it's hard," replied the student, "but it's worth it!"

Bruno Bettelheim stated, "We should concentrate on awakening the will to read. We cheat the child of what it should gain from the experience of literature, a greater understanding of itself and others, and help in solving life's problems." It is not enough to awaken the appetite for reading; we as teachers must do all we can to make sure we do not produce "lapsed literates." I once read a publication which stated, "Every student is expected to pass a content test on each book. This way I make sure that the books have been read. My students learn about theme characterization, imagery, etc." I added, "And to hate reading." I feel so often that a fog of content, tests, literacy terms, workbooks, skill sheets and dittoes, have obscured the vision and distracted thought.

Bill Martin wrote books for children; they enjoyed them and wanted more. I introduced my Tulare class to Roald Dahl and the school library could not keep one of his books on the shelves. The children even wrote to him asking him to write more. He wrote saying he would try but he was getting old!

A worthwhile strategy in my school was to encourage my children to take home books from the library. Many of their homes did not have books and it was an added bonus to find that both Dad and Mum had also read the books. I quote Orville Prescott who said, "Few children learn to love books by themselves. Someone has to lure them into the wonderful world of the written word. Someone has to show them the way." I know that one of my strategies is to "lure!"

Another strategy that I used was to encourage children to become authors. There was always a writing corner in my classrooms as well as a reading corner. It was a fact that if a child could write a story, using its own words, then it could read it. Each child, having written a story, would make a cover for it and on the outside write the name of the story, e.g.

> *Nelly the Elephant.*
> Written by Beatrice Millar
> Illustrated by Beatrice Millar
> Published by Mrs. Thompson, Birches Press.

I wish I had space to include this story. Like so many others written by my children, they were used as library books. The "authors" read them to each other and to younger children in my school. It was always a joy to me to observe children writing their stories. Sometimes they would know that I was watching them and tell me not to look until they had finished. Even the less able reader would write a simple book, and was thrilled to be able to read it. It was encouraged to take it home to share with the family. Elizabeth's story was simple.

The Dog and the Bone
Page 1   Once upon a time there was a dog called Jo. He was brown.
Page 2   One day he found a bone and he was happy.
Page 3   Then Jo started to bury the bone.
Page 4   The sun came out.
Page 5   Then he went to bed and went to sleep.

"Listen," she said to me, "I can read it!"

I quote Engelmen, "We must enlist the child's creativity by letting him write his own words and stories from the beginning. In this way his own drive is harnessed, he proceeds at his own pace, and so far as is possible, in his own way." I have followed this strategy; I got children to think, to write, and then read what they had written.

Another strategy, which encouraged children to read, was the wall story. My children loved to make up stores and tell them in the school assembly. I thought it a good idea to begin a kind of "Tom & Jerry" adventure.

"Once upon a time there was a cat called Tom and a mouse called Jerry. They had lots of adventures."

This would be the first page and I would print it and display it. I would suggest that the children could think what we could put on the next page. The next morning I would accept the suggestions orally, and the class would choose which was the best. "Tom was a very mean cat. Jerry lived in a hole in the wall." I would print this on another large sheet and add it to the first one on the wall. Next day I would ask the children what they thought happened next. "Jerry was very hungry. He saw some cheese on the table. Tom was watching." I would print this and add it to the other sheets. Each morning we would read those pages as a class and get the next suggestion. "Tom pounced on to the table to catch Jerry but the mouse was too quick. Tom decided to wait outside the hole in the wall." So the story would develop and so would the class reading. The less able child had the satisfaction of reading through daily repetition of those wall sheets. I had wall stories that went on and on for weeks, and there was always great competition between the more able to tell you what would happen next.

I have to admit that one of my favorite strategies to get children to read was through drama. It played a very important part in the language activities in my school. Stories came to life when they were acted. In Tulare I used Roald Dahl's *James and the Giant Peach*. We enjoyed reading it chapter by chapter and then they asked me if they could act it. Together we scripted the play and every child had a copy. They learned their parts without realizing and were soon word perfect. If I had called it "reading" they did not comprehend it as such. They built a set and made their costumes. As there was great competition for the best parts they learned them all. Children, who until they had read this book had shown little interest as readers, came alive as grasshoppers and earthworms. "Are there any other books like this?" They asked. The super principal made sure after this that the library was open every day.

High School children in Montebello fell in love with Shakespeare through exposure to *Romeo and Juliet*. I have memories still of the scene in the tomb. No Hollywood actors died with more feeling than my Romeos. "Here's to my love! O true apothecary thy drugs are quick. Thus with a kiss, I die." No actresses died more courageously than my Juliets did. "Oh, happy dagger. This is thy sheath. There rest and let me die." If I had gone into that class and asked them to take out their reading books I doubt whether I should have received such a response.

In Visalia we acted *St. George and the Dragon*. I had told the story as dramatically as I could and they wanted to act it. So we made our script—a copy for each child—and we read it. They, too, did not think they were "reading" for their scripts were not basals! They demanded another such story so I chose *William Tell* which was an excellent choice, for the whole class could be involved in the scenes. By this time they quickly scripted it, acted it, and gave performances to other grades in the school. This was the reading that had meaning for them and they enjoyed it.

At a high school in Tulare, I had a roomful of students who, when I asked them in my best English accent what they wanted me to do with them, hadn't a single suggestion. As I had about twenty teachers observing my session with these children I suggested that I do some drama. Having some idea about the type of student in that room I knew it had to be a dramatic story. So, I suggested that we had all been hijacked and that we were prisoners in that room. We had to find a way out. We had no telephone. We shouted but nobody heard us. Eventually it was decided by one bright student that we write a note and put it through an airbrick near the ceiling. The teachers who were observing were amazed to see how quickly they wrote their notes. The students chose one which said "We are being raped, please rescue us as soon as possible. Help!" They decided that the best pitcher should throw it through the airbrick. As he was about to pitch it, the bell went for recess. They assured me that they did not want to go out so we began to make a script of the hi-jack. Imagine my surprise as I was leaving that afternoon when I was told that they had finished the script and their teacher had said they could act it and he would make it into a film.

There are many such Californian stories I could tell of using drama. In my own school I used poems, nursery rhymes and all the traditional stories like *The Three Bears*, *Cinderella* and later historical stories for drama. One of my favorite poems by Harold Monro gave me the opportunity for choral speech.

"Nymph, nymph, what are your beads?
GREEN GLASS GOBLIN. Why do you stare at them?
Give them me
NO!
Give them me. Give them me.
NO!
Then I will howl all night in the reeds.
Lie in the mud and howl for them.
GOBLIN, WHY do you love them so?
They are better than stars or water.
Better than voices of winds that sing
Better than any man's fair daughter
Your green glass beads on a silver ring.
HUSH! I stole them out of the moon.
Give me your beads. I want them
NO!
I will howl in a deep lagoon
For your green glass beads
I love them so.
Give them me

Give them me
NO!"

So much drama; so much reading too!

I used jingles, songs and poetry in much the same way. I would
copy poems on to large wall sheets and the children would read and learn
them. These sheets would give us a class anthology. The children had
their own anthologies and often would add their own choice of poems
from books in the library corner, which appealed to them. Through
reading these poems, vocabularies were increased. A particular favorite
was *The Brook* by Tennyson.

> "I come from haunts of coot and tern
> I make a sudden sally
> And sparkle out among the fern
> To bicker down the valley
>
> By thirty hills I hurry down,
> Or slip between the ridges.
> By twenty thorps, a little town
> And half a hundred bridges
>
> I chatter over stony ways
> In little sharps and pebbles.
> I bubble into eddying bays
> I babble on the pebbles."

There is far more reading and exciting words in this poem than in a
basal.

I was once asked to teach some elderly Jamaicans to read. They met
regularly in a church and I knew they could sing all the hymns from
memory. I copied out a few favorite ones on to large sheets and as they
sang I pointed to the words. They became aware that if they could read a
phrase in a hymn they could recognize the same phrase in another one. It
was a revelation to them, but not to me who had used such a method with
young children.

In *Why Johnnie Can Read* by Rosina Spitzer, a handout at the Reading Conference, she talks about my school theme of "Water." Each class contributed writing and artwork on the subject and these were mounted in classrooms and in the corridors for all to read. The whole school was excited over "Space" and this was another theme. I had taken my oldest children to an industrial science exhibition where they were able to touch moon rocks. The writing and the reading from this experience had to be seen to be believed.

Our local newspaper *The Express* and *Star* was used as a strategy and we made our own *Express* and *Moon* for all to read. Parents came in specially to read our newspaper, which appeared every two weeks. I must admit I did censor some of the news; but at least it was well read. I had produced a similar newspaper when I was consulting in California Hot Springs. That, too, was very exciting and I think the children made some money selling copies.

I was a firm believer in teacher, parent association, and therefore you can imagine that I would use them as a strategy. They were encouraged to come into school to see their children's work and to attend a Friday afternoon assembly when the school week was reviewed. After the assembly they would go into the classrooms to read the news books. They were also encouraged to hear their children read. Children who were to enter the school could come into school to listen to stories at the end of the day. It was hoped that parents would catch the habit and read to their children at home. They were allowed to borrow books to do so.

Reading stories aloud to children was always part of everyday practice in my school. Good literature, our heritage, was always used. Stories like those from Beatrix Potter have to be read to be appreciated and can be used over and over again. Literature should be encouraged and used to incubate a love of books and reading, and to master the skill for themselves. One of my children told me that when she read she told stories to herself in her head. The Plowden Report, one of our educational bibles, stated "We are convinced of the value of stories for children; stories told to them, stories read to them and the stories they read for themselves." As children choose books from the book corner, they may, as Graham Greene suggests in *The Lost Childhood*, be choosing their future and the values that will dominate it.

So, writing about how I used strategies in my school, I am realizing that I never had a problem getting children to read. I only hope that any young teachers who have a problem could use a few of my suggestions. I once listed the needs of the learner; there should be expectations of success; confidence to take risks and make mistakes; a willingness to share and to engage; the confidence to ask for help. On the same list there were the needs of the teacher; respect for and interest in the learner's language, culture, thoughts and intentions; the ability to recognize growth, strengths and potential; the appreciation that mistakes are necessary to learning; the confidence to maintain breadth, richness and variety, and to match these to the learner's interests and direction, i.e. to stimulate and challenge; a sensitive awareness of when to intervene and when to leave things as they are.

I hope that as teachers we can strengthen the mind of the young child rather than just fill it. I hope that children will grow in their own way into creative, imaginative and interesting people able to talk, listen, read and write. I hope they will be like Oliver Twist asking for more and more books to enjoy and becoming excited and enthralled by them. My hope is that they will have interesting, enthusiastic teachers to encourage them. I hold onto hope; it is a gift, and I hope that those who care about children are hoping for all these things for them too.

I usually begin with a poem. This time I will end with one. It is called Etcetera.

In the beginning
someone gave us
two hands, ten fingers,
two ears, one mouth,
two eyes and a few million nerve ends.

We learned to
handle wood, wool, glass, stone, etc.
hear music, laughter, birdsong, Beatles, etc.
see skies, blue, vast, shining, etc.
to love, hate, want, need, cry, etc.

So now we sit

in wooden boxes
on wooden boxes
at wooden boxes
and wait.........
for the O.K. list of rules
to be handed out by someone
who some years ago went through the same process.

If you put a coin in a slot machine
And pull the handle - you get an answer,
The answer you put in in the first place
It's a wonderful thing - Education.

Cynical? Yes! My hope is that it does not apply to anyone attending the Claremont Reading Conference.

An extra note: I was told that because of a deep vein thrombosis I could not fly to California. I had so hoped that I would be able to attend. I was sincerely grateful to Jane Carrigan for suggesting that I should be bounced off a satellite. I did enjoy it, but missed all the friends I have made over the last twenty-six years. Claremont has meant a lot to me.

POETRY FOR HOPE

Janet S. Wong

A couple of months ago a serious and quiet boy came into the library of a school I was visiting. I had performed my poems in a large assembly in the morning, and then had moved on to doing a metaphor workshop with his class, among others. But he hadn't had any time to share his own poems. So he made a special trip, during recess, into a library full of adults who had gathered to talk to me. He carried a few sheets of paper rolled up in his hands, and asked to show me some poems he had written in the weeks before my visit. They were elaborate and deep, careful rhyming poems that obviously had taken time to craft. I made a few suggestions here and there, gave words of praise. The boy smiled a little. As he left, I was told that he was heavily medicated for ADD, in the sort of sorry tone that seems to come with these kinds of whisperings. "Heavily medicated," I thought. "But all this boy needs is *poetry*!"

This, obviously, is too simple a view. But wouldn't it be a nice addition to the medication to have a doctor prescribe "two poems a day"? Why not take a bit of poetry the way we take our vitamins, first thing in the morning or last thing at night, or both, or at least the way my friend pops her ginkgo, "each time she can remember." In the world of Harry Potter, perhaps the nurse at Hogwarts could dispense a dollop of "Haiku Horseradish" to cure people who'd been cursed to speak in flowery breathless rhyming verse. One gulp might produce short bursts of plain non-rhyming talk, only the very most necessary and basic utterances about the natural world. Those afflicted with "Dull and Serious Thought" could be slipped "Limerick Lozenges." The irresponsible would be assigned four minutes of Myra Cohn Livingston to fill the recommended daily requirement of reflection. Two minutes of Cynthia Rylant for those who keep their jaws clenched tight, twitching; a minute of William Stafford to bring the flighty down to earth; thirty seconds of Valerie Worth to remind the hurried to take a look around. And Langston Hughes for perseverance, for hope.

I have a poem in my third book, *The Rainbow Hand: Poems About Mothers and Children* (1999), called "Hope." I wrote the poem when my son was three years old, at a time when I finally had started to see how amazing my mother was, to have done all that she did for me. I wrote it mainly for the adults in my audience. But a surprisingly large number of children have embraced it. Using the poem as a model, sixth grade boys, even, have spoken up in poetry workshops to compare their own mothers to similarly heroic plants and animals and objects. Mother as Ocean, full of life and mystery and power; Mother as Lion, a tough and fierce hunter, looking to provide for her children. Here is my poem:

Hope

In my own mother
I can see

I will need the strength of a bear,
strength to threaten those who would hurt my child—

Give me this strength.

I will need the softness of a deer,
to nudge my child down the right path—

Give me this softness.

I will need the courage of a fox
to leave my child behind, drawing harm my way—

Give me this courage.

I will need the calm of a tree,
knowing fires will happen,

and I will need to keep the hope I hold inside myself,
knowing that after the fires,

things grow again.

—from *The Rainbow Hand: Poems about Mothers and Children* by Janet S. Wong, illustrated by Jennifer Hewitson (1999).

My books are full of a range of poems, silly ones but also serious ones. When I visit schools, I tend to perform the more cheerful ones, so I am often surprised when children choose, as their favorite poem of mine, one of the "difficult" poems—poems about teasing and hurt feelings, hard times. But they do choose them, all the time. They seem to want to talk about things like fairness and death and lousy days, talk about them so they can understand, maybe, sort and solve their own crazy puzzles, too. Perhaps it is because of this that children like the image in "Hope" of the tree engulfed by fire—and surviving.

Once I met a woman at the airport who told me, "Isn't it horrible, the books they use in schools? I went to my child's classroom and they were reading a book about—death!" I nodded in agreement, adding, "And isn't it terrible how death is in all the Disney movies! Just think of poor Simba shouting 'Mufaaaasaaaa!' as his father falls and he sees the wildebeests trample him flat!" The poor woman thought I was a lunatic.

How could anyone malign a Disney movie? But this was not my intention. I wanted simply to point out that most children are exposed to these serious issues when they are just toddlers, thanks to Disney and other cartoons—so why not encourage them to think and talk—and read—about these things once in a while at the primary level, too?

Children like my difficult poems, poems like "Funeral," "To Caged Birds at the Poultry Store" and "Waiting at the Railroad Cafe" because they know the world can be dangerous and rotten and beyond our control—full of death, and bullies, and unfairness. Or, in the case of "Joyce's Beauty Salon" from *A Suitcase of Seaweed* (1996), children know that sometimes nothing feels more hopeless than a bad hair day. To read and write and talk about unpleasant feelings and experiences is to learn to deal with them. There is, of course, a danger that comes with reading a poem about bad things, just as there is a danger in getting the chickenpox vaccine. Poems about teasing and taunting—maybe my poem "Noise" from *Good Luck Gold* (1994)—might backfire and cause a child to invent cruel things to say. But if I were the doctor, I would push those poems as part of a T&T vaccine, facing the terrible, swift and contagious condition of Teasing and Taunting head on and early, when a child is strong, before he is exposed to such intolerance. First grade is not too soon.

In *Towards Multiple Perspectives on Literacy: The Fifty-Ninth Yearbook of the Claremont Reading Conference*, edited by Philip H. Dreyer (Claremont Graduate School, 1996), I wrote about the experiences that shaped my poem "Noise." Apparently I had forgotten—perhaps out of self-protection—the "Ching chong Chinaman" sort of teasing that I had suffered as a child. The first time I performed this poem for a group of children, it was at the request of their teacher. I had just finished a fun assembly, and these second graders let out a cheer when they heard me agree to read yet another poem. They probably expected another fun poem, though, and the room grew quiet as I read this very serious poem. When the poem was done, the only Asian child in the room raised his hand. Softly, matter-of-factly, he said, "That's happened to me." A blond boy sitting in back of him tapped his shoulder quickly and brusquely, and asked, "Who did it?"—with body language suggesting he would go find the offender and beat him up that instant. The next thing I knew, it was as if we were in a group therapy session. Every single child had something to say. "People make fun of my clothes," one said. "People make fun of my name," another added. "People make fun of the way that I talk;" "people make fun of my freckles." Seven years old, and each had been wronged by the world—and wanted to tell all about it.

I am writing now with a happier voice, I have been told. The biggest problem in *The Rainbow Hand* is the desperation of a teenage girl in "Mother, May I?"—a girl who feels she needs to do what her friends are doing, but whose mother is spoiling her plans. "So you have to do *everything* / they do, then?" the wicked mother asks. (I wrote this remembering the old "so you'll jump off a bridge, too" line.) Or maybe the biggest problem in the book is that of the boy whose mother hugs him in public. Surmountable problems, anyway. When I wrote the poems for *The Rainbow Hand*, I hoped to write a book that a child—eight or forty-eight—would want to share with a mother, maybe with a mushy little note tucked inside. Not all the poems in it are loving and sweet, though, and a few of the poems are even a bit angry at this creature capable of ruining the best of plans. As one title, "Crazy Mother," suggests, I think my mother can be downright mad. But the poem "Crazy Mother" is also a poem full of admiration for my mother's quirks. I want young readers to finish that book and think, "Yeah, I love my crazy mother, too," as they sit down to write a poem of their own.

My fourth collection, *Behind the Wheel: Poems About Driving* (1999), also contains several poems with a more consciously hopeful voice, such as "Ask a Friend." There is a fine line between "hopeful and meaningful" and "preachy and didactic" writing—and no one wants to be labeled didactic—so writing this sort of poem is to bring a certain risk upon oneself as a writer. Yet I feel that poets have a special opportunity, and perhaps obligation, to examine meaningful subjects and to dare to present "lessons" in their work. Reading a whole preachy picture book or novel might be overwhelming to a child, and each turn of the page presents another opportunity to put the book down or to shut it out. But poems are short, seldom longer than a page or a minute long. A child listening to a preachy poem might allow that poem to take hold before he realizes he's supposed to resist. By then, the "damage" is done; the message has become part of the child.

Who would not agree that we need more poems like Langston Hughes' classic "Mother to Son" from *The Dream Keeper* (1994)—and yet isn't this a preachy poem, a poem that exists mainly for its message of inner strength and perseverance? When I first heard the line "Life for me ain't been no crystal stair" I thought instantly of my own parents, and felt a tremendous surge of guilt, as I am the kind to "set down on the steps / 'Cause you finds it kinder hard." From time to time I remember this poem and allow the guilt to build until it propels me to do something productive. Messages can be good.

Ask A Friend

You don't always need
to go it alone.
Ask a friend
to give you a ride,
to help you out,
to get you home.

When you've found some better times,
you won't forget, you'll pay him back.

Let your friends be good to you.
Go along for the ride,
face in the wind.
—from *Behind the Wheel: Poems about Driving* by Janet S. Wong
(1999).

"Let your friends be good to you" is the message there, simple
words. So why do we forget—or so often refuse—to ask for help? I
pursue this idea of connections, our need for connecting and re-
connecting with friends, in my forthcoming collection, *Night Garden:
Poems from the World of Dreams*, illustrated by Julie Paschkis (in press).
The poem "Old Friend" attempts to put down the feeling I have when I
wake up from a dream in which an old forgotten friend has chosen to
visit. The message here is that we owe it to ourselves to keep in touch, to
write letters, to ask for letters, not to forget each other. Here is that
poem:

Old Friend

I had forgotten you, friend.
Is that why you came
into my dream?
I had forgotten you.

When I fall asleep again,
will you leave your address
on my pillow?

—from *Night Garden: Poems from the World of Dreams* by Janet S.
Wong, illustrated by Julie Paschkis (in press).

My first picture book, *BUZZ*, illustrated by Margaret Chodos-Irvine
(in press), follows this pattern of hope and light, too. As I wrote the free-
verse story poem that makes up this book, I became a child again,
hearing the buzzing sounds of the morning, from the buzzing of a bee to
the buzzing of snoring to Daddy's silver razor to the blender to the lawn
mower outside the window. And as it sometimes happens when we
writers are lucky, the process of writing this book transformed me, as I
buzzed out loud to the song of my hair dryer, buzzed in unison with the

coffee grinder, buzzed in sync with the computer's low hum. It was pure and silly fun, to buzz with my six-year-old son, to become sponges soaking up the sounds of the neighborhood.

This is the best I can do as a writer, to send children buzzing into the world with wonder, buzzing with ideas, buzzing with hope for another good day.

Note: Janet S. Wong's first two books, *Good Luck Gold* and *A Suitcase of Seaweed*, received the 1999 Recognition of Merit, awarded by the Stone Center for Children's Books.

TO REWARD OR NOT TO REWARD: EXAMINING A READING INCENTIVE PROGRAM FOR THIRD GRADERS

Gail L. Thompson

Abstract

This article examined the efficacy of an after-school reading incentive program for third graders who were reading below grade level. Three questions were addressed: (1) Did the students in the program say that their reading-related attitudes changed in any positive way? (2) Did the students' teachers notice any positive reading-related changes in the students? (3) Did the students' parents notice any positive reading-related changes in the students? The results revealed several positive reading-related changes. More students became equally comfortable with both silent and oral reading, whereas they had previously cited a preference for one or the other. The number of students who said that they were reading at home on a daily basis increased. Moreover, both parents and teachers agreed that the program had helped students to become better readers and to enjoy reading more. At least half of the parents and some of the teachers also noted that the program had improved the students' attitudes about school. The major finding is that reading incentive programs may be beneficial to young children who are poor readers.

Introduction

In today's post-modern society, literacy is one of the most important tools that individuals can posses. Literacy—or the "Literacy Club" as Smith (1992, p. 434) refers to it—is the foundation on which academic success rests (Chall, 1967; Flesh, 1955; Smith & Dechant, 1961). Despite numerous benefits of good reading and writing skills, many children throughout the nation—particularly those who are poor and from minority groups—tend to be less likely than White children and children from a higher socioeconomic status (SES) to have the reading and writing skills that are needed to be successful in school and consequently, to improve the quality of their lives. Several researchers maintain that the educational system has failed and is continuing to fail poor and minority children (Au, 1993; Darder, 1991; Kozol, 1991; Kunjufu, 1985; and Morgan, 1980). Since African American and Hispanic children comprise a disproportionate percentage of America's poor, the failure of public schools to improve the quality of life for many of these children has been an ongoing topic of concern for educators, politicians, and social scientists.

The National Assessment of Educational Progress's (NAEP) *Reading Report Card*, which examined reading trends from 1971-1984, revealed that although African-American and Hispanic students showed improvement in their reading performance, "the average reading proficiency levels of Black and Hispanic *17 year-olds* were only slightly greater than those for White *13 year-olds*. Though great improvements have been made, there is still a long way to go" (p. 33). More recently, the U.S. Department of Education (1997) published the reading proficiency scores of nine, thirteen, and seventeen-year-olds for several years from 1971 to 1996. For every year under review (for which there were scores listed for each ethnic group), African-American and Hispanic children had lower reading scores than White children (p. 114). Moreover, children who read daily had higher proficiency scores than children who did not (p. 116).

Kozol (1986) found that in proportion to population, African-American and Hispanic adults have higher illiteracy rates than Whites, with Whites comprising 16 percent, African Americans 44 percent and Hispanics 56 percent of the "functional or marginal illiterates" (p. 4). Although a disproportionate number of minority children and adults tend to have lower reading scores and poorer reading skills, White children and children from suburbia are not exempt from these problems. Honig (1999) reported that "as many as 30 percent" of the upper-elementary level students in some suburban schools "are reading below grade level" (p. 7). Au (1993) stated " . . . some of the weakest readers and writers at all age levels are European American students" (p. 2).

In an effort to improve the reading scores of children who were "at risk" for academic failure and grade retention, the "Literacy Club" was created. Numerous studies have indicated that there are strong correlations between grade retention and dropout rates, low self-esteem, and further academic failure. Moreover, minority children and lower-socioeconomic status (LSES) children, particularly those who are African-American or Hispanic males, are at a greater risk of being retained or placed into Special Education classes. The primary goal of the Literacy Club was to motivate poor readers to read by providing them with incentives and after-school tutorial services through a balanced literacy curriculum. One of the characteristics of poor readers in the upper-elementary school grades is a lack of motivation (Honig, 1999). Although many researchers agree that motivation is a crucial component of learning (Ruddell, 1999), and teachers should strengthen students' intrinsic motivation, there is some question about the efficacy of motivational programs that focus on external rewards (Cunningham & Allington, 1999; Kaplan, 1990). For example, Kaplan reported that extrinsic rewards can actually decrease intrinsic motivation "when prizes are given as a reward for performing activities students already enjoy . . ." (p. 287). Conversely, "extrinsic incentives are most useful when students are first learning a skill or when a teacher tries to get students involved in an activity in which they would not normally participate" (p. 287).

In light of the questions that have arisen about the efficacy of motivational programs that are based on external rewards, the current study seeks to examine the role of one reading incentive program in improving the reading-related attitudes of poor readers. Three questions will be addressed in the current article: (1) Did the students in the Literacy Club say that their reading-related attitudes changed in any positive way? (2) Did the students' teachers notice any positive reading-related changes in the students? (3) Did the students' parents notice any positive reading-related changes in the students?

Method

A 12-week session of the Literacy Club was offered at a California elementary school during the 1998-99 school year. The purpose of the program was to motivate third graders who were reading below grade level to read by offering after-school tutorial services and rewards. Several sets of data, questionnaires from teachers, students, and parents were collected to determine the efficacy of the program. An elementary school in southern California was selected as the appropriate school site because the school's administrators expressed a willingness to have the program conducted there. Moreover, the school is ethnically diverse and is populated by children from lower, middle, and upper-class households. Table I provides more information about the demographic make-up of the school.

Table I
1997-98 School Enrollment by Race/Ethnicity

Race/Ethnicity	Percent
American Indian	1.1
Asian	4.0
Pacific Islander	.24
Filipino	4.9
Hispanic	39.1
Black	15.5
White	35.2
Total	100.0

Students were selected by teacher recommendation as a result of their below-grade level reading test scores. Letters and permission slips were sent to their parents. Twenty-five permission slips were returned by a heterogeneous group of children from diverse ethnic and socioeconomic backgrounds, including children whose primary language was Spanish. Third graders were targeted because researchers have found that children who are not reading at grade level by the end of third grade are likely to remain academically behind for the rest of their years in school (Queen, 1999, p. 132). Cunningham and Allington (1999) found that older children who are poor readers are more likely than second and third graders to adopt avoidant behavior and negative attitudes towards reading and writing. Therefore, third graders were deemed to be the most appropriate group for the program.

On the first day of the program, parents attended an informational meeting. They were given an overview of the program and a list of strategies to use to help their children improve their reading and writing skills. Parents were also encouraged to sign up as volunteers. Additionally, graduate students were invited to serve as tutors. Two parents and 44 graduate students volunteered to work with the students. Students who were enrolled in graduate reading courses that were taught by the program director, earned extra credit for volunteering. An average of four graduate students attended each session, excluding the first and last sessions. The tutors worked with small groups of third graders and followed a lesson plan that was designed by the program director. The lesson plan was based on a balanced approach to literacy, with phonics and whole-language activities.

On the first day of the program, the third graders were given an overview of the program, nametags, and club rules. A questionnaire regarding their attitudes about reading and related reading practices was administered to each student. Because it was an after-school program, snacks were provided.

Each session thereafter consisted of several activities. In small groups, students participated in a phonics activity, listened to a story that was read orally, discussed the story, completed a related worksheet about the story, drew a related picture, handed in book reports that they completed at home, returned any books that they borrowed the previous week, selected new books, and received rewards (books, school and art supplies, activity kits, candy, and toys) if they had reached a Reading Milestone. Reading Milestones (see Appendix A) were reached when students took home books, completed related book reports, and turned them in to the program director. Over 400 books of increasing levels of difficulty for children and adolescents were on-site each week. Each student was permitted to borrow as many books as he/she desired. Students also read self-selected books orally with the tutors and their group members.

During the 11th session, a second questionnaire was administered to students. As a result of absenteeism and the fact that some students left early, only 17 copies of the second questionnaire were administered to students. For this reason, only the pre- and post-program questionnaires of the 17 students to whom both questionnaires were administered, were used for the current study. Parents and teachers also completed a related questionnaire. The last session ended with a Closing Ceremony. Parents, administrators, and school board members were invited to celebrate the Reading Milestones that each child had achieved and students received certificates.

The Questionnaires

The first student questionnaire, which was administered at the beginning of the 12-week program, consisted of 17 questions (see Appendix B). The second student questionnaire, which was administered at the end of the program, consisted of 18 questions (see Appendix C). The following questions were included on both questionnaires to determine if any change had occurred in the students' reading-related attitudes:

1. Do you like to read?   a)yes b)no c)don't know
2. Do you own any books?   a)yes b)no c)don't know
3. How often do you read books at home?_____
4. Do you read to your parents/guardians?   a)yes b)no
If so, how often do you read to them?_____
5. Do your parents/guardians read to you?   a)yes b)no
If so, how often do they read to you?_____
6. Do you read to anyone else at home?   a)yes b)no
If so, who?_____
7. Do you like to read a) orally b) silently c) both d) neither
8. How many times have you checked out books from the school library during the current school year?_____
9. How many times have you checked out books from the public library during the current school year?_____

The following questions only appeared on one of the questionnaires:

1. Did you enjoy being a member of the Literacy Club? a)yes b)no
If so, what did you like about the club?_____
If not, what did you dislike about the club?_____
2. Would you like to be in the club again next year? a)yes b)no

3. Do you think you will keep reading books at home after the club ends?   a)yes   b)no

Six third grade teachers recommended students for the program. All of the teachers responded to a questionnaire, consisting of four questions and space for additional comments. The following questions were on the questionnaire for teachers:

The Literacy Club Teacher Questionnaire

Date_____ Teacher_____

Student's name_____

Student's name_____

Student's name_____

Student's name_____

Student's name_____

Student's name_____

1. Do you think the Literacy Club has helped the aforementioned students?   a)yes   b)no

If you answered "yes," in what ways has it helped them? (Circle all that apply.)

a) to become better readers   d) to like school more

b) to enjoy reading more   e) other_____

c) to earn better grades _____

2. Would you recommend this program to parents?   a)yes   b)no

3. If you do not think that the program has helped your student(s) in any way, please explain why._____
_____

4. How can the program be improved?_____
_____

Ten parents returned questionnaires (see Appendix D). The following questions appeared on their questionnaire:

1. Do you think the Literacy Club has helped your child? a)yes b)no
If you answered "yes," in what ways has it helped your child? (Circle all that apply.)

a) to become a better reader   d) to like school more
b) to enjoy reading more   e) other_____
c) to earn better grades _____

2. Would you recommend this program to other parents? a)yes   b)no

3. If you do not think that the program helped your child in any way, please explain why._____
_____

4. How can the program be improved?_____
_____

Results

Student Questionnaires

Students' Attitudes About Reading

When the pre-program questionnaire was administered, all 17 third graders said that they enjoyed reading. When the post-program questionnaire was administered, however, one student said that he disliked reading and four said that they did not know if they liked to read. Four of the five students who gave different answers on the post-program questionnaire were boys. One of these boys, the only child who said that he disliked reading, was a Special Education student who entered the program two weeks after the program began.

Do you own any books?

On the pre-program questionnaire, 16 students said that they owned books and one did not answer. On the post-program questionnaire, 15 students said that they owned books, one said that he did not, and one said that he was uncertain. Both students who gave conflicting answers on the pre- and post-program questionnaires were boys who also gave conflicting answers to the previous question. One of these boys was the Special Education student who entered the program late.

Table II
Students' Pre-Program Responses to
"How often do you read at home?"

Response	Number
Daily	8
Weekly	5
Monthly	2
No Answer	1
Don't Know	1
Total	17

How often do you read at home?

On the pre-program questionnaire, answers to this question ranged from "daily" to "monthly." Nearly half of the students said, however, that they were reading at home on a daily basis (See Table II). On the post-program questionnaire, the majority of students said that they were reading at home on a daily basis. Three students gave vague answers (see Table III).

Do you read to your parents/guardians?

At the time when the pre-program questionnaire was administered, 14 of the students said they were already reading to their parents or guardians. Three students said that they were not. When the post-program questionnaire was administered, the same number of students answered "yes" but there were inconsistencies. One student who had previously stated "yes" said "no" on the post-program questionnaire. One who had previously stated "no," stated "yes" on the second questionnaire. A third student who had previously stated "no" did not answer this question on the post-program questionnaire.

Table III
Post-Program Responses to
"How often do you read at home?"

Response	Number
Daily	13
Weekly	1
Monthly	0
"Not Often"	1
"A Little Bit"	1
"A Lot"	1
Total	17

Table IV
Pre- and Post-Program Responses to
"Do your parents/guardians read to you?"

Pre-Program Response		Post-Program Response
Yes	10	12
No	7	5
Total	17	17

Do your parents/guardians read to you?

On the pre-program questionnaire, most of the students said that their parents or guardians read to them (see Table IV). On the post-program questionnaire, the number increased by two. Four students who had previously stated "yes" said "no," however, on the second questionnaire. One student who gave inconsistent answers elsewhere, also gave conflicting responses to this question (see Table V). Six students who had previously stated "no," said "yes" on the second questionnaire.

Do you read to anyone else at home?

When the pre-program questionnaire was administered, nine students said that they read to someone else at home besides a parent or guardian. At the end of the program, 10 students said that they were doing so. Three students, including the Special Education student who repeatedly gave conflicting answers, gave inconsistent answers to this question. On the pre-program questionnaire, each of the three said that he/she was reading to someone else at home but later said "no."

How do you like to read?

On the pre-program questionnaire, an almost equal number of students said that they liked to read orally or silently and very few said that they preferred both methods.

Table V
Inconsistent Responses to
"Do your parents/guardians read to you?"

Pre-Program Response	Post-Program Response	Number
Yes	No	4
No	Yes	6
Total		10

Table VI
Pre- and Post-Program Responses to
"How do you like to read?"

	Pre-Program Response	Post-Program Response
Orally	6	4
Silently	8	4
Both	3	9
Total	17	17

On the post-program questionnaire, however, the majority said that they liked both methods (see Table VI).

How many times have you checked out books from the school library during the current school year?

On the pre-program questionnaire, the majority of students said that they had used the school library, two said that they had not used it at all, and three said that they did not know if they had or not. On the post-program questionnaire, however, more students said that they did not know how often they had used the school library (see Table VII). Five students indicated that they were using the library more frequently but nine gave inconsistent or vague answers.

Table VII
Pre- and Post-Program Responses to
"How many times have you checked out books from
the school library...?"

	Pre-Program Response	Post-Program Response
0	2	0
1-9	1	1
10 or more	11	8
Unknown	3	8
Total	17	17

How many times have you checked out books from the public library during the current school year?

On both questionnaires, most of the students said that they were using the public library. On the post-program questionnaire, however, a greater number of students expressed uncertainty about how often they had used the public library.

Other Student Questionnaire Results

When asked if they enjoyed being members of the Literacy Club, all of the students said "yes." When asked what they liked or disliked about the program, no dislikes were mentioned. All students mentioned at least one aspect of the program that they liked best and several gave multiple answers regarding what they liked best. "Reading and improving reading skills" was the most commonly cited answer and "rewards/treats" was the second most commonly cited answer. When asked if they would like to be in the program the following year, however, one student said "no" and another student said that he was not sure. When asked if they thought that they would keep reading books at home after the program ended, three students said "no." These three students, including the Special Education student, repeatedly gave inconsistent answers on other sections of the questionnaires.

Teachers' Questionnaire Responses

All of the teachers said that the program had helped the students in at least one way, particularly to enjoy reading more. All but one teacher said that the program had helped the students to become better readers (see Table VIII). All of the teachers also said that they would recommend the program to parents. One teacher mentioned that the program was less effective with two of her Special Education students than with others. Another teacher suggested that the program be expanded to include a greater number of students.

Table VIII
Teachers' Responses to
"In what ways has the Literacy Club helped . . .students?"

Response	Number
To become a better reader	5
To enjoy reading more	6
To earn better grades	2
To like school more	2

N = 6

Parents' Questionnaire Responses

When asked if they thought the program had helped their children, all of the parents answered "yes." The two most commonly cited ways in which the parents thought the program had helped their children were "to become a better reader" and "to enjoy reading more." The third most commonly cited answer was "to like school more" (see Table IX). All of the parents said that they would recommend the program to other parents. In addition to suggesting that the program be expanded to include more children, one parent suggested that the program could be improved by requiring the students to read more chapter books. All of the parents said that they planned to encourage their children to read books at home after the program ended. When asked what they planned to do to ensure that their children would continue to read at home, most parents checked a number of responses. The most commonly cited answer was that parents would ask their children to read to them regularly. The second two most frequently cited answers were that parents would take their children to the public library and read to their children on a regular basis (See Table X).

Table IX
Parents' Responses to
"In what ways has the Literacy Club helped . . .students?"

Response	Number
To become a better reader	8
To enjoy reading more	7
To earn better grades	3
To like school more	5

N = 10

Table X
Parents' Responses to "What do you plan to do to ensure that your child will continue to read at home?"

Response	Number
Buy books for him/her	7
Buy magazines for him/her	5
Take him/her to the public library	8
Encourage him/her to use the school library	7
Read to him/her on a regular basis	8
Ask him/her to read to you regularly	9

N = 10

Discussion

The results of the questionnaires that were used to determine the efficacy of the Literacy Club, a reading incentive program for third graders who were reading below grade level, yielded several interesting findings. The main finding was that some of the reading-related attitudes of the students did change in positive ways. This was verified by parents, teachers, and the students themselves.

When the pre- and post-program questionnaires were administered to students, most of the third graders said that they enjoyed reading, owned books, were reading at home, and that their parents/guardians read to them at home. A number of students also said that they read to another family member at home, in addition to reading to their parents/guardians. All of the students said that they enjoyed participating in the program and most indicated that they would like to participate the following year. Most of the students also said that they planned to continue reading books at home after the program ended. One of the most obvious changes in the students' responses to the pre- and post-program questionnaires concerned the type of reading that they preferred. When the first questionnaire was administered, an almost equal number of students said that they preferred to read silently or orally and very few said that they preferred both types of reading. At the end of the program, however, most of the students said that they preferred both ways of reading. This implies that the oral reading that they did in their small-groups with the college tutors may have increased the confidence levels of some students. Another positive change was that the number of students who said that they were reading at home on a daily basis increased.

The fact that several students gave conflicting or inconsistent responses to questions is cause for concern. It appears that the questionnaire, as a data-gathering method, may not be as effective as other methods in gathering data from young children. Another possibility is that some of the questions were worded in a way that confused some of the children, particularly the Special Education student, who among other children, gave inconsistent answers on numerous questions. A third possibility is that the conflicting responses could have been an indicator of a negative change in some of their reading-related behaviors. Nevertheless, one of the main conclusions that can be drawn from the students' questionnaires is that even though a child may be reading poorly or below grade level, that child might still find pleasure in reading. Cunningham and Allington's (1999) assertion that poor readers in the upper-elementary school grades are more likely than second and third graders to adopt avoidant behavior and negative attitudes toward reading and writing, seemed to be validated by the current study.

Although there were inconsistencies in some of the students' questionnaire responses, when some of their answers were analyzed along with the questionnaire responses of parents and teachers, strong positive correlations surfaced. For example, all of the teachers and parents said that the program had benefited the students in at least one way. All of the teachers and most of the parents said that the program had helped the children to enjoy reading more. All of the teachers, except for one, and most of the parents also said that the program had helped the students to become better readers. Furthermore, all of the teachers and all of the parents said that they would recommend the program to other parents.

The results of the current study, particularly the data from the parents and teachers, indicate that reading incentive programs that use external rewards to motivate students to read can be beneficial to children in at least two ways: To help them to become better readers to help them to enjoy reading more. Nevertheless, caveats are necessary for a number of reasons.

First of all, the study relied on small student, parent, and teacher samples. Larger samples are needed to test the validity of the current findings. Additionally, a comparison of the parents' versus the students' responses to various questions, such as how often the students used the school and public libraries, how often they read at home, to whom if anyone they read at home, etc., might have revealed additional useful information. Moreover, the fact that at least one Special Education student gave conflicting responses on a number of questions and that one teacher said that the program seemed to be less effective with her Special Education students, implies that the reading-related attitudes of poor readers who have not been placed into Special Education programs and those of children who have, might differ in some ways. These findings warrant additional research.

Appendix A

The Literacy Club

Reading Rewards System

Club members will earn rewards for reading books and completing related book reports. During club meetings, members will have an opportunity to share this information with other club members. Rewards will be given according to the following **Reading Milestones**, as long as club members are reading books of increasing levels of difficulty. For example, once students have handed in 14 book reports, they should be reading chapter books to earn rewards thereafter.

Reading Milestones

Number of Books Read

1. One
2. Three
3. Five
4. Eight

10. Twenty
11. Twenty two
12. Twenty four
13. Twenty six

5. Ten
6. Twelve
7. Fourteen
8. Sixteen
9. Eighteen

14. Twenty eight
15. Thirty

Appendix B

The Literacy Club Questionnaire

Student's name_____Grade_____

Date_____School_____Teacher_____

Age_____Date of Birth_____Reading Level_____

Place of birth_____Ethnicity_____

1. How long have you attended this school?_____

2. How many brothers & sisters do you have?_____

3. Birth order?_____

4. Do you like school?   a)yes   b)no   c)don't know

5. Do you like to read?   a)yes   b)no   c)don't know

6. What are your favorite subjects in school?_____

7. Which subjects do you dislike?_____

8. What types of books do you like?_____

9. Do you own any books? a)yes   b)no   c)don't know

10. How often do you read books at home?_____

11. Do you read to your parents/guardians? a)yes   b)no
If so, how often do you read to them?_____

12. Do your parents/guardians read to you? a)yes   b)no
If so, how often do they read to you?_____

13. Do you read to anyone else at home?   a)yes   b)no
If so, who?_____

14. Do you like to read a) orally b) silently c) both   d) neither

15. How many times have you checked out books from the school
library during the current school year?_____

16. How many times have you checked out books from the public
library during the current school year?_____

17.   What do you want to be when you grow up? _____

Appendix C

The Literacy Club Questionnaire (2)

Student's name_____Grade_____
Date_____Teacher_____

1. Do you like school? a)yes   b)no   c)don't know
2. Do you like to read? a)yes   b)no   c)don't know
3. What are your favorite subjects in school?_____
4. Which subjects do you dislike?_____
5. What types of books do you like?_____
6. Do you own any books? a)yes   b)no   c)don't know
7. How often do you read books at home?_____
8. Do you read to your parents/guardians? a)yes   b)no
If so, how often do you read to them?_____
9. Do your parents/guardians read to you? a)yes   b)no
If so, how often do they read to you?_____
10. Do you read to anyone else at home?   a)yes   b)no
If so, who?_____
11. Do you like to read a) orally b) silently c) both   d) neither
12. How many times have you checked out books from the school
library during the current school year?_____
13. How many times have you checked out books from the public
library during the current school year?_____
14. What do you want to be when you grow up?_____

15. Did you enjoy being a member of the Literacy Club? a)yes b)no
If so, what did you like about the club?_____
If not, what did you dislike about the club?_____
16. Would you like to be in the club again next year? a)yes   b)no
17. Do you think you will keep reading books at home after the club
ends?   a)yes   b)no
18. If you have (or had) younger brothers or sisters would you like for
them to be in the club? a)yes   b)no

Appendix D

The Literacy Club Parent Questionnaire

Student's name_____
Date_____Teacher_____
1. How long has your child attended this school?_____
2. Does your child like school? a)yes   b)no   c)don't know
3. Does your child like to read? a)yes   b)no   c)don't know
4. What are your child's favorite subjects in school?_____
5. Which subjects does he/she dislike?_____
6. What types of books does he/she like?_____
7. Does your child own any books? a)yes   b)no
8. How often does he/she read books at home?_____
9. Does he/she read to you? a)yes   b)no
If so, how often?_____
10. Do you read to your child? a)yes   b)no
If so, how often?_____
11. Does your child read to anyone else at home? a)yes   b)no
If so, who?_____
12. Does he/she like to read a) orally b) silently c) both d) neither
13. How many times has your child checked out books from the school
library during the current school year?_____
14. How many times has your child checked out books from the public
library during the current school year?_____
15. Do you think the Literacy Club has helped your child? a)yes   b)no
If you answered "yes," in what ways has it helped your child? (Circle all
that apply.)
a) to become a better reader   d) to like school more
b) to enjoy reading more   e) other_____

c) to earn better grades _____

16. Would you recommend this program to other parents? a)yes
b)no
17. If you do not think that the program helped your child in any way,
please explain why._____

_____

18. How can the program be improved?_____

_____

References

Au, K. (1993). *Literacy instruction in multicultural settings*. Fort
Worth, TX: Harcourt Brace College Publishers.

Chall, J.S. (1967). *Learning to read: The great debate*. NJ: McGraw-
Hill Book Company.

Cunningham, P.M., and Allington, R.L. (1999). *Classrooms that work:
They can all read and write* (2nd ed.). NY: Addison Wesley
Longman, Inc.

Darder, A. (1991). *Culture and power in the classroom*. NY: Bergin
& Garvey.

Flesch, R. (1955). *Why Johnny can't read and what you can do about
it*. NY: Harper & Brothers, Publishers.

Honig, B. (1999). "Reading the right way: What research and best
practices say about eliminating failure among beginning
readers." In *Reading research anthology: The why of reading
instruction* (pp. 7-12). Novato, CA: Consortium on Reading
Excellence, Inc., Arena Press.

Kaplan, P.S. (1990). *Educational psychology for tomorrow's teacher*.
NY: West Publishing Co.

Kozol, J. (1986). *Illiterate America*. NY: Penguin Books USA, Inc.

Kozol, J. (1991). *Savage inequalities*. NY: Harper Perennial.

Kunjufu, J. (1985). *Countering the conspiracy to destroy Black boys*.
Chicago, IL: African-American Images.

Morgan, H. (1980). "How schools fail Black children." *Social Policy*,
January-February, pp. 49-54.

Queen, J.A. (1999). *Curriculum practice in the elementary and middle
school*. Upper Saddle River, NJ: Prentice Hall.

Ruddell, R.B. (1999). *Teaching children to read and write: Becoming an influential teacher* (2nd ed.). Boston, MA: Allyn and Bacon.

Smith, F. (1992). "Learning to read: The never-ending debate." *Phi Delta Kappan*, February, pp. 432-441.

Smith, H.P., and Dechant, E.N. (1961). *Psychology in teaching reading*. NJ: Prentice-Hall.

The Reading Report Card. (1971-1984). Princeton, NJ: National Assessment of Educational Progress at Educational Testing Services.

U.S. Department of Education. National Center for Education Statistics. *Digest of Education Statistics, 1997*, NCES 98-015. Washington, D.C.

BOOKS GO EVERYWHERE
ACROSS THE CURRICULUM

Carolyn Angus and Charlotte Van Ryswyk

In developing our book list, we have read widely among recently published children's books and selected titles that are good choices for both reading aloud and reading alone. We have indicated ways to enliven read-aloud sessions by linking music to some of the books, made curriculum connections, and suggested ways to encourage independent reading. (Note: We have listed only the composers and/or performers and the titles for the music tie-ins. Most of the recordings are available both on cassette and CD. An annotated bibliography of the recommended books is appended.)

Begin With Mother Goose: Nursery Rhymes and Songs

Here are our favorites of the new collections of nursery rhymes and songs and single-rhyme picture book editions.

- Allan Ahlberg's *Mockingbird*

Recordings:
Peter, Paul, and Mary. "Mockingbird" on *Peter, Paul and Mommy.*
McCutcheon, John. "Hambone" on *Mail Myself to You.*
—Listen to Peter, Paul, and Mary's performance of this traditional lullaby, then sing along with them. Compare the direction *Mockingbird* takes in Ahlberg's version with the traditional lyrics.
—Now listen to John McCutcheon's "Hambone." Compare this version with the traditional lyrics.
—Students may be inspired to write their own versions.

- Mary Ann Hoberman's *Miss Mary Mack: A Hand-Clapping Rhyme*

Recordings:
Jenkins, Ella. "Miss Mary Mack" on *This a Way, That a Way.*
Jenkins, Ella. "May-ree Mack" on *Multicultural Children's Songs.*

—Hoberman's book has directions for this hand-clapping game. Do the children know other versions?

—Listen to Ella Jenkins' recording of the traditional song, then play "May-ree Mack" from her album of multicultural children's songs.

—Read Hoberman's book again and sing her additional verses.

• Steven Kellogg's *A-Hunting We Will Go!*

—The tune and Kellogg's variation of the lyrics of this traditional English fox hunting song are included in his *A-Hunting We Will Go!*

—This is another song for which children can write original lyrics, using their knowledge of rhyming words. John Langstaff's *Oh, A-Hunting We Will Go* (Atheneum, 1974; Aladdin Paperbacks, 1991) is a good picture book for inspiring children to make illustrations to go with their lyrics.

• *One, Two, Skip a Few!: First Number Rhymes*
• Cooper Eden's *The Glorious Mother Goose*

Poetry, Please

We have selected collections of poems noteworthy for their imaginative and beautiful language and thought-provoking content as well as some light, playful verses.

• Kristine O'Connell George's *Little Dog Poems*
• Alice Schertle's *I Am the Cat*
• Francisco X. Alarcón's *From the Bellybutton of the Moon and Other Summer Poems/Del Ombligo de la Luna y Otros Poemas de Verano*
• James Stevenson's *Candy Corn*
• Kristine O'Connell George's *Old Elm Speaks: Tree Poems*
• Richard Wilbur's *The Disappearing Alphabet*
• Constance Levy's *A Crack in the Clouds and Other Poems*

Some Perfect Pairs

Read a picture book and a related nonfiction book, a poem and a nonfiction or picture book, a picture book and a novel, or other books that go together in some way.

- Uri Shulevitz' *Snow* and Jacqueline Briggs Martin's *Snowflake Bentley*
- Belinda Hollyer's *Dreamtime: A Book of Lullabies* and Kimiko Kajikawa's *Sweet Dreams: How Animals Sleep*
- Baba Wagué Diakité's *The Hatseller and the Monkeys* and Esphyr Slobodkina's *Caps for Sale*
- Naomi Lewis' *The Emperor's New Clothes* and Kathryn Lasky's *The Emperor's Old Clothes*
- Edward Lear's *The Owl and the Pussycat* and J. Patrick Lewis' *Boshblobberbosh: Runcible Poems for Edward Lear*
- Sallie Ketcham's *Bach's Big Adventure* and Jeanette Winter's *Sebastian: A Book about Bach*

Recordings:
Mr. Bach Comes to Call. Classical Kids.
—This recording is a story biography of Bach with interludes of his music.

- Verla Kay's *Gold Fever* and Sid Fleischman's *Bandit's Moon*

Recordings:
Beall, Pamela Conn and Nipp, Susan Hagen. *Wee Sing America.*
—*Wee Sing America* has three Gold Rush songs: "Sweet Betsy from Pike," "Old Settler's Song," and "Sacramento."

- *Simple Gifts: A Shaker Hymn* and Janet Hickman's *Susannah*

Recordings:
Copland, Aaron. *Bernstein Century-Copland: Appalachian Spring Suite, Rodeo, etc.*
Sharon, Lois, and Bram. "Simple Gifts" on *Elephant Party.*
—The Shaker hymn "Simple Gifts" is the best-known song from this sect. Aaron Copland used the hymn in his orchestral suite *Appalachian Spring.*
—After listening to "Simple Gifts " sung by Sharon, Lois, and Bram, play *Appalachian Spring* in which different instruments repeat the melody of "Simple Gifts." Do the children recognize the tune?

I Have a Tale to Tell

Make folktales, myths, and legends a part of your read-aloud sessions. We have included some new picture book editions of old favorites as well as collections of tales.

- Jim Aylesworth's *The Gingerbread Man*
- Jeanne Steig's *A Handful of Beans: Six Fairy Tales*

Recording:
My Favorite Opera for Children. (Pavarotti's Opera Made Easy Series).
—This fabulous CD anthology has five songs from Humperdinck's opera *Hansel and Gretel*: "Brother, Come Dance with Me," "I Am the Little Sandman," "Children's Prayer," "Song of the Gingerbread Children," and "Ral-la-la-la, ral-la-la-la." Listen to these songs after reading "Hansel and Gretel" in Steig's book.

- Nancy Van Laan's *So Say the Little Monkeys*

Recording:
Raffi. "Sambalelê" on *More Singable Songs for Children.*
—Van Laan's mischievous monkeys come from Brazil. The Brazilian song "Sambalelê" is perfect to pair with the book. With one hearing, children will be both chanting the folktale's refrain and singing the song.

- Suzanne Crowder Han's *The Rabbit's Tail: A Story from Korea*
- Mary Hoffman's *A Twist in the Tail: Animal Stories from Around the World*
- John Bierhorst's *The Deetkatoo: Native American Stories About Little People*

This Land Is Your Land: Social Studies Connections

- Woody Guthrie's *This Land Is Your Land*

Recording:
Guthrie, Woody and Guthrie, Arlo. *This Land Is Your Land.*

—You'll want to listen to this recording (and some of Guthrie's other classic folk songs) after reading this book.

• Harriet Ziefert's *When I First Came to This Land*

Recording:
Diamond, Charlotte. "When I First Came to This Land" on *Diamond in the Rough.*
—Folk songs, passed along orally, have various versions. Charlotte Diamond changed the first line of this song from "I was not a wealthy man" to "Not much money in my hand."
—Children enjoy creating motions for the cumulative verse of the song.

• Laurie Keller's *The Scrambled States of America*

Recording:
Beall, Pamela Conn and Nipp, Susan Hagen. "The United States" on *Wee Sing America.*
—Help children learn U.S. geography with this song that lists the 50 states in nearly alphabetical order.

• Candace Fleming's *The Hatmaker's Sign: A Story by Benjamin Franklin*
• Julius Lester's *Black Cowboy, Wild Horses: A True Story*

Recording:
Beall, Pamela Conn and Nipp, Susan Hagen. *Wee Sing America.*
—You will find six cowboy songs (some with horse sounds) on this recording of American songs. Choose one or all to accompany Lester's book.

In Celebration of Women

These are our picks of the new biographies of women. All are good choices for reading aloud during Women's History Month—and all year long.

• Jeanette Winter's *My Name Is Georgia: A Portrait*

- Laurence Anholt's *Stone Girl, Bone Girl: The Story of Mary Anning*
- Josephine Poole's *Joan of Arc*
- Milton Meltzer's *Ten Queens: Portraits of Women of Power*

I Love Guinea Pigs: A Science Connection

Here are two new picture books to read along with Dick King-Smith's *I Love Guinea Pigs*, a favorite of ours.

- Holly Meade's *John Willy and Freddy McGee*
- Margaret Shannon's *Gullible's Troubles*

Googols, Möbius Strips, and Rhombicosidodecahedrons: A Math Connection

- David M. Schwartz's *G Is for Googol: A Math Alphabet Book*

Music, Music, Music

Use these books to introduce children to jazz, gospel, popular, and classical music.

- Toyomi Igus' *i see the rhythm*
Recordings:
Joplin, Scott. *Greatest Hits.*
Ellington, Duke. *Hot Summer Dance.*
—These are two good recordings for exploring the rhythms of black music.

- Andrea Davis Pinkney's *Duke Ellington*

Recording:
Ellington, Duke. *Hot Summer Dance.*
—You will want to listen to some Duke Ellington music after reading this biography.

- Ysaye Barnwell's *No Mirrors in My Nana's House*

Recording:

Sweet Honey In The Rock. "No Mirrors in My Nana's House" (on the
    CD included with the book).

—This infectious song will have children singing along before they have
    finished hearing it the first time.

• Deborah Hopkinson's *A Band of Angels: A Story Inspired by the
    Jubilee Singers*

Recording:
Fisk Jubilee Singers. Vol. 1, 2 & 3.

• Amy Littlesugar's *Shake Rag: From the Life of Elvis Presley*

—Those interested in exploring the many musical influences on the
    young Elvis Presley will want to listen to recordings of the Grand
    Ole Opry, gospel music, and the Beale Street Memphis blues sound.

• Candace Fleming's *Westward Ho, Carlotta!*

Recordings:
Prokofiev, Sergei. *Peter and the Wolf.*
Britten, Benjamin. *Noah's Flood.*
Puccini, Giacomo. *Girl of the Gold West.*
—Carlotta sings songs from these three works of music in *Westward Ho,
    Carlotta!*

It's As Good As—Or Better Than Or Almost As Good As—The First Book!

Read aloud a sequel or the latest book in a series. Children will turn
to the earlier books for independent reading.

• Paul Brett Johnson's *The Pig Who Ran a Red Light*
• Diane Stanley's *Raising Sweetness*
• Sonia Levitin's *Taking Charge*
• Jean Van Leeuwen's *Amanda Pig and Her Best Friend Lollipop*
• Cynthia Rylant's *Mr. Putter and Tabby Take the Train*

- Cynthia Rylant's *Henry and Mudge and Annie's Good Move*
- Ursula K. Le Guin's *Jane on Her Own: A Catwings Tale*
- Amy Hest's *The Great Green Notebook of Katie Roberts (Who Just Turned 12 on Monday)*
- Avi's *Poppy and Rye*
- Geraldine McCaughrean's *The Bronze Cauldron: Myths and Legends of the World*
- Kathleen Krull's *Lives of the Presidents: Fame, Shame (and What the Neighbors Thought)*

Classic Connections

New books can serve as links to classics and other popular titles.

- Jane Johnson's *My Dear Noel: The Story of a Letter from Beatrix Potter* and Beatrix Potter's *A Tale of Peter Rabbit* and Potter's other little books
- Jon Scieszka's *Summer Reading Is Killing Me!* and a "Summer Reading List" (The list at the back of Scieszka's book is a good starting place.)
- Mordicai Gerstein's *The Absolutely Awful Alphabet* and other alphabet books for older readers

Old Favorites in New Editions

- H. A. Rey's *The Original Curious George*
- N. M. Bodecker's *Hurry, Hurry, Mary Dear*
- Jerry Pinkney's *The Ugly Duckling*
- Louis Untermeyer's *The Golden Books Family Treasury of Poetry*
- Edgar Eager's *Half Magic*

Picture Books

Here are our favorite new picture books. Children will want to hear these stories again and again or to read them on their own, after you have read them aloud.

- Jane Simmons' *Come Along, Daisy!*

- William Steig's *Pete's a Pizza*

Recording:
Diamond, Charlotte. "I Am a Pizza" on *10 Carrot Diamond*.
—Diamond's "I Am a Pizza" is the perfect song to go along with Steig's
    Pete's a Pizza. (Also in Spanish on Diamond's *Soy Una Pizza*.)

- John and Ann Hassett's *Cat Up a Tree*
- David McPhail's *Mole Music*

Recordings:
Beethoven, Ludwig van. *Symphony No. 6* and *Symphony No. 9*.
—McPhail's charming book has snippets of music printed above Mole in
    the illustrations. These come from actual musical scores. Much of it
    is from Beethoven, including his sixth and ninth symphonies.

- Janet Stevens and Susan Stevens Crummel's *Cook-a-doodle-doo!*
- Laura McGee Kvasnosky's *Zelda and Ivy*
- Alexis O'Neill's *Loud Emily*
- Stephanie Stuve-Bodeen's *Elizabeti's Doll*
- Mordicai Gernstein's *The Wild Boy: Based on the True Story of the
    Wild Boy of Aveyron*

Novels

   All of these books are great read-aloud/read-alone choices.

- Eva Ibbotson's *The Secret of Platform 13*
- J. K. Rowling's *Harry Potter and the Sorcerer's Stone*
- Gary Blackwood's *The Shakespeare Stealer*
- Louis Sachar's *Holes*
- Iain Lawrence's *The Wreckers*
- Susan Fletecher's *Shadow Spinner*

Recording:
Rimsky-Korsakov, Nicolas. *Schehrazade*.

—Rimsky-Korsakov's symphonic suite provides excellent mood music
for this story of a young girl who helps Schehrazade (Sharazad in the
book) gather stories to tell her husband.

• Gary Paulsen's *Soldier's Heart*

Books Go Everywhere Across the Curriculum
A Bibliography of Read-Aloud/Read-Alone Books
compiled by Carolyn Angus

Ahlberg, Allan. *Mockingbird.* Illus. by Paul Howard. Candlewick,
1998. In this playful variation of a traditional nursery song, family
members and friends offer gifts for baby's entertainment throughout
the day, ending with a birthday cake baked by Papa and a loving
tucking-in-bed by Mama. (folk song)

Alarcón, Francisco X. *From the bellybutton of the moon and other
summer poems/Del ombligo de la luna y otros poemas de verano.*
Illus. by Maya Christina Gonzalez. Children's Book Press, 1998.
Alaracón shares memories of his childhood summers in Mexico in
22 bilingual poems. Gonzalez's brightly colored folk art illustrations
are as spirited as the verses. (poetry)

Anholt, Laurence. *Stone girl, bone girl: The story of Mary Anning.*
Illus. by Sheila Moxley. Orchard, 1999. A picture book biography of
a fossil hunter. In 1811, at the age of 12, Mary Anning of Dorset,
England, discovered the skeleton of an ichthyosaur—the most
important fossil discovery of that time. (biography)

Avi. *Poppy and Rye.* Illus. by Brian Floca. Avon, 1998. Poppy the deer
mouse and Ereth, her prickly porcupine friend, join Rye in rescuing
Rye's large family of golden mice when their home alongside a
brook is destroyed by beavers. A sequel to *Poppy* (1995). (novel)

Aylesworth, Jim. *The gingerbread man.* Illus. by Barbara McClintock.
Scholastic, 1998. "No! No!/ I won't come back!/ I'd rather run/
Than be your snack!" shouts the sassy gingerbread man as he eludes
pursuers in this retelling of a classic nursery tale. A gingerbread man
recipe is included. (folklore)

Barnwell, Ysaye M. *No mirrors in my Nana's house.* Illus. by Synthia
Saint James. Harcourt, 1998. A young African American girl comes
to know the beauty in herself and the world around her by looking

into her grandmother's eyes. Saint James' boldly colored, stylized acrylic paintings combine with the lyrics of "No Mirrors in My Nana's House" to create a stunning picture book. The author reads the text and Sweet Honey In The Rock sings the song on the accompanying CD. (picture book)

Bierhorst, John (Ed.). *The deetkatoo: Native American stories about little people.* Illus. by Ron Hilbert Coy. Morrow, 1998. Bierhorst's introduction, straightforward retellings, guides to tribes and cultures and their lore, and extensive source notes and references make this collection of 18 stories a valuable addition to folklore collections. (folklore)

Blackwood, Gary L. *The Shakespeare stealer.* Dutton, 1998. Widge, an orphan, is sent by his master to London to steal the script of *Hamlet.* A great introduction to Shakespeare's Globe Theatre and 16th century London. (novel)

Bodecker, N. M. *Hurry, hurry, Mary dear.* Illus. by Erik Blegvad. McElderry, 1998. Blegvad's watercolor illustrations are a perfect match for Bodecker's humorous verse about a harried housewife who rushes to get ready for winter, while her lazy husband does nothing but give orders. (Originally published with Bodecker's own pen and ink drawings by Atheneum, 1976.) (poetry)

Diakité, Baba Wagué. *The hatseller and the monkeys.* Scholastic, 1999. Diakité retells an African version of the story of a hatseller whose wares are stolen by monkeys and illustrates the tale with beautiful paintings on ceramic tiles. The pages are bordered with stylized bands of mischievous monkeys. (folklore)

Eager, Edgar. *Half magic.* Illus. by N. M. Bodecker. Harcourt, 1999. Four children find an ancient coin that grants half of any wish and, once they master the art of double-wishing, the children embark on marvelous adventures in time and space. This is an updated edition of Eager's classic tale of magic (originally published in 1954). Eager's *Knight's Castle, Magic by the Lake,* and *The Time Garden* are also available in 1999 editions. (novel)

Edens, Cooper (Ed.). *The glorious Mother Goose.* Atheneum, 1998. Edens has selected illustrations by famous illustrators from the past—Randolph Caldecott, Arthur Rackham, Kate Greenaway, L. Leslie Brooke, and others—to accompany the 42 traditional rhymes in this collection. A glorious history of children's book illustration as well as a treasury of Mother Goose rhymes. (nursery rhymes)

Fleischman, Sid. *Bandit's moon.* Illus. by Jos. A. Smith. Greenwillow, 1998. Annyrose, a 12-year-old orphan, tells of her adventures with Mexican bandit Joaquín Murieta, the "Robin Hood of the California Gold Rush." (novel)

Fleming, Candace. *The hatmaker's sign: A story by Benjamin Franklin.* Illus. by Robert Andrew Parker. Orchard, 1998. To lift the spirits of his friend Thomas Jefferson after the Continental Congress changes his draft of the Declaration of Independence, Ben Franklin tells a story about the troubles a hatmaker has in trying to create the perfect sign for his shop. (picture book)

Fleming, Candace. *Westward ho, Carlotta!* Illus. by David Catrow. Atheneum, 1998. In this outrageous western adventure, world famous opera singer Carlotta Carusa becomes bored with opera houses and heads west to Deadeye, North Dakota, where her powerful voice pacifies snarling wolves, calls forth rain for the parched country, and tames outlaws. (picture book)

Fletcher, Susan. *Shadow spinner.* Atheneum, 1998. When Marjan, a 13-year-old crippled orphan with a gift for storytelling, enters the Sultan's harem, she helps Shahrazad gather the new stories that she must tell her husband each night to keep the Sultan from killing her. (novel)

George, Kristine O'Connell. *Little Dog poems.* Illus. by June Otani. Clarion, 1999. Thirty short poems and watercolor illustrations provide glimpses into a day in the life of a young girl and her pet, Little Dog— from being awakened by a cold nose to snuggling together under the covers at bedtime. (poetry)

George, Kristine O'Connell. *Old Elm speaks: Tree poems.* Illus. by Kate Kiesler. Clarion, 1998. George's short, beautifully-crafted poems offer striking images of trees. Some of the poems are descriptive; others reflect the relationship between humans and other animals and trees. (poetry)

Gerstein, Mordicai. *The absolutely awful alphabet.* Harcourt, 1999. Gerstein has something alliterative to say about each letter in the alphabet, and he cleverly links the letters: "A is an awfully arrogant Amphibian annoyed at.../ B who is a bashful Bumpkin bullied by.../ C a cruel, cantankerous Carnivore craving to consume..." and so on

Gerstein adds a pleasingly perfect painted portrait of each letter. (alphabet book)

Gerstein, Mordicai. *The wild boy: Based on the true story of the wild boy of Aveyron.* Farrar, 1998. This engaging picture book tells the story of a wild boy who was captured and taken in 1800 to Paris, where he was looked on as an oddity by the citizens and studied by scientists. (picture book)

Guthrie, Woody. *This land is your land.* Illus. by Kathy Jakobsen. Little, Brown, 1998. The folk-art paintings that accompany the lyrics of this well-loved American folk song take readers on a cross-country journey in the 1940s. A tribute to Woody Guthrie by folksinger Pete Seeger, a biographical sketch of Guthrie, and the music for "This Land Is Your Land" are appended. (folk song)

Han, Suzanne Crowder. *The rabbit's tail: A story from Korea.* Illus. by Richard Wehrman. Holt, 1999. A delightfully tangled tale involving a crying baby, an eavesdropping tiger, a thief, and a dried persimmon tells why rabbit has a stumpy tail. (folklore)

Hassett, John and Hassett, Ann. *Cat up a tree.* Houghton, 1998. Nana Quimby can't reach anyone by phone who is willing to help with her ever-increasing cat problem: more and more cats stuck up in a tree. There's a math lesson, too—the cats keep increasing by fives. (picture book)

Hest, Amy. *The great green notebook of Katie Roberts, who just turned 12 on Monday.* Illus. by Sonja Lamut. Candlewick, 1998. Katie Roberts introduced herself to readers at the age of seven in *Love You, Soldier* (1991) and continued her story in *The Private Notebook of Katie Roberts, Age 11* (1995). In this latest book in the series, Katie is in seventh grade, and her journal entries, letters, photos, and drawings reveal her preteen feelings about family and friends. (novel)

Hickman, Janet. *Susannah.* Greenwillow, 1998. Fourteen-year-old Susannah finds it difficult to accept the beliefs and ways of the frontier Shaker community that her father has joined following the death of Susannah's mother. She longs to be a part of a real family once again. (novel)

Hoberman, Mary Ann. *Miss Mary Mack: A hand-clapping rhyme.* Illus. by Nadine Bernard Westcott. Little, Brown, 1998. In this expanded version of a popular play rhyme, the elephant who "jumped so high,

high, high/ He reached the sky, sky, sky" lands in the middle of a
Fourth of July picnic. The melody and directions for the hand-
clapping game are included. (folk song)

Hoffman, Mary. *A twist in the tail: Animal stories from around the
world.* Illus. by Jan Ormerod. Holt, 1998. Hoffman retells ten
traditional animal tales, including an Anancy story from the
Caribbean, a variant of Aesop's "The Hare and the Tortoise" from
China, and a Turkish variant of the cumulative story "The Old
Woman and Her Pig." Source notes. (folklore)

Hollyer, Belinda (Ed.). *Dreamtime: A book of lullabies.* Illus. by Robin
Bell Corfield. Viking, 1999. For this dreamtime collection, Hollyer
has selected traditional bedtime rhymes and lullaby verses by
popular poets, including Eleanor Farjeon, Walter de la Mare, Felice
Holman, and Eve Merriam. (poetry)

Hopkinson, Deborah. *A band of angels: A story inspired by the Jubilee
Singers.* Illus. by Raúl Colón. Atheneum, 1998. Ella Sheppard, born
a slave in Nashville in 1851, helped to organize the chorus that went
on tour to raise money to save Fisk School and became the
successful Jubilee Singers. An author's note tells about the people
and real events that inspired *A Band of Angels.* (picture book)

Ibbotson, Eva. *The secret of Platform 13.* Illus. by Sue Porter. Dutton,
1998. Odge Gribble, a young hag, leads an ogre, a wizard, and a fey
through a magical door (open for only nine days every nine years)
under Platform Thirteen of King's Cross Railway Station, London,
on a mission to rescue the Prince of their fantasy island kingdom,
who was stolen as a baby nine years earlier. (novel)

Igus, Toyomi. *i see the rhythm.* Illus. by Michele Wood. Children's Book
Press, 1998. Striking art, poetic text, and a time line of historical
events are combined in a joyous celebration of African American
music. (nonfiction)

Johnson, Jane. *My dear Noel: The story of a letter from Beatrix Potter.*
Dial, 1999. Johnson tells the story of the origin of *The Tale of Peter
Rabbit* as an illustrated story in a letter to a sick child named Noel
Moore. (biography)

Johnson, Paul Brett. *The pig who ran a red light.* Orchard, 1999. In this
sequel to *The cow who wouldn't come down* (1993), Miss Rosemary
has a new problem: George the pig keeps trying to imitate Gertrude
the cow. Whether he is leaping from the porch in an attempt to fly

like Gertrude or behind the wheel of the pickup truck following the tractor-driving cow, George always ends up in trouble. (picture book)

Kajikawa, Kimiko. *Sweet dreams: How animals sleep.* Holt, 1999. A brief rhyming text and striking color photographs present the sleep habits of animals—orangutans, lions, sharks, black bears, koalas, sea otters, sloth, bats, hippos, flamingos, chipmunks, horses, and people. Endnotes offer additional information about the sleep behavior of the animals. (nonfiction)

Kay, Verla. *Gold fever.* Illus. by S. D. Schindler. Putnam, 1999. With dreams of riches in his head, Jasper leaves his family's farm and heads west with other miners seeking their fortunes during the days of the California's Gold Rush. The brief rhyming text and detailed colored pencil illustrations communicate the dreams and realities of thousands of forty-niners. (picture book)

Keller, Laurie. *The scrambled states of America.* Holt, 1998. What happens when the states get bored with their locations in the United States? They decide to swap sites—and readers get a fun-filled geography lesson. (picture book)

Kellogg, Steven. *A-hunting we will go!* Morrow, 1998. Kellogg has updated the fox hunting game of English folklore into a riotous bedtime romp organized by two not-ready-for-bed-yet children. The tune is included on the endpapers. (folk song)

Ketcham, Sallie. *Bach's big adventure.* Illus. by Timothy Bush. Orchard, 1999. Ketcham's fictional tale is based on a story that Bach liked to tell about the long walk he took as a child to hear the famous organist Jan Adam Reincken (1623-1722) play in St. Catherine's Church in Hamburg. (picture book)

King-Smith, Dick. *I love guinea pigs.* Illus. by Anita Jeram. Candlewick, 1995. A trip to the pet store may very well be the outcome of reading King-Smith's chatty guide to this "chunky and chubby and cuddly" rodent. (nonfiction)

Krull, Kathleen. *Lives of the presidents: Fame, shame (and what the neighbors thought).* Illus. by Kathryn Hewitt. Harcourt, 1998. Biographical sketches combine amusing anecdotes with information on the lives of the U.S. presidents. Hewitt's intriguing watercolor caricatures show the presidents with symbols of their terms in office, interests, and idiosyncrasies. (biography)

Kvasnosky, Laura McGee. *Zelda and Ivy.* Candlewick, 1998. Three short stories about a pair of fox sisters explore sibling rivalry—and loyalty—with warmth and humor. (picture book)

Lasky, Kathryn. *The emperor's old clothes.* Illus. by David Catrow. Harcourt, 1999. In this continuation of Hans Christian Andersen's classic story of "The Emperor's New Clothes," Lasky tells what happened to the old clothes that the emperor discarded before parading through the streets naked. (picture book)

Lawrence, Iain. *The wreckers.* Delacorte, 1998. Fourteen-year-old John Spencer survives a shipwreck on the coast of Cornwall, England, in 1799, only to learn that the villagers are wreckers: pirates who lure ships to the treacherous shores to plunder their cargoes. (novel)

Lear, Edward. *The Owl and the Pussycat.* Illus. by James Marshall. HarperCollins, 1998. Marshall's fanciful illustrations for Lear's nonsense verse feature a dapper Owl and an elegant Pussycat. (poetry)

Le Guin, Ursula K. *Jane on her own: A catwings tale.* Illus. by S. D. Schindler. Orchard, 1999. Not heeding the warning that "being different is difficult and sometimes very dangerous," Jane uses her catwings to fly off to the city. The fourth slim volume in an enchanting fantasy series: *Catwings* (1988), *Catwings Return* (1989), and *Wonderful Alexander and the Catwings* (1994). (novel)

Lester, Julius. *Black cowboy, wild horses: A true story.* Illus. by Jerry Pinkney. Dial, 1998. The true story of Bob Lemmons, a former slave who gained legendary status as a Texas cowboy. (picture book)

Levitin, Sonia. *Taking charge.* Illus. by Cat Bowman Smith. Orchard, 1999. When Mama takes a trip back to Missouri to care for her ailing mother, young Amanda takes charge of the family. She is determined to manage the household without any assistance, but hasn't counted on all the mischief Baby Nathan can get into. This is the third adventure for Amanda, the heroine of *Nine for California* (1996) and *Boom Town* (1998). (picture book)

Levy, Constance. *A crack in the clouds and other poems.* Illus. by Robin Bell Corfield. McElderry, 1998. With this collection of 38 poems, Levy invites readers to explore and marvel at our natural world. (poetry)

Lewis, J. Patrick. *Boshblobberbosh: Runcible poems for Edward Lear.* Illus. by Gary Kelley. Creative Editions/Harcourt, 1998. As Lewis suggests, this collection of poems (some based on actual events in Lear's life; others fanciful) is a way of "tipping a runcible hat and swashbuckling a grateful bow to the memory of a poet in return for the many pleasures he has given readers the world over." (poetry)

Lewis, Naomi. *The emperor's new clothes*. Illus. by Angela Barrett. Candlewick, 1997. Barrett's eloquent (and humorous) paintings for this retelling of Hans Christian Andersen's famous tale are set in pre-World War I Europe. Lewis provides an interesting foreword about Andersen and this story. (picture book)

Littlesugar, Amy. *Shake Rag: From the life of Elvis Presley*. Illus. by Floyd Cooper. Philomel, 1998. A poor 11-year-old Elvis Presley, whose proudest possession is a second-hand guitar, is introduced to soulful "good news" music when the Sanctified Church, a traveling church, pitches its tent in the town of Shake Rag. Bibliography. (picture book)

McCaughrean, Geraldine. *The bronze cauldron: Myths and legends of the world*. Illus. by Bee Willey. McElderry, 1998. McCaughrean retells 27 tales in her third collection of myths and legends from around the world. Notes on the origins of the stories are included. The earlier volumes are *The golden hoard* (1996) and *The silver treasure* (1997). (folklore)

McPhail, David. *Mole music*. Holt, 1999. Feeling that something is missing from his life, Mole learns to play the violin. As he creates beautiful music alone in his underground home, Mole wonders what it would be like to play for others ("Why, maybe his music could even change the world!"). It is through the illustrations that readers know that Mole does just that. (picture book)

Martin, Jacqueline Briggs. *Snowflake Bentley*. Illus. by Mary Azarian. Houghton, 1998. Azarian received the Caldecott Medal for the hand-colored woodcuts in this picture book biography of Wilson Bentley, a self-taught scientist who used photography to study the unique formations of snowflakes. Sidebars provided additional information about Bentley and his study of snowflakes. (biography)

Meade, Holly. *John Willy and Freddy McGee*. Cavendish, 1998. John Willy and Freddy McGee, a pair of guinea pigs who find life as pampered pets boring, get a little more adventure than they bargained for after they scamper out of their cage when the door is left open by mistake. (picture book)

Meltzer, Milton. *Ten queens: Portraits of women of power.* Illus. by
     Bethanne Andersen. Dutton, 1998. Milton offers brief biographies
     of ten queens: intelligent, courageous, and independent women "who
     held power in their own hands and used it." Included are Esther,
     Cleopatra, Boudicca, Zenobia, Eleanor of Aquitaine, Isabel of Spain,
     Elizabeth I, Christina of Sweden, Maria Theresa, and Catherine the
     Great. Source notes and bibliography. (biography)
One, two, skip a few!: First number rhymes. Illus. by Roberta Arenson.
     Barefoot, 1998. Arenson adds brightly colored collage illustrations
     to the counting rhymes, songs, and chants in this collection that will
     have children singing and chanting—and learning to count, add,
     subtract, and more. (nursery rhymes)
O'Neill. Alexis. *Loud Emily.* Illus. by Nancy Carpenter. Simon and
     Schuster, 1998. A young girl with a BIG voice may not fit into an
     ever-so-proper 19th century household, but she's a great hand to have
     on board a sailing ship. It is Emily who saves the ship from crashing
     on the rocky shore during a storm: Her loudly voiced "DANGER!
     PLEASE HELP! DANGER! PLEASE HELP!" calls forth whales
     that cradle the ship to safety. (picture book)
Paulsen, Gary. *Soldier's Heart.* Delacorte, 1998. Paulsen's short novel,
     loosely based on the experiences of a 15-year-old boy who lied about
     his age to fight for the Union in the Civil War, recreates the terrors of
     the battlefield. (novel)
Pinkney, Andrea Davis. *Duke Ellington: The piano prince and his
     orchestra.* Illus. by Brian Pinkney. Hyperion, 1998. A glowing
     tribute in word and art to "the jazz-playin' man"—"King of the
     Keys./ Piano Prince./ Edward Kennedy Ellington./ The Duke."
     Includes sources: bibliography, videography, and museum
     exhibitions. (biography)
Pinkney, Jerry. *The ugly duckling.* Morrow, 1999. Pinkney offers
     readers a glorious picture book edition of Hans Christian Andersen's
     classic tale. Pinkney's retelling is lively and his watercolor
     illustrations are beautiful. (picture book)
Poole, Josephine. *Joan of Arc.* Illus. by Angela Barrett. Knopf, 1998.
     An engaging picture book biography of Joan of Arc. Chronology.
     (biography)

Potter, Beatrix. *The tale of Peter Rabbit.* Warne, 1902. A nursery classic tells of disobedient Peter's misadventures in Mr. MacGregor's garden. (picture book)

Rey, H. A. *The original Curious George.* Houghton, 1998. The original watercolors produced by H. A. Rey for *Curious George* (paintings that were not used in the edition published in 1941) have been reproduced for this new collector's edition. (picture book)

Rowling, J. K. *Harry Potter and the sorcerer's stone.* Scholastic, 1998. The great destiny of Harry Potter, a neglected orphan, is revealed when Harry enrolls in Hogwarts School of Witchcraft and Wizardry. (novel)

Rylant, Cynthia. *Henry and Mudge and Annie's good move.* Illus. by Suçie Stevenson. Simon and Schuster, 1998. Cousin Annie moves in next door to Henry in this 18th adventure of a boy and his big dog in a superb easy-to-read series. (beginning reader)

Rylant, Cynthia. *Mr. Putter and Tabby take the train.* Illus. by Arthur Howard. Harcourt, 1998. In this latest book about elderly Mr. Putter and Tabby, his old yellow cat, plans for a pleasant afternoon trip with their neighbor Mrs. Teaberry and her dog, Zeke, get complicated when the ticket master informs them that pets can't go on trains. (beginning reader)

Sachar, Louis. *Holes.* Farrar, 1998. Stanley Yelnats is sent to a camp for juvenile delinquents in an arid Texas desert, where he is forced to dig large holes. So begins this well-crafted novel that has everything: an engaging main character, an unusual setting, an intriguing plot, a satisfying blending of the realistic and fantastic—and humor. Newbery Medal book. (novel)

Schertle, Alice. *I am the cat.* Illus. by Mark Buehner. Lothrop, 1999. A celebration of cats in well-crafted poems and expressive paintings. (poetry)

Scieszka, Jon. *Summer reading is killing me!* Illus. by Lane Smith. Viking, 1998. In this latest book in the Time Warp Trio series, Joe, Sam, and Fred get trapped inside their summer reading list. (novel)

Schwartz, David M. *G is for googol: A math alphabet book.* Illus. by Marissa Moss. Tricycle Press, 1998. A wealth of information about mathematical terms—A is for Abacus, B is for Binary, C is for Cubit, and so on—is offered in an interesting (and frequently humorous) way. (nonfiction)

Shannon, Margaret. *Gullible's troubles*. Houghton, 1998. Gullible Guineapig is just that—gullible. He believes everything his Uncle Bernard, Aunt Sarah, and Cousin Lila tell him. In the end, however, one of their outrageous suggestions (eating 50 carrots one after another will make you invisible) turns out to be just what Gullible needs to escape from the cellar monster, and it is the relatives who are in danger. (picture book)

Shulevitz, Uri. *Snow*. Farrar, 1998. With the fall of one snowflake, a young boy and his dog begin their celebration of the first snowfall of the season while adults declare that it will come to nothing. "Snowflakes keep coming and coming and coming," however, until the whole city is blanketed with snow— much to the delight of the boy. Caldecott honor book. (picture book)

Simmons, Jane. *Come along, Daisy!* Little, Brown, 1998. Ignoring the "Come along, Daisy!" of her mother, a charming yellow duckling gets lost when she goes exploring around their pond. (picture book)

Simple gifts: A Shaker hymn. Illus. by Chris Raschka. Holt, 1998. Raschka used oil crayon on pastel paper to create boldly colored illustrations, which he says were inspired by Paul Klee's *Dark Voyage*. The illustrations are not in the style usually associated with the Shakers, but they definitely are pleasing. A note about the Shakers and the music for "Simple Gifts" are included. (hymn)

Slobodkina, Esphyr. *Caps for sale*. Harper, 1940. Thieving monkeys imitate a cap peddler in this classic "tale of a peddler, some monkeys and their monkey business." (picture book)

Stanley, Diane. *Raising Sweetness*. Illus. by G. Brian Karas. Putnam, 1999. Sweetness once again saves the sheriff (now Pa to Sweetness and the seven other orphans he adopted in *Saving Sweetness* (1996)). The problem: Pa's completely inept at cookin' and housekeepin'. The solution: He needs to think about gettin' married. And, of course, Sweetness is just the one to help things along. (picture book)

Steig, Jeanne. *A handful of beans: Six fairy tales*. Illus. by William Steig. HarperCollins, 1998. Fresh retellings of six fairy tale classics: "Rumpelstiltskin," "Beauty and the Beast," "Hansel and Gretel," "Little Red Riding Hood," "The Frog Prince," and "Jack and the Beanstalk." (folklore)

Steig, William. *Pete's a pizza.* HarperCollins, 1998. It's raining and Pete is in a bad mood. His father knows just what to do to cheer Pete up—make him into a pizza! (picture book)

Stevens, Janet and Crummel, Susan Stevens. *Cook-a-doodle-doo!* Illus. by Janet Stevens. Harcourt, 1999. Big Brown Rooster decides to bake a strawberry cake using a recipe in Great-Grandmother Little Red Hen's *The Joy of Cooking Alone.* He, however, has the not-so-expert help of friends Turtle, Iguana, and Potbellied Pig. Information on ingredients, cooking utensils, and baking instructions are given in sidebars. The recipe for "Great-Granny's Magnificent Strawberry Shortcake" is included. (picture book)

Stevenson, James. *Candy corn: Poems.* Greenwillow, 1999. The short, illustrated poems in *Candy Corn* are diverse in form and subject. A special treat for those who have enjoyed Stevenson's *Sweet corn* (1995) and *Popcorn* (1998). (poetry)

Stuve-Bodeen, Stephanie. *Elizabeti's doll.* Illus. by Christy Hale. Lee and Low, 1998. Elizabeti, a young Tanzanian girl, has a baby doll (actually a rock) named Eva, which she lovingly nurtures while Mother cares for Elizabeti's new baby brother. (picture book)

Untermeyer, Louis (Ed.). *The Golden Books family treasury of poetry.* Illus. by Joan Walsh Anglund. Golden Books, 1998. Untermeyer collected more than 400 poems and organized them by theme. His introductory notes and commentaries on the poets and the writings add interest. This is a new edition of the Golden Books anthology originally published in 1959. (poetry)

Van Laan, Nancy. *So say the little monkeys.* Illus. by Yumi Heo. Atheneum. 1998. This Brazilian folktale explains why the tiny "blackmouth" monkeys sleep in tall palms which are full of sharp thorns: they are too busy having fun and munching on bananas to build suitable shelters from rain, wind, and the jaguar. The language of the text and the stylized illustrations are both as playful as the monkeys. (folklore)

Van Leeuwen, Jean. *Amanda Pig and her best friend Lollipop.* Illus. by Ann Schweninger. Dial, 1998. In this latest book in the Amanda Pig easy-to-read series, Amanda and Lollipop share the fun of playing at each other's house. A sleepover at Lollipop's, however, proves to be too much for young Amanda. (beginning reader)

Wilbur, Richard. *The disappearing alphabet.* Illus. by David Diaz.

Harcourt, 1998. What would happen to the world we know if the letters of the alphabet began to disappear? Wilbur explores some possibilities in 26 short, humorous poems. Diaz's imaginative computer-generated illustrations match the wit and whimsy of the verses. (poetry)

Winter, Jeanette. *My name is Georgia: A portrait.* Silver Whistle/Harcourt, 1998. In this portrait of Georgia O'Keeffe, Winter treats the painter's life as autobiography. Winter's illustrations include images O'Keeffe often used. Selected bibliography. (biography)

Winter, Jeanette. *Sebastian: A book about Bach.* Browndeer/Harcourt, 1999. "The first Voyager spacecraft was launched in 1977. On the spacecraft there is a recording of sounds from Earth. Should the spacecraft encounter any life beyond our galaxy, the first sound that will be heard is the music of Johann Sebastian Bach." This foreword establishes the tone for Winter's picture book biography of Bach—a tribute in simple words and striking paintings. (biography)

Ziefert, Harriet. *When I first came to this land.* Illus. by Simms Taback. Putnam, 1998. A poor immigrant begins to build a life in America by buying a farm. Taback's brightly colored illustrations add to the fun of Ziefert's retelling of this traditional song. (folk song)

HOPE OF THE NEW CENTURY: EARLY LITERACY, THE EMPOWERMENT OF TECHNOLOGY

Jean M. Casey

Imaginative progressive teachers who had computers in the classrooms and were prepared to give students the time and support to learn often created wonderfully fertile learning environments--children can learn to use computers in a masterful way; learning to use computers can change the way they learn everything else (Seymour Papert, 1993, *Mindstorms*).

The first question administrators, teachers and parents ask is, "Will computers make a difference in the learning that occurs in the classroom?" Past studies failed to answer this question or answered it negatively because they used standardized reading test scores as their only measure. The Simi Star Project, a collaborative grant between six school districts and IBM tested the effectiveness of computers in the classroom and effects of integrating technology into the curriculum. As a university researcher and reading professor, I was asked to be the evaluator of the Simi Star Project. It resulted from a grant between IBM and Simi Valley, Ventura, Oxnard, Santa Barbara, Orcutt and Point Hueneme school districts all located in Southern California. Six networked computers were placed in 24 kindergarten and first grade classrooms to test integration of technology in the curriculum and measure the effect on writing and reading development of the students. I worked with a team of educators and developed a qualitative study to examine these classrooms. The software used in the study was Writing to Read, Stories and More, Children's Writing and Publishing. The teachers were carefully trained, parents were informed as partners, and students were given daily access to the computers for writing their own language experience stories. The students also were given phonemic awareness and systematic phonics support. The researchers used observations, interviews, questionnaires, portfolio assessment as well as reading attitude tests to measure the students writing and reading development. The experimental classrooms were compared to control classrooms without computers but a similar approach to teaching. The results were significant. All students in the experimental classrooms using Writing to Read, averaged at least two writing levels higher based on a holistic evaluation than those in the control classrooms. The experimental group had a significantly higher positive reading attitude score than the control group (Casey, 1997). Teachers and parents all rated this program excellent on a 5 point rating scale.

These classrooms became writing, reading and publishing labs; the teachers kept samples of the children's daily writing in portfolios that were used as assessment and in parent conferencing.

That was just the beginning. One computer in each room was connected to the Internet and children chose pen pals from other states and Europe. One kindergarten child proudly wrote his daily message to his friend in Alaska. A fifth grade classroom was working on a project about the world environment online with a fifth grade classroom in Paris, France. Children were not only experiencing the meaningful use of writing and reading, but developing life long friendships and understanding of children like them all over the world.

The teachers quickly were caught up in the enthusiasm they saw in their student writers. They produced more communications and newsletters for their parents than teachers in the control classroom were able to do; they also designed lessons and modeled stories that they wrote specifically on the computer and shared on the projection monitor with their students. Teachers became hooked on e-mailing each other, finding lesson ideas on the Internet, asking questions of the university people pertaining to certain theories and ideas. The teachers spent time reflecting on their teaching with the university researcher and also building a community of support with their peer teachers in the project.

The six computers were busy all day. When the language arts block was over and children had written their own stories, it was time to use the computers with HyperStudio, a software-authoring program for children to design their own multi-media research reports in science and social studies. Math, art, graph making was all a part of the daily curriculum; there never was an empty seat in front of a computer.

Children received 90 percent more time using computers then those who visit a lab once a week for an hour.

The teachers also discovered that the daily writing of their students offered the best assessment possible of the skills the child had already mastered and those that were needed. Look at Brandon's work in the figure below. He is a first grade student. Without the computer, based on his immature drawing, a teacher would conclude (using Gesell Developmental Scales) that he was at a 3-year-old maturity level. He would be mislabeled and misplaced. But given the use of the computer we can see that Brandon has the phonemic awareness skills, sentence structure, punctuation and story sense of a six-year-old or older. How many students have we misjudged in the past based only on their underdeveloped motor coordination with a pencil. Giving them a new tool unlocks the intelligence they have and allows them to express it for all to see.

Figure 1

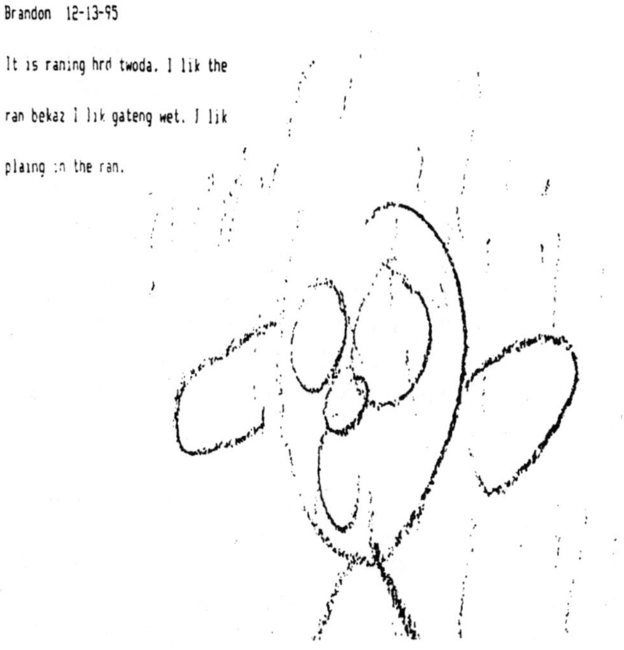

Brandon 12-13-95

It is raning hrd twoda. I lik the

ran bekaz I lik gateng wet. I lik

plaing in the ran.

At What Grade Level Should We Have Computers in the Classroom?

Some administrators and parents might think that high school is the time to start computer use, some third grade. As the evaluator of the Simi Star Project, reading one thousand writing samples from five- and six-year-olds was enlightening and taught me a valuable lesson. These young children could write much more than we ever imagined that children that age were capable of doing. It proved that they had many more ideas than they had been able to express with pencil and paper.

The time to have computers in the classroom is the first day children enter school. The computer is a sophisticated writing tool that gives students auditory feedback, a visual display and control of their learning. It is a tool that can allow any student to feel like an author on the first day of school!

When I taught first grade twenty years ago and a child entered the classroom and said, "Teacher when will I learn to read?" we had to say, "Not until you have mastered the three hundred fifty skills on our district reading scope and sequence chart. The first one is consonant b, there are three hundred forty nine more." The discouraged child went back to his seat.

Today when a child enters kindergarten and says, "When will I learn to read?" The professional teacher says, "Today!" Using KidWorks Deluxe (Knowledge Adventure) the talking word processor, a child can sit down write his name, mom's name, his dog's name, letters of the alphabet, whatever he wants to write. He prints it out and has immediate proof of his literacy and authorship. He can take home his printed piece that very day and have it posted on the refrigerator for all to see. He can write; he can read!

Another important aspect in integration of computers into the curriculum is meeting the needs of the mainstreamed students. Some are students who in the past, because they had not yet developed adequate motor coordination, were often mislabeled learning disabled, dyslexic, or attention deficit disorder (A.D.D.). The computer really is essential for changing the lives of these children. The following stories are about two of the many children I worked with using the talking word processor.

Dyslexic Nicholas: The Heavy Label

Nicholas taught me the next lesson. He was coming to the remedial reading clinic at the university. He was flunking his subjects at school and his parents were frantic. I trained the reading clinicians and then they worked weekly one hour a week with the children labeled "remedial readers." Rose was Nicholas's tutor and she came to me distressed. She felt she had been trying all the ideas we spoke about in class but they were not working with Nicholas. I agreed to work with him at the next session and Rose would observe through the two-way mirrors. The next week I was waiting for Nicholas. When he arrived, I told him I would be his tutor for this one session and asked him to tell me about himself. He said, "My name is Nicholas and I am twelve years old. When I was six they told me that I have dyslexia and would never learn to read, and I have not ever learned. I not only cannot read, I get an F in handwriting and math." He couldn't understand it because he liked math. He was good at it and knew all the answers through mental calculation and could respond with them orally. However, the teacher insisted on written responses on timed tests. This approach made Nick nervous and with his poor handwriting he was always destined to get an F. Because of these grades his dad would not let him play with his friends after school, he was ordered to stay in his room and do homework. Nicholas was a very depressed twelve year old as he stated, "I hate my life; I wish I was dead!"

Amazingly, Nicholas had just diagnosed his problem. He was not learning to read because he believed he could not. He was bright and could respond orally but had trouble with handwriting and got tense under pressure. My first step was to work on this attitude of failure that he had held on to for the past six years. I told him about Albert Einstein, Nelson Rockefeller, Tom Cruise, to name a few who were dyslexic. Nicholas was very surprised to hear that and certainly did not think those men were dumb. I reassured him that he was not dumb either, but had not been given opportunities to learn the way he could most effectively. Nicholas was a case just like Patrick in Denny Taylor's book, *Learning Denied*, the school system had failed him (Taylor, 1991).

As we continued to work together, I asked Nicholas if he had ever used a computer? "No," was his reply. I introduced Nicholas to the talking computer with KidTalk software (Casey, 1983). He immediately began to compose his life story. Then he was able to read it and print it out. "You are a very bright boy Nicholas, you just needed a more sophisticated writing tool to help you put all your great ideas down on paper," I told him. It took more than a talking computer, it took a teacher who understood Nick's particular learning strengths and needs and cared enough to encourage him and help him learn in other ways. But it was definitely a breakthrough and turned Nick on to learning once more.

David was a student in the first grade at one of the Simi Star Project schools. I entered his classroom and saw a 10-page story on the bulletin board. I began to read it. David walked up to me and said, "Do you like that story? It's mine? Follow me to the computer and I will show you more, it is twenty-six pages long now." I followed him with great interest. He took me to a computer, put headphones on my head and proceeded to play the story for me. I listened in awe as the computer began to read his long story of the dinosaurs' lives, George Washington's life, and his grandma's life.

At recess I could hardly wait to go to the teachers' lounge and speak with his teacher. "Mary," I said to her, "David must be a gifted first grader. His story is outstanding, well above what you would expect from an average first grader." She laughed, "Oh no, "she said, "you should have seen him at the beginning of the year, he was identified as A.D.D. and he couldn't hold a pencil or write and he hated school. Now he doesn't want to go out even for recess when he is in the middle of one of his great stories!" I drove home thinking about a technology that had made a student write in a gifted manner even though he had been labeled a poor writer. A technology that compelled a student, who had been labeled with attention deficit disorder, to sit for long periods of time thinking, creating, imagining a twenty-six page story. If he could sit that long writing something of interest to him, then sitting still was not the problem, having something worthwhile to attend to seemed more probable. Something is wrong with the labels, I concluded. The students are fine when given the right tools and environment.

Thomas Armstrong, psychologist, teacher, and consultant has years of experience working with children who have attention and behavior problems. He has the belief that these children are at core fully intact, whole, and healthy human beings...that the best way to help them is to provide the kinds of nurturing, stimulating, and encouraging inventions that are good for all kids (Armstrong, 1995). The computer provides the motivation, stimulation, and control in the learning environment. All you need to provide is nurturing and encouragement. I worked with ESL, LEP, and Down's syndrome students and the computer was equally empowering, an essential learning tool for them. For gifted students the computer finally freed them from the boredom of classroom work too easy for them and allowed them to create, imagine and write far beyond anyone's expectations.

In summary, the time has come for us to integrate computers as tools in every classroom. Six networked computers worked well in a classroom of twenty-five students, but one per student as envisioned by Seymour Papert (1993) should certainly be our goal. We must help teachers recognize the power of the computer as a problem solving tool when used by the learner to construct his own literacy. They are as empowering to five-year-olds as they are to you once you discover you can use PowerPoint to produce a presentation that will impress your staff and parents. They need to be in every classroom, and in every school. Money must be set aside for training to help teachers understand that this is a new paradigm, one in which students create stories directly from their mind into the computer and then have the control and power for easy editing. Untrained teachers think stories must be written out in pencil first, then corrected and then laboriously typed by the child into the word processor. There is no surer way to make children dislike technology than to use the approaches designed for the pencil. It is as if you had to wash your clothes on the washboard by hand before you put them in your washer! Wouldn't you hate that?

John Henry Martin, educator and creator of Writing to Read summed up the benefits of computer use for literacy for all students, he said, "The computer can give the learner the world's most beautiful feeling, the Greek 'Eureka,' I got it, I know it, I can see it, I can understand it! That's a transforming feeling; to be awakened from dormancy, from sadness to strength, to dignity. I can write; I can read! Do this for your students today!"

A 21st Century technology equipped classroom, trained teachers, a risk-free learning environment, and you are ready; when the three and four-year-olds doing Broderbund's Living Books on their home computers today come to your classroom door next year and ask, "Where is the CD-ROM?" "When do I learn to read and write?" Your teachers will say, right over here! Right now!

References

Armstrong, T. (1995). *The myth of the ADD child: 50 ways to improve your child's attention span without drugs, labels, or coercion.* NY: Dutton.

Casey, J. M., and M. Cron. (1983). *KidTalk.* Long Beach, CA: First Byte.

Casey, J. M. (1991). "The language machine: Technology can be a ticket for entry into the literacy club." *The California Reader,* 24:4, pp. 12-15.

_____. (1992). Simi Star Project Report. Long Beach, CA: California State University.

_____. (1997). *Early literacy: The empowerment of technology.* Libraries Unlimited: Englewood, CO. P.O. Box 6633, Englewood, CO 80155-6633 or 1-800-237-6124 or lu-books@lu.com

Knowledge Adventure. (1990). KidWorks Deluxe, Talking Word Processor and Graphic Design Software, 4100 West 190th St. Torrance CA 90504 1-800-545-7677

Papert, S. (1993). *Mindstorms: Children, computers and powerful ideas.* NY: Basic Books.

_____. (1993). *The children's machine.* NY: Basic Books.

Taylor, D. (1991). *Learning denied.* Portsmouth, NH: Heinemann.

TEAM GAMES IN THE SECONDARY LANGUAGE ARTS CLASSROOM

Pete C. Menjares

Introduction

"Ok, contestants. Prepare to answer the following question for your team. Who was the author of the short story entitled the "Black Cat?" At the sound of a bell three students leap out of their seats and run to the white board and proceed to write the answer to the teacher's question as fast as they can and with correct spelling. Each student writes "Edgar Allan Poe" as the answer to the teacher's question. The first student to write the name first without error is proclaimed correct and his team awarded a point. As the teacher declares the representative from "Team Two" the first to write the answer to the question correctly, one of the three teams celebrates the awarding of the point with shouts of "Yes," "Alright" and with "high fives" as members of the other two teams sigh with disappointment. The disappointment is short-lived, however, as there are plenty of additional opportunities to answer questions before the review game is over. From that point the teacher proceeded to a second question, and a third, and a fourth, and so on until all of the questions written on index cards have been asked, but not before each team member had been given a chance to answer at least one question. The game is intense as students from each team have a chance to answer a question. The contestants are cheered on by their teammates as they await the reading of the next question. Finally, after a period of about 20 minutes, the score keeper appointed by the teacher tallies the points and notes each team's earnings on the board with the team having the highest total being declared the first place winner. The other two teams in the game earn the distinction of being the second and third place winners. In this class, no one loses, everyone wins. The use of team games similar to one just described in the Language Arts classroom is not uncommon. As a supervisor of student teachers, I regularly walk into secondary classrooms to observe the instruction of student teachers engaging their students in a variety of collaborative learning techniques such as the use of team games for the review of text material or for pretests. The effective use of a variety of cooperative group approaches is an important instructional approach in the secondary classroom (Vacca & Vacca, 1999). Through my observations, I have come to find that some of these efforts are successful while others are not. Therefore, the purpose of this paper is to (1) share the findings of my observations of the use of team games in the middle and senior high school Language Arts classroom, (2) note a few of their benefits as well as their limitations, and (3) propose a number of practical suggestions for their use.

Background

The observations that were made of student teachers and their master teachers in 9th and 10th grade English/Language Arts and English Language Development classrooms took place over the course of two semesters. The schools in which the student teachers were intentionally placed were high in student diversity and represented a broad range in academic ability. During this period I had observed student teachers in mostly low ability classrooms and in classrooms that contained high concentrations of English language learners. Of these English language learners, the majority were from Latino backgrounds with Spanish being the language primarily spoken in the home. In each of these contexts, the student teachers observed utilized a form of team games of the "Jeopardy" or "Trivial Pursuit" type with evenly matched teams, a score keeper, points earned, and sometimes prizes. The games were primarily used for the purpose of reviewing text material and as pre-tests. In each of the observed instances the teacher generally divided the class into groups of approximately seven to ten students (depending on the size of the class) with each of these groups forming a "team." The materials used for the review game were taken directly from the text material used in the classrooms and were age and reading level appropriate. These text materials were usually in the form of a reading or literature anthology or other trade book, such as a novel or other teacher selected materials, such as articles or newspaper clippings.

Once the information or concepts used for review were identified, the teacher or students set out to prepare anywhere from 25 to 30 questions for each unit of study. The student teachers in most cases generated the questions but at times received assistance from their master teachers. In some instances the learners generated some of the questions themselves or in teams. The student teacher would then verify the correctness of the student questions and incorporate them into the total pool of questions used for review. These questions were written on 3"x5" index cards and were read by the teacher. For a unit on Greek and Roman Myths, for example, questions such as, "Who was the author of the Iliad and the Odyssey?" or "The story of the Trojans was told in what great epic poem?" and "He was the chief god of Mount Olympus--who was he?" were typical of those questions asked in a review session. Rules were important to help ensure the success of the game and so the teams were asked to not talk during the reading and answering of the questions. In addition, offering help to the students selected to answer the question was generally not allowed. Students getting the questions correct were awarded points that were recorded on the white board or notepad. If a team violated the rules of the game, the teacher would deduct a point from the team's total score. The game continued until the teacher asked each of the questions or until each student had a chance to participate. The team earning the most points at the end of the review period was declared the winner with the other teams earning second, third, or even fourth place.

Benefits

During each observation period, notes were taken of the review game being played. These notes were then analyzed and examined for themes. Over time it became evident that a number of benefits were being found with respect to cognitive (problem solving skills, recall versus recognition tasks, strategizing, etc.) and affective (team building, cooperation, sportsmanship, etc.) outcomes, and in the enhancement or reinforcement of basic literacy. A select number of these latter benefits are noted below and briefly explained.

Review of Learning Material

One of the more obvious benefits found to be of particular value was the frequent review of learning material. In the process of preparing for a review game, students were required to reread texts and class lecture notes for information and other facts that were to be included in a review session. It was not uncommon for the teachers to report that prior to the use of these games students would barely work through the required reading in the first place and that the expectation that the students would reread materials was remote. In addition, students were not known to review class lecture notes once they had been taken and stored in their notebooks. The games created a culture of competition within the classrooms observed, but also of cooperation; and it was within these cooperative learning groups that teams reviewed course materials that would have otherwise not been reviewed. Because students were aware that the contents of the reading and study materials were to be asked of them, it was in their best interest to revisit facts and concepts, and the teachers created an environment in which they were allowed to do so. The possibility of a team game could almost assure that the students would review course learning materials at a greater level.

Note-Taking and Study Skills

Another benefit observed in the classes was the reinforcement of the value of note-taking and other study skills needed to be successful in a game or other learning situation. The use of lecture and study notes for a review game gave the notes a new meaning and purpose in the minds of the students. Because the questions and answers used in the games came from the lectures and reading materials, the teachers reported that students worked diligently at generating a set of usable and reliable notes that could be used to assist them in their study. As a result, some of the teachers were able to introduce lessons on note-taking techniques and text outlining skills. Still others took advantage of the students' interest to introduce lessons on the memorization and organization of learning materials. Opportunistic teachers were able to teach and reinforce valuable learning skills that would have benefit in their classrooms as well as in others.

Homework

A benefit in an area similar to that above was the improvement in the quality and completion rate of homework. It was observed amongst the 9th and 10th grade students in this study that homework was not completed at an acceptable rate, and that the quality of the homework turned in for credit was poor. As a result of the review game environment, students would rewrite class lecture notes and would improve the overall quality of their homework knowing that the information in the homework would be used in the games. Homework would include the independent reading of course materials as well as written summaries of the reading to be used in class for discussion and in reviews for tests or quizzes. Credit was given to the students for homework, yet once the students realized that completing the reading and written summaries enhanced their memory which assisted them in the team game, it added a new value to the homework required for class. This was an unplanned but welcomed benefit to the teachers, since the students themselves realized the value of completing homework in order to ensure their success in the game.

Increased Interest and Motivation

An additional value observed in the students was an increased interest in learning and a greater degree of motivation demonstrated in the classroom. Within the team game format, it appeared that reading and writing took on new meaning for the students. Reading and writing were viewed as a means to an end. For some students, regular classroom attendance was an indication of increased interest and motivation but for others, reading and writing, for the purpose of getting questions correct in a game, was the reason for increased interest and motivation. A higher level of enthusiasm and energy exhibited in the classroom also indicated increased interest. Students appeared to enjoy the class more than previously. It was not uncommon at the start of the class to hear students ask if they were going to play Jeopardy that day. If they learned that they were not going to play, they were visibly disappointed, but if they learned they would be playing, they were pleased. To what degree this increased interest and motivation was the result of the team game environment is unknown; however, it was clear to this observer that the students were interested and motivated to learn.

Feedback on Learning

Feedback of student learning by the teacher was important. Often times in the Language Arts classroom, feedback on student comprehension of reading material is delayed until a teacher has finished grading papers or tests. In some cases, this turnaround period could be a matter of days or even weeks. In the game format, students were asked questions directly. As a result, the teachers were able to provide immediate feedback as to whether or not a student had gotten the question right or wrong. This had value for the individual student as well as for the team. In the cases I observed, teachers allowed the students to return to their groups after the completion of a game to rewrite their notes and to verify information based upon the feedback given to them in the game situation. If certain facts were missed with regularity, the teacher was able to identify this deficiency and draw the students' attention to it. This reality also had the added benefit of providing the teacher with feedback on his or her teaching. This information was useful when evaluating lessons and teaching.

Literacy Reinforcement

One of the greatest benefits observed had to do with the fact that basic literacy skills like reading, writing, spelling, and basic math skills like addition, subtraction, division, and estimating were frequently reinforced. The students were not always aware of the literacy benefits gained from their participation in a review game, but the reading and rereading of course materials, writing and rewriting class notes, writing and spelling at the chalkboard, adding and subtracting points earned became routine and part of the total game experience. This, of course, was a novel way of getting the students to read and write that may not have otherwise been possible. The students observed were reading and writing at a rate higher than was previously noted. The team game approach also served as a reminder to the teachers that there were numerous possibilities for teaching or reinforcing reading and writing skills.

For the Teacher

For the student teachers observed for this paper, there was practice in writing test and review questions that may not have otherwise been possible. The game format also provided the teacher with an opportunity to check for understanding in reading, assess weaknesses and strengths of students, evaluate teaching and learning objectives, help students prepare for tests and quizzes, and, perhaps most importantly, provide the students with additional opportunities to practice their literacy skills. In total, the benefits in using a team game format for review were substantial for both the student and teacher and served to enhance an environment that helped to facilitate learning.

Limitations Question Writing

Some teachers, especially new ones, sometimes find the art of question writing difficult. Often team games, such as those used for review, consisted of questions that were of the "who" or "what" type that generally had a one-word answer. These convergent questions were often not sufficient to take learners to the higher levels of Bloom's taxonomy of thinking skills. A teacher may have been content only to assess knowledge at the most basic levels or lacked the experience to take his students to more complex levels of thinking through the use of objective questions. Secondly, questions were often poorly written and not well planned. Still others offered little benefit to literacy beyond simply spelling words or names. Thirdly, questions tended not to be weighted equally. The degree of difficulty that existed between questions varied substantially, yet the teacher may have only allowed one point per question when it was obvious to the students that some questions were more difficult than others. Students were quite astute at recognizing the degree of difficulty for questions and were disappointed if they perceived that there were inequities being reinforced as a result of the teacher giving some students or teams easier questions than others. This presented a challenge to the teachers to write test questions that were fair as well as valid. In addition, some questions were poorly conceived and may have had more than one right answer. This was particularly true when students were asked subjective questions pertaining to the interpretation of a piece of literature with no one correct or incorrect answer.

Winners and Losers

Some teachers unintentionally created or reinforced a system of winners and losers with the use of review games that emphasized competition over cooperation. Once again, students were able to discern this reality when the teacher used words such as "winners" and "losers" and the teams were rewarded accordingly. On one occasion, I observed a teacher declare one team the winner and the rest of the teams were losers and then proceeded to give the winning team candy while the remainder of the class received none. At that point, the students who did not receive the candy became quite upset and resolved not to participate in a review game again. This unfortunate turn of events could become a case of classical conditioning in which the students pair "losing" with literacy type activities and, therefore, lose their desire to read and write. On the other hand, some students may have only engaged in reading and writing when they were assured that they would receive a tangible reward for their participation.

Game Rules

In some instances, the rules of the game were not thought out very well. Unrealistic rules or poorly written or stated rules, were not well received by the students. In some instances, the teacher did not consistently maintain or reinforce the rules equally for all of the teams involved in a game. Once again, the students in this case were quite astute at pointing out the inconsistencies to the teacher or in indicating a point of inequity. These students would tune out a teacher or they refused to participate in a future team game as a result. In the example given at the top of this paper, a question related to the author Edgar Allan Poe was cited. While observing the same teacher in another class, a debate arose amongst the students about the teacher awarding a team one point when the contestant simply wrote the name "Poe" while the others were busy writing the full name. It appeared that the teacher had bent a rule for the one team whereas the others did not receive the same benefit. Once again, this resulted in discouragement and disappointment on the part of the other teams, thus resulting in a loss of enthusiasm and desire to participate.

Student Differences

It had been my experience that not all students responded equally well to the game setting. Even with an emphasis upon cooperation, second language learners, special needs students (such as those with learning disabilities), noncompetitive students, or highly anxious students may not have performed as well in this environment as others. In these instances, these students would choose not to participate and withdraw from the activity. They may also have feigned illness or come up with other reasons in order to be excused from the competition. In such instances, teachers needed to demonstrate a higher degree of sensitivity to these students and work hard to create an environment where all students would feel safe and successful in learning.

Suggestions for Using Group Games

The following suggestions for using group games have grown out of my experience as a classroom teacher, university professor, and student teacher supervisor, as well as from extensive reading in the area. While the following suggestions are by no means exhaustive, I would encourage teachers who might consider using team games to implement them in their own classrooms and to read in this area of research:

1. Plan ahead. One of the best things any teacher considering the use of team games or other cooperative learning strategies can do is plan ahead. Perhaps there is nothing worse than having a teacher decide that morning to engage his or her class in a complex activity with little or no advanced preparation. The inability to plan ahead is a sure recipe for disappointment or even disaster in the classroom.
2. Be clear on the information to be reviewed. I suggest that teachers review clearly their unit goals and lesson objectives. The content to be addressed and questions used in a game setting should be taken from the reading materials used in class and from the student's writing. An inability to attend to this matter could result in a review or test question being content invalid.
3. Apply the principles of good test-item construction for game questions. Any introductory text on teaching or educational psychology will provide instructions on writing test questions. These sources will also assist the teacher in avoiding obvious pitfalls. For example, avoiding trick questions is obvious, as is asking questions that are too lengthy to be processed aurally by many students. However, if a teacher is not confident in his ability to write valid questions I suggest taking advantage of commercially available test banks or questions often found in the teacher's packet that accompany many of the reading materials used in class or text.
4. Clearly state the objectives and rules of the game before participation and reinforce the rules consistently. If a teacher finds that the rules established prior to the game are difficult or impossible to maintain,

he or she should agree together with the students to create rules that are agreeable to everyone.

5. Clearly state the advantages or purposes of participation in group games. A teacher's ability to state the value of any learning activity is always advantageous. It is not necessary to give every reason or rationale for engaging students in an activity but students should have an idea of the value associated with their participation in any learning activity.

6. Involve each of the students as much as possible. This suggestion is sometimes the most difficult to implement. There are some realities, such as those stated above, which prohibit some students from participating in a game. However, the student who chooses not to participate for whatever reason should be required to participate or else pay the consequences for his nonparticipation. Unless students have a valid reason for not participating, the teacher should have a reasonable expectation that all students will become actively involved in the learning.

7. Use discretion in the use of tangible rewards for achievement. Tangible and edible reinforcers can be used effectively. However, as stated previously, a misuse or over reliance on these reinforcers can result in students only participating when they are assured they will be given a treat. In the case of only rewarding the team with the most points, I have always suggested that every team receive something for its participation. In this case, the teacher may decide to give every team member one reward whereas the team with the most points may receive two rewards. But once again I advise teachers to use discretion in the distribution of tangible or edible reinforcers for learning.

8. Solicit and incorporate student suggestions for information to be learned, game questions, and rules and procedures. There is a saying that people have a tendency to support that which they help to create. This saying applies to the use of team games. When students have an opportunity to contribute to the creation of the game, this involvement may help to increase their interest and motivation. This suggestion also assists the teacher by placing a great part of the responsibility for learning on the shoulders of the student.

9. Vary the game format. Jeopardy and Trivial Pursuit type games are not the only forms available for these purposes. Explore as many other formats as you desire. In addition, the use of bells, whistles,

buzzers, lights and props significantly enhance the quality and feel of the game. Be creative.

10. Allow the students to create their own games. I have observed a unit on Greek and Roman myths, such as the one mentioned earlier, converted nicely into a game board type created exclusively by the students. Empower your students and trust them to create truly wonderful games that result in learning and literacy.

11. Every student is a winner. Do your best as a teacher to ensure that every student is successful. Work hard to create an environment where students feel safe and valued. Never label a student or team a "loser." Rather, regularly affirm the abilities and capabilities of every student to succeed in learning and literacy.

12. Have fun! Regardless of the activity, there is nothing less convincing than a teacher who does not enjoy teaching or trying a new method or strategy. This is especially so in the use of team games. If a teacher chooses to engage his students in group games, it would be hoped that there is enjoyment in it. Laughter, smiles, surprise and enthusiasm go a long way. If teachers are able to do this, one should not be surprised when students begin to take on this very same enthusiasm for learning.

Conclusion

To conclude, it is important to note that the use of the techniques described in this paper is not all fun and games--it is learning too! The use of cooperative learning in the classroom is a viable means of enhancing and reinforcing academic achievement in a way that is highly engaging and that serve a number of cognitive and affective needs as well (Slavin, 1987, 1988, 1996). As suggested, there are many benefits associated with the use of team games in the secondary Language Arts classroom. The use of team games also allows the secondary student to become engaged in classroom activities in a spirit of fun, to experience success in reading and writing and to demonstrate comprehension of text material in a novel format. "Ready teams? Let's begin!"

References

Slavin, R.E. (1987). "Synthesis of research on cooperative learning." *Educational Leadership*, 48,(5), pp. 72-82.

Slavin, R.E. (1988). "Cooperative learning and student achievement." In R.E. Slavin (Ed.). *School and Classroom Organization*. Hillsdale, NJ: Erlbaum.

Slavin, R.E. (1996). "Research on cooperative learning and achievement: What we know, what we need to know." *Contemporary Educational Psychology*, 21, pp. 43-69.

Vacca, R.T., and Vacca, J.L. (1999). *Content area reading: Literacy and learning across the curriculum* (6th ed.). Longman.

LITERATURE CIRCLES:
PROMOTING A LOVE FOR READING

Janet Ghio

One School's Story

Lincoln High School sits in the Central Valley of California in Stockton, California. Our school community, like most California schools is made up of a diverse student population. Like every school, we have readers with a wide range of reading experience. However, several years ago, as we implemented the Learning Record Assessment System, formerly called the California Learning Record, (Barr, 1995) and began to carefully examine what and how our students read, we became somewhat alarmed. As part of this assessment system, we needed evidence of how and what students read. We asked students to keep reading lists, lists that included assigned school reading as well as what students read for pleasure or for solving problems (Barr, 1994). We discovered that many of our students did not read for pleasure. When asked for written reflection about their reading, we read comments like "I read what is assigned. If you ask me to read for pleasure, I wouldn't even know what to choose" or "The books we read in school aren't that good" or "Why don't we ever get to choose what we want to read?"

Of course, we found students who loved to read and read avidly, but it was almost as if they were "closet readers." We were not providing enough opportunities for students to select books or enough opportunities for students to talk about books other than the core literature we assigned. As an English Department, we thought of ourselves as being student centered. We had spent a great deal of time revising our core reading list so it was balanced with contemporary, classical, and ethnically diverse literature. For the most part, the books students talked about in class were books the English Department had selected. Of course, we had generated some enthusiasm and awareness of a variety of genres, but we wanted our students to love to read. We wanted reading to be something students did for enjoyment, to get information, and to learn about the world. We wanted reading to be something students would continue to find satisfying throughout their lives.

Why Literature Circles

Our English Department is a collaborative, energetic department of about twenty teachers. More than half of our teachers have attended a California Literature Project Summer Institute. We had read the research, but we were forced to reexamine that research and our classroom practices. Together, we shared an article published in *Educational Leadership* that summarized much of the recent reading research. The article by Linda G. Fielding and P. David Pearson contended that successful reading comprehension programs needed to include four components: large amounts of time for reading text, teacher-directed instruction of reading strategies, time for collaborative learning, and opportunities for students to talk with others about their responses to reading (Fielding & Pearson, 1994). As we examined our curriculum, we recognized that we had included in our instruction the components needed for a successful program, but we needed to expand the amount of time students read and the opportunities for students to share their responses to reading.

We knew students read more when given a choice in what to read, but we also were aware of the reality that we needed to help students discover what they enjoyed reading. We wanted students to be engaged in self-selected books. We reviewed Louise Rosenblatt's description of reading as an interaction between the reader, the author, and the text (Rosenblatt, 1983) and the theory that when readers share their interpretations of what they read, the meaning they construct is enhanced. We talked about the enthusiasm and engagement we experience as adults when we talk about what we read.

As we continued to examine the research, we were reminded of the fact that independent reading is the number one factor associated with reading achievement (Anderson, Wilson & Fielding, 1988). We needed something that could serve as a catalyst for students to want to read independently and for pleasure. Some teachers had tried "book clubs" with their students, but our success with this had been limited to a few teachers. We finally came to an agreement to read during our summer break Harvey Daniel's book *Literature Circles: Voice and Choice in the Student Centered Classroom* (Daniels, 1994).

Staff Development

Our first day back to work in the Fall of 1995 began with small group discussions of Daniel's book. Teachers liked his ideas and the personal accounts of classroom use of literature circles. We decided to spend our "forum" discussions held each Monday afternoon in literature circles and to experience as adult readers the ideas shared in Daniel's book. In order to try some new books that might engage our diverse student population, we divided into groups of no more than four teachers to read and discuss books. We selected from an array of genres and books: *Into the Wild* by Jon Krakauer (nonfiction), *Arranged Marriages* by Chitra Banerjee Divakaruni (short stories), *The Heart of a Woman* by Maya Angelou (an Oprah Book at the time), *How the Garcia Sisters Lost Their Accent* by Julia Alvarez, *Always Running* by Luis Rodriquez, and *Woman Warrior* by Maxine Hong Kingston (a Stockton author). Our principal, who had also read Daniel's book, was invited to participate, and she enthusiastically accepted the invitation.

It was this experience that convinced our English Department to implement literature circles as part of our curriculum. We quickly saw literature circles as a helpful tool for allowing students to have opportunities to choose books of interest that they could read independently. We believed the student-generated discussions and the group presentations at the end of a literature circle unit just might be the catalyst we were looking for to get students reading for pleasure and reading independently.

We also saw literature circles as an opportunity for teachers to take observational notes of how students read. As part of our Learning Record Portfolio Assessment System, (Barr, 1995) we had been discussing methods for collecting observations of students talking about what they read. We saw literature circle discussions as a means for us to collect the evidence we needed to inform our instruction. We wanted to observe what reading strategies students applied in order to make meaning of texts they read independently. We wanted to see if the direct instruction of reading strategies we gave our students when teaching core literature carried over when students read independently. We wondered if students used these strategies to unlock meaning and to think critically about their reading (Ghio, 1998). Because literature circles are student-centered, we recognized that we would have the time to listen and write anecdotal and observational notes.

Literature Circles – A Definition

Introducing the idea of literature circles into our classrooms, we used Harvey Daniel's definition.

> *Literature Circles are small, temporary discussion groups [whose members] have chosen to read the same story, poem, article, or book. While reading each group-determined portion of the text..., each member prepares to take specific responsibilities in the upcoming discussion, and everyone comes to the group with the notes needed to help perform that job. The circles have regular meetings, with discussion roles rotating each session. When they finish a book, the circle members plan a way to share highlights of their reading with a wider community... Once readers can successfully conduct their own wide-ranging, self-sustaining discussions, formal discussion roles may be dropped (Daniels, 1994, p.13).*

We then proceeded to present to our students the features of literature circles and to define the various responsibilities students would have for conducting their own discussions of the books they selected.

Implementing Literature Circles

The features of literature circles are explicitly explained in Daniel's book (1994). Individual teachers and schools might apply these features differently according to what seems to work best. For the past several years, as Lincoln High School has implemented the use of literature circles, we have basically kept the features of literature circles described in Daniel's book; however, we have also discovered what seems to work best at our school.

Feature #1: Students choose their own reading. There are a variety of methods for allowing students to choose what they will read. One method is for the teacher to offer a list of books available at the school. We offer books we have purchased for the purpose of literature circles (this is why it is important to have the support of the principal). Some teachers have brainstormed with students' ideas for books that they want to read. We try to purchase these books; however, our local bookstore has allowed students to buy at discounted prices these self-selected books.

Books of a particular genre or theme might be selected. For instance, our ninth grade English course theme is "Search for Identity." Using this theme, we have now acquired quite a few books for the purpose of literature circles: *Macho* by Victor Villasenor, *Cantora* by Sylvia Medina-Lopez, *The Bean Tree* by Barbara Kingslover, *The Contender* by Robert Lipsyte, *The Chocolate War* by Robert Cormier, *Into Thin Air* and *Into the Wild* by Jon Krakauer, and *Friday Night Lights* by H.G. Bissenger, to name a few. Obviously, when a school or classroom begins literature circles, the teacher can only offer what is available; but the more literature circles are used, the more schools will want to acquire a variety of reading selections for this purpose.

To get students to select books, it is a good idea to talk about the books available. We invite students who have read any of the offered books to share their comments. Students are allowed to examine the books. They are encouraged to read a few pages since much of the reading our students do with their literature circle book is independent reading; therefore, they need to be able to read the book. We try our best to assist students in selecting what is best for them and what they want to read.

Feature #2: Small groups are formed according to student choice. Once students become familiar with what books are offered for the literature circle, we ask students to write a list of books they would like to read and to give their reasons for their selections. We usually can accommodate the student's first book choice; however, on occasion we have to give the student a second choice. We do this with the promise that during the next literature circle session, the student will be given a first choice book.

Some teachers have used a lottery system. Cards are distributed with a number for the round when the student gets to come to the front of the classroom and select a book. However, the disadvantage of this system is that the students who are in the last rounds might be dissatisfied because the books left are not books they want to select. Teachers need to use this method with caution.

We have discovered that a group of four students is best; however, on occasion, depending on the maturity of the students, a group of five or six can be quite effective. A group of only two does not work well because even our best readers have found this not as exciting as hearing the ideas of several of their classmates.

Feature #3: Different groups read different books. Given a choice, students will naturally select a variety of books. We listen to students and have worked to discover and purchase selections from a variety of genres that students want to read. The idea is to create an atmosphere where students take responsibility in locating and selecting books that interest them. We have to be particularly responsive to student ideas for book selections. We offer a list of books each time we conduct literature circles; but if students come up with an idea for a book selection that is appropriate for the school setting, we do our best to acquire the suggested books.

Also, we have discovered that it is important that teachers remain flexible in applying this feature. If, for some reason, there is enthusiasm for a particular title and books are available, we have had success in having two literature circle groups reading the same book. We do not want to defeat our purpose of nurturing a love and enthusiasm for reading.

Feature #4: Groups meet at a regularly scheduled time. The first time the group meets in their book-alike groups, students receive a schedule that they collaboratively complete. We have found it best if students are given a date when the group must finish the selection. They will meet once or twice a week, depending on the literature, the students, and the teacher. We also have discovered that it is important to give students a calendar with the day of each literature circle meeting indicated. It is best to have literature circle discussions on the same day each week. A schedule, such as the one seen below, has proven to be quite helpful to students and teachers. It includes the dates of each meeting, the pages or chapters that are to be read (to be determined by the students), and the student's responsibility for the discussion (also decided upon by the group).

<u>Sample Schedule Sheet</u>
Your Name_____
Book Title _____
Author_____
Group Members_____
Reading Schedule:

WEEK	DATE	Pages/Chapters Read
Week One	_____	_____
Week Two	_____	_____
Week Three	_____	_____
Week Four	_____	Book Completed

Responsibility Assignments: Discussion Direction (DD), Illustrator (I), Connector (C), Literary Luminator (LL), Summarizer (S), or Vocabulary Enricher (VE). Decide what responsibility each group member has each week. Do not repeat discussion responsibility.

Group Members	Week 1	Week 2	Week 3	Week 4

Feature 5: Students use written or drawn notes to guide their reading and discussion. Writing and drawing are important parts of literature circles. Students are asked to respond to what they read. They use the self-assigned responsibility (explained in Feature 8) as a guide or an idea for responding to the reading, but the teacher-facilitator encourages students to not be restricted totally to the responsibility the individual has for that week. Eventually, students can "graduate" from the assigned responsibilities and the discussion can become more natural, with students using their response logs for the scheduled literature circle discussion. However, we have found it best to always have an assigned

discussion director with some written questions for generating
discussion.

On the day of a scheduled literature circle discussion, it is the written
or drawn response that teachers look for on the students' desks. The
second item teachers look for is the book or selected literature. Both of
these are needed because it is the literature and students' responses to the
reading that drives the discussion.

Feature 6: Discussion topics come from the students. The
students in the group have control over the group discussion. It is the
Discussion Director and the group members who bring questions to
group. Teachers do not provide the questions or control the direction of
the discussion. The assigned responsibilities allow the group members
to bring a variety of responses to the discussion. I have listened to
students in a Sylvia Plath's *The Bell Jar* literature circle discussing their
personal experience with depression and their knowledge of current
treatment for depression. I once listened to a group share, with much
laughter, family "ghost stories" as part of their discussion of Maxine
Hong Kingston's *Woman Warrior*. Another time, a student shared with
his group his religious experience to help his group members better
understand the experience Langston Hughes described in his
autobiography *The Big Sea*. His group members asked this student many
questions about his personal experience. It was obvious that the
knowledge he brought to the group helped his group members broaden
their understanding of the literature they had read. The teacher's job is
to listen, observe, and to not interfere with the discussion. The student's
job is to share responses to the literature; this is what creates engagement
for the student.

**Feature 7: Literature circle meetings are aimed at being open
and natural conversations.** This, of course, is not often the case with
our ninth grade students who are being introduced to the idea of
literature circles. These students are much more dependent on the
assigned responsibilities. It is often difficult for students who are new to
the practice of talking about their responses to literature to sustain a
lengthy discussion about what they have read. However, with practice,
the discussion becomes open and natural. We have discovered that with
experience, readers are able to grow and mature in this capacity. It is not
uncommon for juniors and seniors and even younger experienced

students, to spend the entire fifty-minute period discussing what they
have read. Generally, students will discuss twenty to thirty minutes, and
then have some time left for personal written reflection of the discussion
or for silent sustained reading. Literature circles "is based on a faith in
self-directed practice. Literature circles embody the idea that kids learn
to read mainly by reading and to write mainly by writing and by doing so
in a supportive, literate community" (Daniels, 1994, p. 24).

**Feature 8: Students take on a variety of responsibilities for
discussion sessions.** Harvey Daniel's book offers clearly defined
responsibilities, which are especially helpful when first introducing the
idea of literature circles. In his book, teachers will find "role sheets" for
both fiction and non-fiction which describe the responsibility a student
completes and brings to the discussion. Our teachers have sometimes
substituted Daniels' "role sheets" and instead distributed to students a
one-page handout with the specific responsibilities listed and defined.
Students select the "role sheet" or responsibility they will complete for
each literature circle session and bring their written response to the
literature circle discussion. These group assigned responsibilities have
worked effectively in helping students sustain conversation about their
reading.

We have used a variety of these responsibilities with much success:
discussion director, whose responsibility it is to bring questions to the
group for discussion; **literary luminator,** whose job is to locate a few
sections or quotations from the reading that the reader thinks are
significant or interesting; **illustrator,** whose job it is to create some kind
of picture, drawing, sketch, or graphic related to the reading; **connector,**
whose job it is to find connections between the reading, the outside
world, other books on the same topic, current or historical events, or
personal experience; **summarizer,** whose job it is to provide the group
with a brief summary of the highlights or key points or events of the
reading; **vocabulary enricher,** whose job it is to find and define in
context a few important words in the assigned reading. Students share
their "role sheet" or responsibility with the group, and this gives each
student in the group something to say. It serves as scaffolding for
student so they eventually can have a more open and natural
conversation. These assigned responsibilities are often the starting point
for a more open discussion. Also, these roles or responsibilities give

students an opportunity to practice a variety of reading strategies that help them make meaning of what they have read.

Feature 9: The teacher serves as a facilitator and observer. The intent of literature circles is to create a student-centered reading experience. The job of the teacher is to organize the students. The idea is that the teacher is to not teach. Some teachers have even become part of a literature circle group, but for the most part we have used this time to listen and record observations of students reading. The fact that we are busy with a clipboard in hand recording our observations on mailing labels, which we later make part of the students' observational notes in the Learning Record Portfolio Assessment System, keeps teachers from becoming the center of the learning. Our students know that the literature circle is student centered, and we will not interrupt their discussion with our ideas. Also, students know that we will not answer questions, but let the group members reading the literature "do" the discussing and thinking. We encourage students to not be teacher-dependent, and we respect them as learners in the act of discovering and sharing meaning and responses to what they have read.

Feature 10: Evaluation of literature circles is by teacher observation and student self-reflection. While students are discussing, I write observational notes. For instance, I hear Dora ask, "How on earth did she get to watch the birth of a baby. It just doesn't quite seem possible. How could she possibly get in to see that? It's not explained." I write down Dora's words with quotation marks and note that she is questioning the author's craftsmanship or logic. I am observing how Dora reads and how she thinks about what she reads.

Another student, Tristen, who is reading *Black Boy* by Richard Wright, is sharing with his group the fact that he understands Richard's anger. He explains that his own little brother has the same rage that Richard feels because his little brother does not like his step-mom. He tells his group, "Whenever Fred [his little brother] comes home from visiting my Dad and our step-mom, he is just terrible. It's the same thing Richard is going through." Tristen is responding to a group member's question about Richard's anger. I note in my observations that Tristen, who is not generally a motivated reader, is making personal connections to the book and is using his prior knowledge to make sense of what he is reading. I also note that Tristen is keeping up with the groups' assigned reading and is discussing often, which is something I had not noticed during class discussions of core literature.

These observations are later placed in the Learning Record portfolio so that students can reflect about the various reading strategies they use when they discuss what they read. These observations also give the teacher and the students an opportunity to think about the type of experiences and instruction students need to further their ability to read and respond to texts critically.

Usually, at the end of each literature discussion, students are asked to reflect upon the discussion. They might be asked to respond to any of the following questions: What did you do well today during your literature circle meeting? What do you still need to work on during literature circle meetings? What was an important contribution you made to the discussion? How much did you participate in the discussion today? What was an important idea or thought expressed by someone else in the group during the discussion? What other comments would you like to make about today's session?

Students are given time to reflect about their discussion which is often submitted to the teacher weekly. This self-reflection and the student's response log or assigned responsibility response allow teachers to see what went on in groups the teacher did not observe on a given day. This reflection also helps students see themselves as learners and discover what they want to do to grow as readers. This has become rich evidence of student learning as students use their responses and self-reflection as part of their portfolio assessment.

Feature 11: When books or selections are finished, readers share presentations with the class, and then new groups are formed with new reading choices. This has been an important part of the literature circle process and has worked well with short stories as well as with books. Teachers require that certain criteria is met by the group, such as, all members in the group must contribute and participate, the presentation must be well planned and well rehearsed, the presentation must capture the essence or theme of the reading but not "ruin" the book for anyone in the class who chooses to read it, the presentation must be audible and organized.

Students have enjoyed planning these presentations. We have seen a variety of presentations from video presentations to puppet shows. Planning these presentations has brought students together who otherwise would not have spent much time together outside of class. I'll never forget the group that met for several nights, produced a wonderful video, and then got together again to celebrate their success with a pizza at the local pizza parlor. These students had not known each other until they got together in their literature circle group.

The presentation also serves as a way for groups of students to share what they have read with a larger audience. From seeing these presentations, students get ideas about what they want to read independently. This is clearly illustrated when Jessica wrote, "The literature circles have been a huge success for me. I never really had any ideas about what I wanted to read, but now I have lots of ideas about some good books. My reading was really limited. I always read the "same ole...same ole" things I've been reading. I would have never even thought about reading books like *Black Elk Speaks* or *Kitchen God Wife,* but now I know I'll read those books. I think I'll learn a lot about the world other than my sheltered little world. I've got lots of ideas for my summer reading list."

The Results

Implementing literature circles has been a tremendously challenging and rewarding task. Our staff has worked collaboratively to improve the process and to collect a variety of books for the sole purpose of literature circles. We have added classroom libraries as well and have turned to our community for book contributions.

As we examine our students' Learning Record Portfolios, we notice that students' reading lists have expanded into something more than reading only what is assigned school reading. We are beginning to see the evidence that students are reading independently and are discovering what they want to read.

Laurie, a ninth grade student in the spring of 1998, perhaps captured the results of literature circles best when she wrote, "I learned a lot this year and I had fun with it. We've read interesting books and we've done fun activities. I especially like the literature circles where students take on different roles and read different books. It makes learning exciting and I remember more this way. I never really liked to read before. In fact, I use to avoid reading. But now I love it." This is what we hoped for, and this is what literature circles are doing for many of our students.

References

Anderson, R.C., Wilson, P.T., and Fielding, L.G. (1988). "Growth in reading and how children spend their time Outside of School." *Reading Research Quarterly* (23), pp. 285-303.

Barr, M. (1995). *The California learning record.* San Diego, CA: The Center for Language in Learning.

Barr, M., Syverson, M. (1999). *Assessing literacy with the learning record.* Portsmouth, NH: Heinemann.

Daniels, H. (1994). *Literature circles: Voices and choice in the student-centered classroom.* York, Maine: Stenhouse Publishers.

Fielding, L.G., and Pearson, P.D. (1994). "Reading comprehension: What works." *Educational Leadership,* 51 (5), pp. 62-68.

Ghio, Janet. (1998). "Becoming accomplished readers in the high school classroom with the help of the learning record." *California English, 3* (4), pp. 11-13.

Rosenblatt, L.M. (1983). *Literature as exploration*, (4th ed.). NY: The Modern Language Association of America.

CONTENT CONNECTIONS: ASSISTING THE TRANSITION FROM NARRATIVE TO INFORMATIONAL TEXT

Leona J. Manke

The first few years of reading instruction focus on narrative text: fairy tales, folk tales, stories about the little engine that could and stories about our most embarrassing moment or missing the school bus, The stories we read or that are read to us before we enter school and the stories we read and write in the first few grades develop in us a sense of story structure. Most offer little help in understanding informational text. So when reading loads increase as children progress from primary grades through high school, with the subsequent shift to reading for content, students need new strategies to cope with the new text structures.

The first step in the transition from narrative text to expository text is to utilize narrative texts as part of the content curriculum. Picture books like *Molly's Pilgrim* tell a story—in this case the story of a Lithuanian family who comes to America for religious freedom—while discussing the concept—a pilgrim can be anyone, from the Plymouth settlers to Kosovo refugees who come to practice their religious beliefs. Teachers can use fiction, biography, or historical fiction to assist in the transition.

The second step in the transition from narrative text to expository text is the use of tradebooks—books published for the mass market or libraries—instead of textbooks—books published to teach specific subject matter in the schools. There are several reasons tradebooks offer a better source for information. According to Freeman and Person (1998), the three major ones are reading difficulty or concept load, limited information, and the quality of writing.

In an effort to create texts that meet specific reading level criteria, word choices are limited and sentences are shortened. As a result students have no source of color and texture to build the word pictures which can assist in understanding the text. Shorter sentences abandon causal relationships and leave the students with little or no understanding of the connectedness of events. These "dumbing down" decisions may actually hamper the students' understanding of text.

In addition, textbooks often present a survey of issues and events of the subject using technical vocabulary. While there is an amazing amount of information covered in the textbook—the United States history textbook that moves from Native Americans' migration to the Gulf War—there is little in-depth information. And it is the in-depth information which connects us to the past, which makes facts come to life. So students are expected to grasp many concepts—photosynthesis and biomes, for example—from undeveloped definitions; they wind up memorizing the terms, and students and teachers alike believe because they can recite the definitions that they understand the concepts.

Sometimes textbooks are inaccurate. In some cases the inaccuracies are blatant as in the case of a social studies text which placed Puget Sound near Eugene, Oregon. Other times the inaccuracies occur because of the need to generalize: for example, a description of magnets that places the poles at the ends where in some cases, like the ceramic magnet, the poles are on the surfaces (Freeman & Person).

The quality of writing in textbooks is, in the words of most students, boring. While sometimes the topic itself is called boring because students possess inadequate background knowledge or experience with the topic, usually the language keeps students from enjoying and learning from textbooks. The colorless, simplified language and short, choppy sentences combined with a lack of voice create text that disengages the reader. Tradebooks provide a more engaging transition from narration to exposition. Their primary purpose is to involve young people in learning through colorful writing and informed, detailed text.

The concept load issue seen in textbooks is solved in the classroom by using a variety of tradebooks. When covering a topic, magnets, for example, the book selection can include easy-to-read picture books through books written for adults. Students can select the level which challenges without overwhelming them. When my fifth grade class studied Columbus, I selected an easy-to-read passage from a book that chronicled the journey through the eyes of a cabin boy, two mid-level magazine articles and a more-difficult passage from a translation of Columbus' diaries. I distributed the readings according to the levels of the students in each group and each student collected answers to the KWL questions we had previously brainstormed. (KWL is a strategy where students brainstorm what they Know, what they Want to learn and what they have Learned.) The process avoided reading level stereotyping because no student recognized the stratification of the readings. And each reading contained information the others didn't have. The same strategy can be used with any topic.

Tradebooks usually specialize regarding a topic. Rather than presenting concepts from biomes to how plants grow, tradebooks explain only one topic: biomes or how plants grow. There are overview books: Eyewitness Books on plants and trees are books which present topics with simple, "sound-byte" text with extraordinary photographs or drawings. Many teachers supplement these overview books with others focusing on particular subtopics presented in the overview.

Lastly, tradebooks generally use easy-to-understand text, offer explanations which enhance the definitions of technical vocabulary and colorful, attractive artwork to bring the concepts to life. The previously mentioned Eyewitness books have such vivid artwork that the ideas are often grasped by analyzing the photographs.

The most important step, however, is helping students develop the strategies necessary to comprehend informational text. The development of comprehension involves arousing curiosity, activating prior knowledge and predicting. When the reader's curiosity is piqued, she is motivated to continue reading. Another word for this is engagement. It's what happens when we are so involved in a book we can't put it down.

Often students know a lot about a topic, but if they do not use what they know to make sense of new material that they read, they fail to comprehend. Activating prior knowledge allows the reader to connect what is known to new material.

Prediction is another valuable component of comprehension. The ability to make a "guess" on what will come next—the next word, the next sentence, the next concept—leads us to that next word, sentence and concept. For example, a reader of this article will predict from the clues in the introductory paragraph that somewhere in the next few pages strategies to assist the transition from narrative to informational text will be presented. If I didn't present them, that prediction wouldn't be verified, through no fault of the reader's; in fact, a sense of unease or frustration or disappointment could ensue. We use prediction so unconsciously that we tend to only notice it when we fail to verify our prediction.

Four strategies are presented here (yes, the prediction did come true) to help students activate prior knowledge, arouse curiosity and predict with texts that assist in the transition from narrative to informational text. I selected books around the theme of immigration and chose the following four strategies: Brainwriting, categorical overview, anticipation guides, and story impressions.

Brainwriting, a form of brainstorming used in the business world, involves students in writing their thoughts down rather than saying them aloud. To begin the process the teacher asks students to gather in groups of three or four. After the teacher introduces the topic students will be reading about (immigration, for example), students jot down all the words, ideas, or concepts they can think of on a piece of paper. After about thirty seconds the students pass their papers to their left. Then each reads the previous student's thoughts and adds more. After thirty seconds, they shift again. This continues until the students get their original paper back. The ideas are discussed, in small groups or the whole class, and the teacher assigns the reading. After reading, the students compare their lists and add or subtract if it seems appropriate. This strategy obviously activates prior knowledge and assists in prediction. For some students it may even arouse curiosity because they want to read to see if what they brainstormed was actually part of the text. Students might come up with the following ideas in the immigration example: loneliness, poverty, steerage, 1880s, religious freedom, alienation, prejudice, land of opportunity, strength, and acceptance.

The second strategy, categorical overview, can be used to organize the brainwriting results or to brainstorm as a whole class. The class brainstorms a topic, and the teacher writes the ideas on the board. After gathering a number of ideas, the teacher asks the class to consider what categories the ideas might fall into. In our immigration example, the categories could be reasons for emigrating, emotional responses to leaving homeland, physical conditions during and after travel, and other. Then the words are categorized. Reasons for leaving: poverty, religious freedom, land of opportunity. Emotional responses: loneliness, alienation, prejudice, strength, acceptance. Physical conditions: poverty, steerage, Other: 1880s. The reading is then assigned and followed by a discussion of the text. Additional ideas and categories can be added, if desired. Like brainwriting, categorical overview arouses curiosity and activates background knowledge. In addition, the categorization of the ideas can lead to written summaries with the paragraphing structure already in place, each category representing a paragraph.

Anticipation guides (Vacca & Vacca, 1999) also arouse curiosity, activate background knowledge and encourage prediction. The teacher designs a series of statements that focus on the topic, book, or chapter to be read. The statements can be factual, challenge misconceptions or provoke discussion but should include ideas which are explicit or implicit in the text. The statements should also permit dichotomous relationships (agree, disagree; yes, no; true, false). Blanks that express that dichotomy are placed in front of each statement. Before reading, students decide whether they agree or disagree with each statement (Figure 1). After all students have read the text, they compare and discuss the results of their predictions. The teacher can ask students to support their choices by referring to the text.

Figure 1: Anticipation guide for *Grandfather's Journey*

Read each statement. If you believe that a statement is true, place a check in the True column. If you believe it is false, place a check in the False column. Be prepared to discuss your choices.

True _____   False _____   1. Homesickness occurs when we leave and miss places where we have felt comfortable.

True _____   False _____   2. Moving to a new country requires
                                 making many changes.
True _____   False _____   3. Clothes in Japan are the same as
                                 clothes in America.

The fourth strategy, story impressions (Denner, 1992), can help with the transition from narrative to informational text by using it with both kinds of text. To develop a story impressions chain, select between ten and twenty main ideas or events from the story or text. Use no more than three words to describe each of the events. Arrange these in chronological order and connect them by arrows. To engage in story impressions, students are given the chained words and asked to write a story or text using the words as a guide. After finishing the story, students read the original piece and compare their versions with the original. It is important for students to realize there is no judgment regarding how close their version and the original's match, since it was a prediction. Many students also get truly involved in the reading of the text, even exclaiming outloud, "I'm right!" The examples included here deal with the narrative text, *Molly's Pilgrim* (Figure 2), and the informational text *Immigrant Kids* (Figure 3).

Figure 2: Story impression chain for *Molly's Pilgrim*

Molly, teasing
↓
Tears at home
↓
Momma, Yiddish
↓
No Jewish students
↓
No change
↓
Thanksgiving
↓
Pilgrim village
↓
dolls
↓
clothespin

↓

pilgrim?

↓

traveled from Europe

↓

religious freedom

↓

Momma, doll

↓

different, beautiful

↓

still arriving

Figure 3: Story impression chain for *Immigrant Kids*

poor

↓

sail to America

↓

steerage

↓

dark, crowded

↓

Statue of Liberty

↓

herding passengers

↓

Ellis Island

↓

identify tags

↓v

lines

↓

physical, mental disabilities

↓

1 in 5

↓

yes, no

↓

ferry to city

Clearly, the transition from narrative to expository text can be a difficult process for many students. An aware teacher who offers students strategies to bridge the shift can ease that transition.

References

Cohen, B. (1983). *Molly's pilgrim*. Boston, MA: Houghton Mifflin.

Denner, P.R. (1992). Effects of prereading activities on junior high students' recall. *Journal of Educational Research, 86*, pp. 11-19.

Freedman, R. (1980). *Immigrant kids*. NY: E.P. Dutton.

Freeman, E., and Person, D. (1998). *Connecting informational children's books with content area learning*. Needham Heights, MA: Allyn & Bacon.

Say, A. (1993). *Grandfather's journey*. Boston, MA: Houghton Mifflin.

DEMOCRATIC SCHOOL POLICY, PROCEDURES AND PRACTICE IN SOUTHERN CALIFORNIA

Marsha L. Thicksten

What is democratic education? In the state of California in the United States of America, this question is not addressed nearly as often as the present media debate over whole language versus phonics. On campus recently, I told an office staff person of my interest in democracy and she stated she did not have time for such lofty ideas and that our work at hand was to teach students to be teachers, not those other things. How ironic that teaching students is not seen as having something to do with our form of governance as citizens in our workplace community.

Democracy is something that is taken for granted by much of society in the United States of America. The cornerstone of the teacher education program at Claremont Graduate University is democratic educational classroom practice. Does that mean that we vote on everything? No. Rather, it means that we deliberate and struggle to create and modify a program which is as close to our vision as possible. We struggle to share decision-making. We collectively create our agendas. We come together in the face of adversity for what we think is ethical and fair. We challenge one another and ourselves to stand for social justice in our world. This is not an easy task and sometimes we have misunderstandings. Yet we rally together like a family in the face of challenges. These ideas which seemed so lofty are a major part of our vision at the university level.

How do we learn to do this "stuff" called democracy and do we do it very well? Why is it so important? How do we prepare students to be democratic? In what ways do students learn self-governance?

At a recent state conference, a school principal read a description of a class about which I had written. He then stated that a democratic classroom was one where the teacher selects a social justice project which students then organize and plan by using classroom meetings and inquiry-based learning.

When I described an alternative view of democratic classroom practice—a classroom I had been observing for several years that was activity-center based and where student choice and selection in literacy activities was stressed everyday for a period of time—this practice was not seen as democratic. I had shared a description of this class for a steady discussion. This principal, with his particular definition of what democracy in the classroom was, saw no purpose in what was occurring in the student choice activity center class that I was describing. "That is not democratic. It has no purpose," he stated.

In yet another setting, I described a class with teacher-imposed rules. Students worked quietly at their desks or listened to teacher-driven lessons. Instructional strategies were didactic. For participants in this setting, this didactic class was not considered democratic.

If we are to prepare students for democratic governance, then how do we do this? Is there one correct way to become democratic in policy, procedure and practice?

Alma Flor Ada writes in her forward to *Building Communities of Learners: A Collaboration Among Teachers, Students, Families and Community* by Sudia Paloma McCaleb (1994), "too much of what is attempted in education is done *to* students and their parents rather than *with* them. As a result, even some very well intended efforts continue to perpetuate the notion that the capacity to know and to generate new knowledge is a privilege of some, rather than a birthright of every individual, ontologically inherent to every human being. Thus, it is refreshing, as well as a source of hope and inspiration, to center a book on the words of children and their parents. In this book, stories and reflections are shared and dreams and hopes revealed as an invitation to educators to recognize that, while much work remains to be done, schools can become truly democratic spheres for human grown, if we recognize the innate potential all human beings for the construction of an equitable, just and responsible reality" (McCaleb, 1994, page viii).

How the voices of students emerge in the classroom and how that is then articulated into society as our vision and goal is a matter of policy, procedures and practice. The fact that we have such a wide variety of schools and practices is a living example of democracy in action. Parents and students may select from public as well as private schools. Many school districts offer a wide variety of schools with "ability plus," "back to basics," "technology magnet," "fine arts focus," and "whole child" alternatives. Although the actual practices of the school are not necessarily democratic, the existence of these schools and the choice that families have in selecting a school through established policies and procedures, is a democratic act and process to some extent. When school boards and officials include parents and community members in decision-making that is fair and accessible to the diverse needs of families, then this is even closer to democratic practice. However, if these acts and processes were exclusionary, whether by design or unintentionally, then a democratic effort that is ethically grounded would be morally bound to examine and modify its policy procedures and practice to include the diversity represented in our society. This is not easy work. It is the work of a democracy. In democratic communities, we strive to include rather than exclude whether we are faculty members, a teacher working with kindergarten students, or school board members and school staff members.

In terms of democracy in schools, I suggest that individual deeds or actions may not appear to be democratic so we must examine our policy, procedures and practice in order to recognize what is needed to negotiate a more democratic process. If students need to learn to listen to the procedure that will be used for a democratic discussion in a kindergarten class, it may be that the teacher will be didactic to draw their attention to the rules for discussion. If a teacher wishes to teach students in a preschool or university class about freedom to create new knowledge or individual decision making, then the strategy may be one of allowing students to choose and select from a variety of research/resource centers in a very unstructured setting. If a teacher is attempting to teach students to be more actively engaged in social justice activities as an endeavor of community building or moral and ethical responsibility of being a citizen, then it may be that the teacher will select a project that will allow students to decide how to proceed with planning and implementation. The point is that there may be many strategies that lead to democratic classrooms and democratic communities. Research into how democracy is created, taught, negotiated, and practiced both in and out of the classroom and school community is what I propose is needed. Reflection as to what constitutes learning and instruction for democratic citizenship and classroom practice is a continuing dialogue that needs to include classroom teachers and students.

> Ideally, schools should exist as macrocosms of the world in which students can learn, live, and practice democratic principals. Unfortunately, few schools have made this kind of educational experience a priority. Classroom teachers, on the other hand, must be able to create a democratic community of learners in which everyone's voice is heard and in which governing and responsibility are shared so that all have equal opportunity to learn and participate. We must think about educating all of our students, not just to be good citizens but to ultimately govern (Giroux, 1989, in McCaleb, 1994, p. 45).

Dr. Suzi Soohoo and I made a presentation at the full faculty retreat at Chapman University in August, 1996. Below is a list of questions I created for this workshop. This inquiry for reflective educators and communities was abstract for some professors who were in disciplines other than education. The abstract and reflective questioning is vital to the formulation of how we teach and why we teach. Thinking about the structures, the ethic of care, and the negotiation of curriculum needs to be a greater part of our everyday practice. Examining our practice and policy for frameworks, forms and processes that are democratic takes substantial time, energy and thoughtfulness.

Constructivism

How is creation of knowledge viewed by the teacher, student, and community?

How are social context and collaborative student engagement fostered and valued?

How are the students made clearly aware that the responsibility for learning is their responsibility?

How do students construct their own meaning?

In what ways are class activities meaning centered?

In what ways is the teacher willing to modify the syllabus or lesson plan to reflect student requests for modification?

How is the teacher's model of inquiry able to support all learners and ability levels of students?

In what ways does the teacher facilitate and help students scaffold thinking and cognition?

How does the teacher facilitate debate, dialogue, inventing, and creation of original ideas?

Is there a balance of discovery, research, collaboration, and teacher scaffolding of cognition?

Does teacher help a student go beyond a single dimension of research or thinking? Is risk taking encouraged?

How is student voice represented?

What alternatives are provided for student voice to be heard?

How are multiple ways of viewing and solving problems fostered?

Critical Inquiry

How do we challenge students to explore more than one perspective or solution?

How do learners look beyond the immediate to the long-term consequences?

In what manner do we set aside time to create a deep or meaningful discussion?

How is student voice represented?

What alternatives are provided for student voice to be heard?

How are multiple ways of viewing and solving problems fostered?

Power Structures

How does the teacher use his/her position and authority to foster the seeds of democracy?

How do talking and turn taking impact learning in the classroom?

How do voice, gender, ethnicity, and linguistic differences play out in the classroom?

Is referential knowledge (knowledge that is generated by the student about life, ideas, experiences) valued and fostered in the class?

What is the nature of discourse patterns in varying discipline?

Does the teacher have at least some knowledge base?

Is there an ethic of care and a concern for the affective (social, emotional) component?

Do administration and school district staff support each other with time, space for appreciation, validation, resources, continued update of knowledge in current curriculum?

Is the teacher a researcher as well?

Are there adequate benefits and appreciation for students, teachers and administrators who foster constructivism and democratic learning?

Is the curriculum integrated to create student-centered opportunities for connection and empowerment?

For what purposes do the teacher and student use assessment?

What forms of assessment and evaluation foster learning?

Democracy is a process that must be fostered. Examining structures and power roles that we use is a critical part of evaluating this thing called curriculum if students are to learn inside democratic literacy classrooms.

Reference

McCaleb, S.P. (1994). *Building communities of learners.* NY: St. Martin's Press.

CREATING CLASSROOM COMMUNITY THROUGH DEMOCRATIC TEACHING

Greta Nagel

A team of first grade teachers realized that their students were restless, not listening, and acting bored during teacher-directed lessons in Social Studies. They designed an action research project that focused on the children's engagement, and they decided to try a center's approach that incorporated student choice to see what effect that would have. They never went back to their old way of teaching. The children talked and interacted; they were lively and interested. In addition, they learned content beyond the basic curriculum, and they remembered better when they were responsible for various aspects of their learning (Sagor, 1999).

Many educators come to similar realizations when they reflect on their students' learning. Children can make many decisions related to their education. They can become empowered citizens. One veteran teacher explained that she is now willing to have students "live their democracy" before they ever talk about it. Putting students in charge of more means that she communicates expectations for learning more often and more clearly. Resting responsibility upon the shoulders of her students has been a delight (Nagel & Thicksten, 1997).

Teachers who promote democratic practices agree that it takes commitment and perseverance as well as creativity to enact their missions. Democracy in the larger society doesn't just transfer in to schools and classrooms. On the contrary, public schools across the United States are still highly involved in "factory model" educational practices. An overt goal of many educators is to train students to become competent workers who follow directions well. The prominent and dominant voices in classrooms are those of teachers--for amounts of time that exceed 80% of the total class time. Adults in the US tend to envision ideal classrooms as placid places where well-scrubbed children sit quietly and obediently, responding with accuracy to teachers' pointed questions and directions.

In contrast, democracy is full of talk, for citizens are expected to discuss, debate, and ask questions. Activities seldom proceed perfectly according to plans, because individuals have the freedom to discover new ideas and take new paths. Inquiry and problem solving are prominent parts of daily life. Citizens have choices.

Many descriptions of classroom teaching focus on the behaviors of teachers. However, when educators gather to discuss democracy in classrooms, their words focus more on students than on teachers. Democratic teaching means that activity goes from being teacher-driven to student AND teacher-driven. Students are able to express their thoughts and control many aspects of their learning. They appreciate greater independence from the teacher while they engage in work for the common good of the class. They are active, not passive; they learn by doing, and they are encouraged to ask questions. Therefore, this article will highlight children and their teachers and the things they do. In democratic classrooms, children are empowered to think, and they are educated to care about others. In the process, they "grow" community. Community does not evolve without democratic practice. In one teacher's words, "When schools have a vision of students as citizens, they give students a sense of community that helps them make connections with the world" (Wood, 1990).

As I have looked about for democratic education, I hold the following perspectives to be true:

(a) Participation in an effective democracy requires that individuals communicate and think clearly.
(b) Self-fulfillment of individuals and collaborative development of the class as a whole are important.
(c) Learning democracy comes best from doing democracy. Classroom life can serve as a powerful model.
(d) Education for democracy inspires caring and commitment.

In the following pages I present a medley of practices and activities that I have observed and experienced in a variety of classrooms within seven districts of Southern California. I have organized the ideas according to broad attributes of culture that an anthropologist would typically examine: Social Organization, Politics, Economics, Values, Recreation, and Education. The descriptions that follow are from a variety of real classrooms, but they are grouped here as if they were from classes in one K-8 school devoted to democracy. Because many activities and opportunities are open-ended, something that goes on at one level in practice could very well occur at others (K-1-2; 3-4; 5-6; 7-8). For that reason, I eliminate stating in which context I have actually observed them.

Social Organization

Whose voices are heard? Students AND teachers talk often, but they also make a pledge to have quiet times. Children speak with one another in a wide variety of group configurations. They also speak with the teacher in formal and casual ways, and to the class as a whole in formal (news reports, sharing) and dramatic (plays, reader's theatre) ways. Students use the telephone to conduct interviews and do school-related tasks.

What kinds of roles do class members play? Students are influential and active. Roles may be imaginary (primary playhouse, drama), designated (song leader, ball monitor), self-selected (encourager, librarian) or elected (group leader, student council president). Students are, at times, in charge of lesson presentations. When it is time to teach about a science experiment, a student does the directions and the demonstration. Students enjoy having tandem teachers. They interact with each teacher three days a week because Wednesday is the teachers' overlap day. Group work is common, but the type varies from day to day and within each day.

How is status achieved? Students are judged by their ongoing performance, by doing something well in a variety of roles. Home groups of five change the first week of each quarter so that students achieve new relationships. Opportunities to share talents and skills from inside and outside the school context allow each child to achieve status based upon one of multiple intelligence. Bulletin boards are arranged so that each student has a place of honor to decorate and contribute a work of excellence. At the end of each day, students fill out a self-assessment of their work habits and citizenship. At each town meeting, class members join their teacher in assessing how they are doing as a community. The results aren't always positive, but being a learning community is held in high esteem.

Politics (Power)

What decisions are made by students? Many decisions are designated as those of the classroom citizens. Students influence choices from what songs to sing, what subjects to cover at certain times, what assignments to do in what order, to what values to promote and what consequences to uphold. Children use paper from supply drawers appropriate to their projects and they may gather equipment to use from various parts of the room. In order to respond to self-selected literature, students select from a long list of possible creative book reports.

Students maintain personal word banks. Kids are able to sit at the teacher's desk for special projects. They handle laser disks to find the pictures they want to view. Individuals may join schoolwide contests or not as they choose. Children choose where to sit at read-aloud time. They may choose to sit on the couch in the library. Kids may write at any one of the tables.

How is power distributed? There are teams and committees, co-leaders, officers, and monitors. Parents have clear information about how to call or write and are welcome in the classroom. Parent input is elicited through surveys, flyers, tear-offs in newsletters. Students engage in real-life problem solving that involves critical thinking and independent decision-making. Several students go to training sessions in conflict resolution. Peel-off groups meet each week for skill development activities with the teacher. Self-selected activity time includes time to "read the room." Children select their own topics for writing. Students choose items to bring from home for sharing. They select which books they would read from the core list. Students are learning to create their own web pages.

How is control achieved? Peers (team leaders, sergeant-at-arms) are in charge of reminding one another of norms. Class meetings provide opportunities for peer review of rules, procedures, and plans. Students encourage one another with compliments. Class planning and problem solving are handled at regular "Town Meetings." Students have written a class compact and standards to cover a variety of procedures for the class.

How do individuals share ideas and persuade others? Students (and parents) are encouraged to speak and write for a variety of audiences including letters to principals and newspapers, presentations at council meetings, articles for classroom newspapers that go to homes and other classrooms, speak at class meetings, and talk in group work. Students decide how to use the time left at the end of the day by listening to mini-speeches and voting. They design and create flyers to advertise their sale of student artwork during the lunch hour. Children post posters and butcher paper banners on campus as long as they meet standards set by student council. Student council representatives prepare presentations in order to report back to their classrooms.

Economics

What work do students do? Citizens all pitch in to make the classroom run well. They take care of classroom chores and learning tasks. Class members design the classroom jobs and write the job descriptions. They lead groups and create rubrics. They learn how to ask questions and they design questions for one another. Students' questions are incorporated in tests.

How do class members "earn a living"? Children help organize hundreds of books arranged in tubs by color codes. The mail system has student workers delivering messages to student mailboxes. The work crew includes individuals who were in charge of morning opening ceremonies, lunch count, equipment, door and lights, award certificates, mail, paper passing, trash disposal, attendance, and assistance to the mayor (who happened to be the teacher). In addition there was a recycling center, a lost and found, a school supplies center. Student librarians decide upon the placement and storage of books and materials for classroom checkout. They design the system of cards and the rules for borrowing.

Students quiz each other on their individual student spelling tests given to one another. The weekly classroom newspaper is a paper quilt of student-prepared stories and features. The Copying Center keeps track of necessary class assignments for absentees or forgetful students. Students do homework and check it in with the homework monitor, a student who records completion, but does not correct the homework. Individuals later participate in a variety of self-correction strategies, sometimes using keys independently, sometimes working with a group to reflect and discuss. Students are expected to finish assignments or write clear letters of request for extensions.

Values

What ideals are held? Rules must be fair. Students share a feeling of care and respect. Honesty is revered. Talking about things is honored. A part of each day is devoted to expression through the arts. Getting an education is very important. They respect one another.

What is emphasized as meaningful? Students are encouraged to speak out, think for themselves, and take risks. Curriculum is integrated and applications to real life are sought on a regular basis by serving the school community; helping the larger community. Students prepare for the career fair; they give reports, prepare booths, and invite guest speakers. Kids visit the local university. They select and implement various community service projects. They recycle newspapers and donate food and toys for the holidays. They sing holiday carols at the local hospital. They sing and perform mini-dramas at the nearby retirement home. A committee is in charge of designing the room decoration according to themes as the year progresses. Students created bunches of bats who live in a cave and "flew" around the classroom, and assessing also referred to the many pictures of bats that were hung in one corner of the classroom. Students are trained in leading conferences with their parents and teachers. Students talk through agenda items that they contribute to the chalkboard AGENDA section and everything gets handled in orderly discussion, from what constitutes "Nutrition" at nutrition break to where to store backpacks, from rules for students who need to work alone to plans for the holiday party. Students talk about problems, discussing their feelings and making suggestions for possible solutions. They resolve their decisions with votes of "aye" and "nay."

Recreation

Which games, sports, hobbies, enjoyable pastimes are important? Students created a games checkout center so that more choices were available at the recess time. Imaginary playhouse play is a choice activity. Students write plays and act them out for classmates. Students have an opportunity to work with anyone in the class on a challenging jigsaw puzzle that is kept out on a table in one corner of the classroom. Several clubs are available each semester for recess participants.

How does play take place? Many activities involve cooperative, not competitive, spirit. The whole class enjoys activities with the parachute, striving to improve the class record rather than promote individual winners. Students may select a transparency of a favorite song or poem from the notebook of overhead transparencies. Students love to play "hot seat." They get to ask polite questions of the person - student or adult- who sits on the special chair in the front of the room. The arts are an important part of every day: dance, sing, create dramas.

Recess is devoted to multiple activities, including "clubs" such as the walking club, math club, and the newspaper club. Everyone joins in parachute play at P.E.

Education

What is important to learn? Students learn how to ask questions, how to solve problems, how to listen to one another. Many choices about what to learn are made by children and teachers, not just the district or the state. If learning about animals is required, the students decide which animals will go into their individual notebooks. Students read self-selected literature at appropriate levels of difficulty. Research topics center upon student interests. Kids are guided in the use of the Internet to locate information that they need for their research. Students learn about responsibility by engaging in activities that require responsibility.

What ideas are transmitted from one generation to the next? Learning about one another is considered important—the traditions, languages, crafts, and insights of classmates and their families are important to understand. Students learn that content can be learned and remembered through a variety of strategies. Partners take notes from social studies texts, nonfiction books, science chapters, biographies, and various trade books as references for their reports on chosen topics. Children also have a journal time during which they choose their topics and write pieces to the length indicated by their contracts with the teacher. Some guided reading lessons are with small, heterogeneous groups that sit around a table to explore books together. Playhouse roles are determined through group decision making. Some literature circles are student-generated. Students devise standards for book reports. Kids help to design rubrics for their projects, and they participate in designing the assessments while their teacher records information on the overhead projector.

Discussions focus on freedoms: freedom of speech, freedom of movement around the room, selection of how they would approach a subject, choice of strategies and projects, and self-selected research projects. Students are allowed to talk with one another and circulate as long as they are engaged in their designated tasks. Students write book critiques about the new books that arrive. They have a voice in lesson planning. "We want a whole day of Social Studies," they suggest.

The students struggle to answer, "How can we improve in comprehension?" Everyone's contributions go onto post-it notes that are then grouped and photocopied for class discussion. Children write stories in several different ways. Some days they have turns on the classroom computers, sometimes with a partner or sometimes with a parent volunteer. Some students chose to do a poster for their class to enter the drug free contest, making up the slogan and figuring out how to place the pictures.

The children have several slots of time during which they may decide what important things they wish to do. The students may choose from among four centers each Friday. Centers typically last for two or three weeks and they tend to have parent leaders or older student "teachers." Some choices have included Spanish lessons, Reader's Theatre, sign language, stitchery, sand painting, weaving, and drama. Kids keep a log of possible topics to choose from in their writing workshop folders. Each student maintains an individual book list of books read.

Partners work together on literature studies, research projects, TV reviews, and debates. Pairs of children "read the room" to one another in rich with environmental print. At the writing center children create poetry, letters, short stories, narratives, reports, and long stories. Children write letters to their favorite authors as well as to their "buddies" from the fifth grade. Students come to visit in small groups at the end of August before school starts. They interact in groups doing activities typical for that class to give the teacher a jump-start on authentic assessment. Parents fill out questionnaires about student interests and history. Children use their developing sign language to communicate with one another.

As an art activity, students do pencil contour drawings of one another. The students enter information about the focus animal of the week on their big KWL chart. Students build a California mission to scale. Each student has responsibility for deep research about one particular area (for example, courtyard, tannery) or room (dining room, chapel). Students participate in class meetings where problems are solved and plans are made. Literature Circles follow a set format with special roles that students select once their group is set. The kids work in small groups to plan and build a city the size of almost one third of the classroom.

Unfortunately, democratic contexts continue to be rare in terms of the demographics of most districts. Although I have met principals who are devoted to democracy and who encourage their faculty members, and I have met individuals and teams of teachers who plan--and practice--democracy, I have visited no school that is fully engaged. More often than not, democracy is lived in several classrooms that are surrounded by others that learn about democracy. Nevertheless, the efforts of many esteemed individuals with nationwide programs urge us onward. Devoted teachers engage students with authentic experiences and responsibilities. They profess to be "on the way." They are learners.

I have no doubt that possibilities exist in the aftermath of highly publicized school tragedies and with the ensuing examination of student-student, teacher-student, and parent-teacher-student relationships within schools. A school in which the above practices occur regularly is within the reach of all. It is a place where citizens of all ages and roles gather in true community, for each individual feels respected for having knowledge, power, and affection (Nagel, in press).

In Addition ...

The following list, originally prepared for the 1997 Claremont Reading Conference summarizes practices that promote classroom democracy in ways that evoke "learning by doing." It is not meant to be prescriptive, for in the hands of an authoritarian teacher, each and every practice could end up being quite UN-democratic. It is, therefore, necessary that the teacher's overall philosophy and day-to-day guiding beliefs allow for student voices be heard and for their decisions to be the ones that help guide the process of task completion.

Democratic Literacy Practices: A Partial List

Student Speaking/Listening

think / pair / share	councils	coaching
book groups	committees	student radio shows
literature circles	"Share & Stare"	book conferences
cooperative groups	peer tutoring	debates
inclusion opportunities	Speakers' Bureau	plays, reader's theatre
class meetings	author's chair	guest speakers
book talks	student as teacher	student videos, TV shows
conflict resolution	"How To" talks	interviews

Student Writing

Daily News	job descriptions	photo essays
classroom newspaper	scripts	propositions
letters to the editor	constitutions	editorials
policies	class mission	consumer letters
critical essays	books	advertising / posters
prescriptions	Venn diagrams	charting
journals	"Buddy" journals	e-mail
poetry	brainstorms	handbooks

Student Reading

student writings	book clubs	newspapers
self-selected readings	class books	original documents
materials on-line	pamphlets	research materials
reader's theatre	choral readings	poetry readings
cases		

Student Assessment

rubrics	self-correction	taping (audio, video)
peer editing	interviews	accomplishment lists
portfolios	letters	student-led conferencing

References and Recommended Readings

Apple, M., and Beane, J. (Eds.) (1995). *Democratic schools.*
　　Alexandria, VA: Association for Supervision and Curriculum
　　Development.

Campbell, D.E. (1996). *Choosing democracy: A practical guide to
　　multicultural education.* Englewood Cliffs, NJ: Prentice-Hall.

Kohn, A. (1996). *Beyond discipline: From compliance to community.*
　　Alexandria, VA: Association for Supervision and Curriculum
　　Development.

Nagel, G. (in press). *Effective groups for the literacy classroom.*
　　Boston, MA: Allyn & Bacon.

Nagel, G., and Thicksten, M. (1997). *The Claremont Reading
　　Conference yearbook.* Claremont, CA: Claremont Graduate
　　University.

Nelsen, J. (1996). *Positive discipline.* NY: Ballantine.

Porro, B. (1996). *Talk it out: Conflict resolution in the elementary
　　classroom.* Alexandria, VA: Association for Supervision and
　　Curriculum Development.

Sagor, R. (1992). *How to conduct collaborative action research.*
　　Alexandria, VA: Association for Supervision and Curriculum
　　Development.

＿＿＿＿. (January, 1999). Conducting action research. A presentation
　　at California State University, Long Beach, California.

Sapon-Shevin, M. (1999). *Because we can change the world: A
　　practical guide to building cooperative, inclusive classroom
　　communities.* Boston, MA: Allyn & Bacon.

Shor, I. (1992). *Empowering education.* Chicago, IL: University of
　　Chicago.

Wood, G.H. (1990). "Teaching for democracy." *Educational
　　Leadership, 48,* (3), pp. 32-37.

In addition, ongoing issues of these publications are EXTREMELY valuable:

*Educational Leadership, The Journal of the Association for Supervision
　　and Curriculum Development.* 1250 N. Pitt, Alexandria, VA
　　22314-1453.

Issue: Creating a Climate for Learning (September 1996). *Educational Leadership, The Journal of the Association for Supervision and Curriculum Development*. Alexandria, VA: ASCD.

Issue: Exemplary Curriculums (May, 1996). *Educational Leadership, The Journal of the Association for Supervision and Curriculum Development*. Alexandria, VA: ASCD.

Issue: Politics and Literacy (September, 1992). *Language Arts, A Publication of the National Council of Teachers of English*. Urbana, IL.

Language Arts
Primary Voices, K-6
Voices from the Middle: Publications of the National Council of Teachers of English. 1111 Kenyon Road, Urbana, IL 61801.

Rethinking Schools. 1001 E. Keefe Ave. Milwaukee, WI 53212.

Teaching Tolerance. Southern Poverty Law Center. 400 Washington Ave. Montgomery, AL 36104

and materials from   Developmental Studies Center (DSC)
                             2000 Embarcadero, Suite 305
                             Oakland, CA 94606-5300

Taking an Anthropologist's View of Culture

Social Organization
        Whose voices are heard?
        What kinds of roles do students play?
        How is status achieved?
Politics
        What decisions are made by students?
        How is power distributed?
        How is control achieved?
        How do individuals share ideas and persuade others?
Economics
        What work do students do?
        How do class members "earn a living"?

Values

      What ideals are held?

      What is emphasized as meaningful?

      What expressive aspects of living are treasured?

Recreation

      What games, sports, hobbies, enjoyable pastimes are important?

      How does play take place?

Education

      What is important to learn?

      What ideas are transmitted from one generation to the next?

LEARNING TO READ IN ANOTHER COUNTRY: INSIGHTS FROM A LITERACY LESSON IN SENEGAL

Kathryn Z. Weed

In Senegal, West Africa, the children who are fortunate enough to attend school enter the first grade speaking one, two, or sometimes even three of the local languages. Few come with knowledge of the school's language of instruction, French. During the first months of the school year, the children are exposed to oral language and engage in a variety of oral language development activities (Weed, in press). Starting in January of the first grade year, formal reading instruction begins.

This article will reproduce the first reading lesson (translated by the author into English) that a class of 54 first-graders experienced two months after they had started school. The account of the lesson will be followed by an analysis and comments on the lesson. The article ends with two lists, one of recommended readings which provide further insight into working with language and other minority children, and the second of recommended websites which provide articles about working with second language children.

The reproduction of the first reading lesson provides us with insights into the strengths and the constraints that teachers and students face in other parts of the world. It is offered here as an opportunity for us to step out of our own world and to learn about and learn from the experiences of others. The lesson was conducted in French, the language the children had been learning to understand and speak and the one in which they would be learning to read. The teacher provided some explanations in Wolof, the language of the majority of the students, but not of all. I have translated the lesson into English and made note where something was said in Wolof.

The Context for the Reading Lesson: the First Grade Curriculum

Before beginning the lesson, I wish to put reading lessons in their context within the Senegalese curriculum for first grade. The job of the first grade teacher is to help students with language. As previously mentioned, the first two months of the first grade year are devoted to oral language. During this time the children are also exposed to mathematical concepts and to the mechanics of writing, i.e. holding a pencil, making lines, curves, and circles within designated spaces. After this initial period, reading is added. The complete curriculum for first (and second) grade consists of: oral language (French), reading and writing (penmanship), and mathematics. The children spend five hours in school from 8:00 to 1:00 with a single half hour break from 11:00 to 11:30. On two days (Tuesday and Thursday) they come back to school from 3:00 to 5:00 in the afternoon for a review or elaboration of the morning activities. Of the total 26.5 classroom hours per week, approximately 6.5 are devoted to oral language, 6.5 to reading, 6.5 to mathematics, and 3.5 to writing (penmanship). An additional 2.5 hours are spent on language, reading or a combination of the two. The remaining time is programmed for physical education and manual activities although I never observed any lessons of this type during my visits.

The school year began around the first of November so at the time of this reading lesson, Monday, January 5, 1998, the students had been in school for a little less than two months. They were just returning from a two-week break. The school in which this observation was conducted was in a middle-class neighborhood in the capital city, Dakar.

The First Reading Lesson

The 54 students were seated shortly after 8:00 and waited, silently, without fidgeting, their eyes forward as the teacher, Mme. D, briefly looked over her lesson plans. During the next 20 minutes Mme. D. led the students through an oral review of a previously learned dialogue, introduced a new one, and directed the choral and individual recitation of the three new lines. Then Mme. D. said, "Today we are going to begin reading," and gave an explanation in Wolof. She proceeded to get out two of the familiar flannel board figures that were normally used to introduce a new dialogue--the schoolboy Sidi and the school building.

She put them up and, pointing to Sidi, asked, "Who is this?" "Sidi,"
chorused the students. "Where is Sidi going?" "To school!" came the
answer. "Sidi is going to school," said Mme. D., orally giving the
students the very sentence they would be reading (*Sidi va à l'école.*).
The students repeated chorally and a few, designated by Mme. D.,
individually.

Moving to the blackboard, Mme. D. then printed *"sidi,"* saying the
word as she wrote it. The students repeated. "In order to read, you have
to look [at the words]," she admonished them. She then printed the
whole sentence, *"sidi va à l'école,"* saying each word as she wrote it and
the students repeated. Mme. D. insisted that the students include the
punctuation *"point"* (period) at the end of each recitation of the sentence.
This same procedure of writing, naming, and students reciting was
repeated as Mme. D. wrote the same sentence in cursive. (Notice that
"sidi" did not begin with a capital. This detail surprised me at first until I
realized that we, in fact, teach two written forms to our kindergartners
and first graders—capitals and small letters—whereas in schooling based
on the French system, the two types introduced initially are print and
cursive.) "Who is going to read?" Mme. D. asked, following her
question with an explanation in Wolof. Ultimately, eight children,
designated by Mme. D., came up to the front, took a meter stick, used it
to point to each word and read both the print and the cursive version of
"sidi va à l'école." Mme. D. then reviewed by underlining each word,
emphasizing the break between each as she repeated the phrase. She
repeated this explanation in Wolof.

Moving to her table, Mme. D. then held up a 2-sided slate (of
approximately 8" x 10") on which *"sidi"* was printed on one side, and
written in cursive on the other. She showed the students both sides and
asked, "What is this?" "Sidi," came the answer. She then called on a
couple of individuals, gave an explanation in Wolof, and called on a few
more students to tell her what was written on the slate. She repeated the
same procedure with three other slates on which were printed and written
the words, *va, à,* and *l'école.* (Although she only used Wolof once more,
after showing the word *"va".*) Four students were then called to the front
of the room and each given a slate. Mme. D. read, *"sidi va à l'école,"*
pointing to each slate as she spoke. The students repeated. Mme. D.
then mixed up the slates, explaining to the students in Wolof what she
was doing and what she expected of them, i.e. that everyone was to read

the mixed up sentence and that one student would then come and arrange the slates correctly. This procedure was followed twice with all the students reading the mixed up sentence, one student coming to the front, rearranging, and then reading the correct sentence. After the second student had performed, Mme. D. explained in Wolof the differences between print and cursive. (The students had been reading both sides of the slates and in the mixing Mme. D. had made sure to have some in cursive and some in print so that the student who put the sentence back in order also had to correct the written forms at the same time.)

The next procedure began with "who can take *sidi* away?" Mme. D. explained in Wolof about taking the appropriate slate away from one of the four students standing in the front and then erasing the word from the sentences she had previously written on the board. A student came to the front, removed the slate containing *"sidi,"* and erased *sidi* from both the print and cursive versions on the board. "What is left?" asked Mme. D. *"Va à l'école."* came the chorus. "What was taken away?" *"Sidi."* "And what is left?" *"Va à l'école."* "Who's going to take away *"à"*? A volunteer came up, took away *"à"* and erased it from the board. "What's left?" At this point, the student made a mistake, saying *"va à l'école."* Mme. D. explained in Wolof that the *"à"* had been taken away and that the student was to read only what was on the slates. Another student was then asked to take away *"l'école"* and was again reminded of the procedure of taking the slate, showing it to the class, putting it down, and then erasing the word from the board. "And what is left?" *"Va,"* said the class. Mme. D. held up the slate and called on numerous individuals to say the word.

For the last procedure, Mme. D. asked who could show her *"va"* on the board. "You have to show it to me correctly, hold the ruler at the word." She repeated her instructions in Wolof. Three students individually came to the board, took the ruler, and pointed to either the cursive or printed *"va."* "Who can show me another 'va'? " Mme. D. asked. She was referring to the sentences she had written before the start of class which were on the left side of the board:

> *je lis: sidi va à l'école.*
> *je découvre: sidi va à l'école.*
> > *va*
> > (I read: sidi is going to school.

I discover: sidi is going to school.

is going

je lis and *je découvre* were printed in red, the sentences and
"key" word in white.)

She then explained in Wolof that the students needed to search in the
sentences to find *"va,"* they couldn't just choose the isolated word on the
other part of the board. Two students came up and each found a *"va."*
"There it is. And this too is..." said Mme. D. pointing to one of the
sentences. *"Va,"* said the students.

At this point, the reading portion of the lesson ended and the students
were asked to get out their own slates. They were then instructed how to
write *"va"* both in print and in cursive. The step-by-step versions
consisted of four steps for the print version and six for cursive. When
finished, the students were asked to raise their slates and Mme. D
checked them. Mme. D summed up this portion of the lesson by saying
that they now had *"va."* (This was the first of a number of key words
that the students would learn from each of their sentences. These key
words were slowly added over the rest of the year to a list on the extreme
left side of the board, followed by their respective vowels printed and
written in cursive.)

This first reading lesson took approximately 45 minutes. Subsequent
lessons followed the same general pattern although the teacher found it
less and less necessary to use Wolof as students became more familiar
with the procedures.

Outline of the Lesson

The following outline of the lesson divides the procedures into the
stages "into," "through," and "beyond." This overview will help us see
how the teacher proceeded through the points she wanted the children to
learn, how she varied the activities to expose the children to the words in
various ways, how she made the words and concept she was working on
comprehensible.

Into:
1. Teacher introduces the new area of learning—reading (French; Wolof)
2. Teacher uses familiar flannel board cutouts to set the scene, ask questions, and lead students orally to the sentence to be read (French)
3. Students repeat the sentence (*Sidi va à l'école*) orally

Through:
4. Board activity
   a. Teacher pronounces each word while writing it on the board (print) and all students repeat
   b. Teacher pronounces each word while writing it on the board (cursive) and all students repeat
   c. Teacher explains the procedure (Wolof) and students (8) come to the board, use a pointer and read the sentences (French)
   d. Teacher underlines individual words, uses Wolof to explain the concept of "word"
5. Slate activity
   a. Teacher shows 4 slates with one word on each (explains in French, Wolof) and students repeat
   b. Four students come to the front and each hold a slate, teacher reads (French)
   c. Teacher mixes the slates (explains in Wolof)
   d. All students read mixed sentence (French)
   e. One student puts slates back in order, reads (French)
   f. Repeat activity
   g. Teacher explains print/cursive distinction (Wolof)
6. Slate activity
   a. Teacher explains activity (Wolof), calls off one word, student comes and takes it away (French)
   b. Second student erases word from board
   c. All students read the remaining words
   d. Teacher asks which word had been taken away, what is left and all students respond
   e. Repeat activity until only *"va"* remains
   f. Teacher holds up the last slate and the whole group, then individuals repeat *"va"*'
7. Board activity

   a. Teacher invites students to point out key word *"va"* on board
      (French, Wolof)
   b. Students (5) come to board and point out *"va"*
   c. Teacher explains about finding word in sentence (Wolof)

Beyond:
8. Teacher directs students in writing the key word *"va"*

Comprehensibility of the Lesson

After reading through this lesson, it is easy to spot some of the differences from the manner in which reading is introduced to first graders in California: the lesson is conducted to the class as a whole; there are no small groups; none of the students has a book; the children do not hear a complete story; they do not see a book; there are 54 students in the class; etc. However, what is not so evident at first glance is the work that the teacher does to make the lesson comprehensible to the students who are still in the process of learning the language of the classroom, a language which they will not hear outside the school and, further, how she builds success for all students of a concept, reading, which may be foreign to a number of these students. (The literacy rate in Senegal is only 33.1 percent [*CIA Factbook*, 1998].)

In addition, something that is also not so readily apparent is that Mme. D. accomplishes all that she does with few materials. She is the only one with a book. (The reading book is available at bookstores and at the local open air markets but most families are not able to afford the $2-$4 price. In future lessons, Mme. D. will have written the whole page the students are to read on the board.) At her disposal, Mme. D. has the blackboard, a few flannel board figures, and small slates. She also has Wolof, the language of the majority of the children. In analyzing this lesson, I find that Mme. D. skillfully interweaves the use of the visual material available to her with strategic use of Wolof.

Mme. D. takes advantage of this language resource while not taking away from the purpose and intent of the lesson. An analysis of the lesson finds a systematic use of Wolof: to introduce and/or explain reading concepts and to introduce new procedures. The students do not use it. Examples of the first use include the beginning of the lesson when Mme. D. introduces the students to a new area of learning—

reading. First she states briefly in French that they are beginning reading that day and then gives a slightly longer explanation in Wolof. She then uses Wolof at the end of activities 4, 5, and 7. For example, in 4d after the students have seen the sentence on the board, repeated it, and some of them have come forward and pointed out each individual word as they read, Mme. D. reemphasizes the idea of distinguishable units, i.e. words, by underlining each individually and explaining in Wolof the concept of one-to-one matching. She again uses Wolof in 5g, when she wishes to explain and emphasize the print/cursive distinction. And, during activity 6d, when a student makes a mistake, she points out the difference between what the student has said (*va à l'école*) and what is left on the slates (*va, l'école*). She comes back to the one-to-one matching concept in 7c in which students have to find the word *"va"* in the sentences written on the board. This occurs after they have been working with the word in isolation (on the small slate).

To introduce new procedures, Mme. D. again uses Wolof to facilitate the smooth flow of the lesson. For example, in activity 4c when she wants students to come to the board, point to the words, and read them, she explains this new process in Wolof. Slate activity #5 is also new and there are two different procedures in which she wishes the students to engage, 5a and 5c. Likewise slate activity #6 requires an explanation, as does the boardwork #7. Importantly, Wolof is not used to move from activity 3 in which students are repeating the sentence to activity 4a and 4b in which Mme. D. writes the sentences on the board. She is able to direct this procedure without resorting to Wolof. It is not a new activity (the teacher putting something on the board), and because of its visual nature, the students can look at what she is doing and what she is gesturing without needing the more familiar language. And in fact, not all explanations are in Wolof. For example, during 4a, Mme. D. gives students advice regarding reading ("In order to read, you must look [at the words]."), but she says this in French. The latter part of this sentence (*il faut regarder*) is a phrase that she has used frequently to this point, in other contexts, so she is fairly well assured that the students will understand.

In sum, although many of the outward trappings of this lesson are quite different from the California experience, there are numerous things to be learned from this lesson. In the eight activities identified in this lesson, there is a flow that leads the students from the known oral language to the to-be-learned written. Mme. D. makes use of the resources available to her by introducing the lesson with familiar visuals (the flannel board figures) and with familiar procedures (responding to questions and reciting answers). She moves the students to the written representation of the language and provides several different experiences in which the students can work with the words both in a sentence context and in isolation (boardwork 4, slate activities 5 and 6, and boardwork 7). Ultimately, she has the students work with the key word by having them write it. Throughout the lesson, she makes use of the students' primary language in order to emphasize points and to explain procedures.

Over the 45 minutes of the lesson, what have the students experienced? They have repeated the sentence numerous times, they have seen it written as a whole sentence and repeated it while looking at it, they have identified individual words within the sentence, they have worked with individual words by reading them out of order and then fitting them back into their correct order, and they have had to identify a word within the sentence. A lot of work for the first lesson!

What does this Senegalese reading lesson have to say to us as educators in the American context? Two main points can be drawn from it. One is the importance of the lesson process itself, the sequence of varying activities that lead the students to an understanding of the concept to be learned. The eight procedures identified in this lesson clearly divide into an 'into' phase which makes use of the students' background knowledge to introduce the new concept, a "through" phase which provides numerous ways to grasp the concept, and a "beyond" phase which has students work directly with print. Second is the use of all available resources, including the dominant primary language. Mme. D.'s use of Wolof gives us a clear example of a lesson that effectively uses the students' home language to reach the goals of the lesson. Her use of Wolof is not random. It does not detract from the lesson, but rather helps move it along smoothly (procedural use) and helps explain important concepts (conceptual use). Thus, an important lesson for us as reading educators is that we need to use all the resources available to us to help children learn. If we are fortunate enough to have some knowledge of the language of the children, judicious use of this language can only help our children in the long run. Educators should not be denied the use of a resource that has such obvious advantages for students.

Recommended Reading

As a follow-up to this article, I have included a list of books that I recommend as teacher-friendly, eye-opening, and helpful accounts of teachers and researchers working with children whom others may ignore.

Hayes, W. C., Bahruth, R., and Kessler, C. (1998). *Literacy con cariño.* 2nd Ed. Portsmouth, NH: Heinemann.
> An account of a 5th grade class of migrant children in South Texas who had experienced little, if any, academic success. By believing in the children himself, by organizing the year's work around the abilities and needs of the children, Mr. B. was able to help the children achieve and go on to further academic success.

Heath, S. B. (1983). *Ways with words; Language, life and work in communities and classrooms.* New York: Cambridge University Press.
> Heath studied the language, life, and work of two communities in the Piedmont Carolinas. The resulting book, now a classic, opens our eyes to the various uses of language and literacy in a community and how our schooling practices privilege some children and disadvantage others, often those we wish to reach the most.

Igoa, C. (1995). *The inner world of the immigrant child.* New York: St. Martin's Press.
> Igoa maps out her experiences in working with immigrant children and the program she has developed to help them learn English and become successful students. In reading her delightful, anecdote-filled account, the reader gains insights into the worlds of the children and teaching/learning strategies which helped them cross the barrier into American schooling.

Ladson-Billings, G. (1994). *The Dreamkeepers: Successful teachers of African American children.* San Francisco: Jossey-Bass.
> Ladson-Billings portrays eight exemplary teachers of African American students. One of the strengths of the presentation is that the teachers differ in personal style and methods but share a teaching philosophy that affirms and strengthens cultural identity.

Weed, K. and Ford, M. (1999). "Achieving Literacy through Multiple Meaning Systems" in E. Franklin (Ed.). *Reading and Writing in More than One Language: Lessons for Teachers.* Alexandria, VA: Teachers of English to Speakers of Other Languages.

Children in a second-grade class make use of art, conversation, and writing to achieve success in literacy. All chapters in the book center on actual classrooms and the accomplishments of second language chidren.

Recommended Websites

In addition to the books, the following websites are helpful for teachers who wish to know more about working with English language learners.

CATESOL (California Association of Teachers of English to Speakers of Other Languages). (1998). *Position statement on literacy instruction for English language learners, Grades K-12.*
>   http://www.catesol.org/literacy.html

Collier, V. (1995). *Acquiring a second language for school.*
>   http://www.ncbe.gwu.edu/ncbepubs/directions/volume1/04.htm

McLaughlin, B. (1995). *Fostering second language development in young children: Principles and practices.*
>   http://www.ncbe.gwu.edu/miscpubs/ncrcdsll/epr14.htm

Simich-Dudgeon, C. (1989). *English Literacy Development: Approaches and Strategies that Work with Limited English Proficient Children and Adults*
>   http://www.ncbe.gwu.edu/ncbepubs/classics/eld.htm

References

CIA Factbook, (1998). http://www.odci.gov/cia/publications/factbook/sg.html

Weed, K. (in press). *Language Learning in School: Implications for EFL Classrooms, English Teaching Forum.*

LITERACY STRATEGIES IMPROVE CONTENT AREA LEARNING

Linda McCorkel Clinard

Middle and high school teachers today still ask questions similar to the I asked as a seventh-grade student teacher in Science during the mid-1960 i.e., "Why can't these students read and write by now? Why am I hearing that I still need to teach reading? How can I fit teaching reading into an already full curriculum?" Little research and instructional support were available to help teachers explore answers to these questions in the 1960's

This paper will provide (1) a summary of the emergence of content are literacy as a focus for effective learning across the curriculum, and (2) highlights from a content area literacy staff development experience which included student teachers, middle and high school classroom teachers, teac educators and K-12 curriculum leaders in Orange County, California in Spring, 1999.

Content Area Literacy Emerges

Policies and statements about content area reading instruction can be found as early as the 1920's.

...the U.S. Bureau of Education acknowledged that each subject matte area contributes directly to the development of reading competency (Gray, 1925). Accordingly, educators popularized the slogan "Every teacher should be, to a certain extent, a teacher of reading" (Whipple, 1925, p. 6). Although reading educators recognized the importance of providing instruction that would aid students' understanding of subjec matter textbooks, an examination of classroom practice between the 1930's and 1960's failed to provide evidence that this sort of instructio was widespread (Austin & Morrison, 1963). The limited use of readir strategies in the subject matter classroom appears to be a result of the of teacher training in reading methods (Early, 1957; Ryder & Graves, 1994, pp. 2-3).

Many instructional theories and practices about content area learning have emerged over the past 50 years (Bond, 1941; Gray, 1948; Moore, et al., 1992) with a significant increase in research and related policies since the 1970's. Some states began to require coursework in content area reading instruction for secondary teachers in the 1970's. Many other states joined in making this a requirement for a credential by the early 1980's (Estes & Piercey, 1973; Farrell & Cirrincione, 1984). Content area teachers began integrating strategies in more organized and effective ways in the 1980's yielding evidence which demonstrated that they were more confident, and student learning improved (Pearce & Bader, 1986; Conley, 1986; Alvermann & Swafford, 1989; Bean, Singer, & Frazee, 1986).

Currently, professional resources provide a wide-range of support for implementing content literacy strategies at all grade levels (Moore, et al., 1998). Some researchers have focused upon the middle school learner (Atwell, 1987; Duffy, 1990; Beers & Samuels, 1998; Combs, 1997; Irvin, 1998) while others suggest strategies for middle and high schoolers (Lenski, et al., 1999; Cochran, 1993; Silver, 1998; Dupuis, et al., 1989; Tierney, Readence, & Dishner, 1990; Conley, 1995; Roe, Stoodt, & Burns, 1995). Still others offer suggestions for high school and college students (Olson, 1997; Chapman, 1993).

More recently, content area *literacy*, rather than content area *reading,* has been the focus of teacher training resources (McKenna & Robinson, 1993; Alvermann & Phelps, 1994; Readence, Bean, & Baldwin, 1998; Vacca & Vacca, 1999). Emphasis on the integrated nature of the language processes of listening, speaking, thinking, reading, and writing within the context of content-specific classrooms has emerged as a key element for training preservice and practicing secondary teachers (Readence, Bean, & Baldwin, 1998; Postman, 1979; Tierney & Shanahan, 1991).

Content Literacy Expectations in California

Policy-makers, legislators, and curriculum leaders in California have been influenced by the need to improve learning for all students by applying literacy skills across the curriculum. The California Commission on Teacher Credentialing (CCTC) adopted the following *"Standard for the Preparation of Single Subject Teaching Credential Candidates for Reading, Writing and Related Language Instruction in English"* in January, 1997. Single Subject

(secondary) preservice teacher education programs will be held accountabl
to show evidence that...:

The professional preparation program provides substantive, research-
based instruction that effectively prepares each candidate for a Single
Subject (SS) Teaching Credential to provide instruction in content-base
reading and writing skills for all students, including students with varie
reading levels and language backgrounds. The SS Credential Program
includes a significant practical experience component in reading that is
connected to the content of coursework and that takes place during eac
candidate's field experience(s) or student teaching assignment(s). The
program places all candidates for SS Credentials in linguistically and/o
culturally diverse field experience sites and student teaching assignmen
with teachers whose instructional approaches and methods in reading a
consistent with a balanced, comprehensive program and who cooperate
with institutional supervisors and instructors (California Department of
Education, 1997).

California Assembly Bill 1086 in 1997 identified the following specific
skills which current, practicing upper grade teachers (Grades 4-8) are
expected to understand and be prepared to apply:

o Word attack skills
o Spelling and vocabulary
o Comprehension skills
o Research on how reading skills are acquired
o Strategic Reading strategies across curriculum (text-handling)
o Independent, self-selected reading
o Integration of listening, speaking, reading, and writing
o Intervention for, and integration of, low performing readers
o Effective ELL (English Language Learner) reading instruction
o Planning and delivery of appropriate reading instruction based on
  assessment and evaluation

The California *Reading and Writing Content Standards for Kindergart*
through 12th Grade (California Department of Education, 1998) include
expectations that all students will be engaged in strategies across the
curriculum to develop competency in word analysis, vocabulary, literacy
response and analysis, reading comprehension, writing, listening, speaking
and other related literacy skills. The *Reading/Language Arts Framework f*

California Public Schools Grades Kindergarten through Grade Twelve
provides teachers with the blueprint for addressing the standards with all
students (California Department of Education, 1999).

Content Area Literacy Collaboration

Secondary student teachers, classroom teachers, curriculum leaders, and
teacher education faculty representing the UCI Department of Education
Professional Development Schools program (ten districts and 23 secondary
schools), eight Orange County teacher education institutions, and the Orange
County Department of Education participated in a "Content Area Literacy"
preservice collaborative experience in March, 1999. This experience was a
first-step in developing on-going communication among partners for
identifying "best practices" in the content area classrooms in which we
participate.

Four content area literacy professional resources were introduced to
provide the basis for future communication, i.e., *Practical Ideas for Teaching
Writing as a Process at the High School and College Levels* (Olson, 1997);
Content Area Literacy: An Integrated Approach (Readence, Bean, &
Baldwin, 1998); *Reading & Learning Strategies for Middle & High School
Students* (Lenski, Wham & Johns, 1999); *Into Focus: Understanding and
Creating Middle School Readers* (Beers & Samuels, 1998).

Literacy Strategies in Content Classrooms

Funds provided through a Goals 2000 Preservice Reading Grant made it
possible to offer copies of each resource to student teachers and/or classroom
teachers who signed a commitment to (a) implement a minimum of one
"new" strategy and (b) offer feedback:

Please write/type a half-page journal reflecting upon your experience in
planning and implementing this strategy. Journal content may include
your reflections about (1) planning experiences; (2) observations of
students' responses to the strategy; (3) use of strategy with different
classes; (4) evidence you saw of various levels of student performance
(independent, instructional, frustration/challenging) AND/OR (5) future
goals for use of the strategy.

The journals submitted represented middle and high school teachers from Social Science, Language Arts, Math, Science, and World Languages. Eac journal provides insights into the ways in which the teacher matched the strategy to curriculum expectations and the students.

Social Science

Middle and high school teachers in Irvine, California, explored "new" strategies for Social Studies classrooms.

"Content Reading Inventories" (Readence, Bean, & Baldwin, 1998, p) 66-70) were developed as assessments by a committee of Irvine Unified School District teachers after being introduced to a sample inventory creat by Kathy Wanchek (a middle school Language Arts teacher) and Anne Ru (a middle school Resource Teacher). An excerpt from Kathy's journal stat

This idea/template was presented to the committee of teachers who wi teach the Summer "I'M RAD" (Irvine Model Reading Advancement Development) program. The teachers saw the many possibilities presented by the use of this tool and wanted to create a collection of C for use in our summer school programs.

The "People Search" (Lenski, Wham, & Johns, 1999, pp. 13-14) serv to generate interest in a reading selection that would begin a unit studying China in Candy Peleaux's diverse freshmen *Global Perspectives* class at University High School in Irvine.

...Traditionally, we begin a unit with background reading from a textbook. To begin the China unit, I introduced the reading with the " the signature of..." activity, hoping to simultaneously access students prior knowledge and to get the class excited about the unit. The activi itself was incredibly easy to construct and to integrate. I figured that t response would be positive, but it was better even than I anticipated. Students enjoyed getting out of their seats, and they enjoyed the "soci aspect of the activity; also, those who already knew about China were proud to share their expertise. ...Comments such as, "This is fun." a "I like this" were often heard, and the competitive and cooperative m the atmosphere was refreshing. Next time I incorporate this activity, I will make it a bit longer and more complex. I plan to use this activity introduce each reading assignment throughout the year.

Language Arts

Four Language Arts teachers described strategies implemented in their classrooms. Two who used *Practical Ideas for Teaching Writing as a Process at the High School and College Levels* (Olson, 1997) were an adjunct English professor and a high school English teacher. A UCI student teacher and a high school teacher found strategies which are described in *Reading & Learning Strategies for Middle & High School Students* (Lenski, Wham, & Johns, 1999) and *Content Area Literacy* (Readence, Bean, & Baldwin, 1998).

April Moore (Vanguard University, Costa Mesa) used the "Showing, Not Telling"(Olson, 1997) strategy with a freshman college class.

I used the "Showing, Not Telling" strategy, pp. 39-45 in *Practical Ideas* after I noticed that my students were not using enough examples in their writing. I presented "good" examples of "showing" paragraphs and "bad" examples (taken from the textbook) and explained that this writing activity would help them use more examples and be able to support their writing points. ....As they continued to use this strategy until the end of the semester, all of the students continued to improve in their writing....

Christine King's sophomore English class at University High in Irvine used "clustering" and a "sharing/revising process" to scaffold instruction and improve their essay writing skills.

I used a prompt from an old AP exam and modified some of the ideas for pre-writing and sharing/revising in Carol Booth Olson's *Practical Ideas for Teaching Writing as a Process* (Olson, 1997). I was able to do the modifications and have all the materials ready after one evening of work- a very quick and easy strategy....

Students in two of my American Lit. classes were very accepting of the pre-writing and revision strategies...I had all but four students hand in each step of the process - the clustering, the introductory paragraph, the rough draft, the revision, and the final copy. They were actively engaged in the pre-writing with 100 percent of students on-task the first day...I would certainly use the strategies again. I did learn that my typical revision/editing cover sheet was far too demanding. I usually have students looking for correctness, as well as ideas and support. This new

revision/editing sheet was much easier for students and less
intimidating…

Keri Kemble, a UCI student teacher at Los Alamitos High School, used
"Knowledge Rating Scale" (Lenski, Wham, & Johns, 1999, pp. 37-38;
Readence, Bean, and Baldwin, 1998, pp. 73-74). The scale was used to
activate her English III students' prior knowledge of vocabulary words in Z
Neale Hurston's "How I Got to be Colored Me."

I asked for a show of hands to see if any students had used a rating sca
like this before. None had. I instructed students to look at the five
vocabulary words listed on the scale and rate them according to their l
of understanding: "Know It Well," "Have Heard It/Seen It," and "No
Clue." Students needed no other direction to complete the scale and ev
seemed to carefully deliberate prior to their choices. I then directed th
students' attention to fill-in-the-blank sentences taken directly from the
story…We completed the close activity as a class, going back and forth
between sentences to find the right matches…

I used the Knowledge Rating Scale strategy with two classes and the
results were clear. Students finished the introduction with an
understanding of the vocabulary words and were intrigued to begin the
essay. I will definitely use this strategy again, but perhaps next time I
might adapt it to include a brief response space so that students will ha
to record their pre-lesson answers to check post-lesson (knowledge).
What a great (and quick) assessment!

Jennifer Davis used an "Anticipation Guide" (Lenski, Wham, & Johns
1999, p. 143; Readence, Bean, & Baldwin, 1998, pp. 159-61) with English
students at University High School, Irvine, to introduce the issues in Rome
and Juliet.

The Anticipation Guide was a nice opportunity for students to examin
their beliefs prior to beginning the play Romeo and Juliet. In a non-
threatening way, it also presented the issues the students discuss while
reading the play. Often, especially with the classic love story, student
"buy into" what they are presented without thinking for themselves fir
personally liked the fact that the students were forced to decide how tl
think/feel about an issue which they never encountered prior to readin
about it in the play.

Creating the questions was easy because there were only five…We spent approximately thirty minutes sharing and discussing the various beliefs in the room…students willingly participated….

This strategy seemed easy for all levels of students. The only complaint I received was from some of my special education students. They had no problem circling an answer, but some had problems trying to justify their answers…

Mathematics

Three high school and middle school Mathematics teachers chose strategies from three different resources (Olson, 1997; Readence, Bean, & Baldwin, 1998; Lenski, Wham, & Johns, 1999).

Freshmen in Ryan Dahlem's Math A class at University High School, Irvine reviewed vocabulary through competition on a day prior to taking a test.

…The unit I was teaching was full of vocabulary terms that are similar and often confusing to students, e.g., "area, surface area, square, square units, cube, cubic units…" I used "Teaching Vocabulary through Competition" (Olson, 1997, p. 276) as a review the day before a test. I have used competition strategies before and knew the students would enjoy this type of activity. The most successful part of the lesson was "Vocabulary Charades," which was new for both the students and me. Seeing a student "gesture" a math term really showed whether s/he understood it or not…. I will use this strategy again in Math A, and perhaps try it in my functions, statistics, and trigonometry courses.

Jo Ann Byars demonstrated the importance of the communication skills of listening and writing in her math lessons at University High.

The idea of having students record their thoughts was based on the rationale that writing is a powerful tool for learning and questioning across the content areas. The students wrote about their reflections, reacting to what they observed and learned from going through the class activity. Information about writing as a tool for learning can be found in Content Area Literacy (Readence, Bean, & Baldwin, 1998, pp. 183-203).

The students seemed to enjoy the activity that made them aware of the importance of literacy development in the study of mathematics and in life in general.... Students had some very interesting insights. One stated, "I am a better listener than a speaker." Another student wrote, " also realized how I could be hearing something my friend or someone i saying to me in a different perspective."

Lois Hoshijo, a middle school math teacher at Spring View Middle School in Huntington Beach, used the "Magic Square" strategy.

I used the Magic Square example from Art Scholastic (1993) that was found in *Reading & Learning Strategies for Middle & High School Students* (Lenski, et al, 1999, pp. 43-45) to assess students' knowledge mathematical terms.... The students found this review challenging and interesting. It took just a few minutes for students to complete the activity...There are many uses for Magic Square in math literacy. Mag Square can be used as a warm-up to review previously-learned content, a pre-test for future lessons, or as a post-test...Students' responses to th activity were favorable ...(1) "It was fun studying definitions with the Magic Square;" (2) "This was a different activity. I think I'll rememb the definitions of the terms that were difficult for me to learn;" (3) "I like this. It was more challenging than just writing the definitions for each vocabulary word."

Science

Tinh Tran and Ingrid Chlup teach Science at University High, Irvine. T used a "Word Sort Assessment" (Lenski, Wham, & Johns, 1999, pp. 53-54 with eleventh and twelfth grade chemistry classes.

I selected this strategy because I wanted to see if the students could ma connections between concepts and ideas. Also, it was a way to see if th students remembered information from the previous chapter. I made a (Gas Laws Word Sort) of terms, concepts, equations, and ideas arrange in a random manner. I then instructed the students to group the words i way that made sense...I intentionally made the assignment open-ended, because I did not want to limit the students' thinking. Throughout the monitoring process, I heard students propose different ways to group th terms.... I will use this strategy again as an individual assignment, instead of a group one. There were some students in the groups who ju "went along for the ride," and contributed little. Assessing each student individually would provide a better indication of exactly what percentage of the class retained the information...

Ingrid Chlup used a "Knowledge Rating Scale" (Lenski, Wham, & Johns, 1999, pp. 37-38; Readence, Bean, & Baldwin, 1998, pp. 73-74) with her "sheltered" sophomore Science students to assess prior knowledge and provide students an opportunity to preview upcoming topics and vocabulary.

I believe this strategy was beneficial for students, assisting them to identify significant vocabulary and concepts... I found this activity useful for both myself and my students since I was given the chance to assess what students already knew...and students previewed where the unit was going with the amount of vocabulary they would need to learn.

World Languages

A UCI Student Teacher majoring in French and two high school Spanish teachers provided examples of three different strategies for students studying a second language.

UCI student teacher Lauri Resnikoff used the "Deceptive Definitions" strategy (Olson, 1997, p. 274) in a French I class at Ocean View High School in Huntington Beach.

Based on the suggestions in *Practical Ideas*, I divided the class into groups of three or four and distributed the twelve vocabulary cards... After students played the game, I gave them a matching quiz to assess how much they had learned. The students did not complain about the activity and I believe that it helped them learn new words, because they all scored from "very good" to "excellent" on their pre-quiz.

Michelle Natan used a "Pre-Writing Graphic Organizer Strategy" (Olson, 1997, pp. 14-17) with her intermediate Spanish students at University High School, Irvine.

This is a great prewriting strategy for any level language learner. The essay topic this day involved the students writing a letter full of recommendations to a student who would be visiting them from Costa Rica. The strategy was easy to explain and model in Spanish. I drew a center circle with the main topic of the essay and then asked students to help me connect ideas (supporting ideas, examples, further ideas) to the center idea with more circles. This center circle expanded outward as ideas were connected to it.... Students then created their own clusters. The best part of this strategy for me was that students, regardless of ability level, could all find something to write so that their job of writing the actual essay at home was less daunting....

Marjie Toops used a different type of graphic organizer ("sunflower organizer") in her intermediate Spanish class to organize information read the text (Lenski, Wham, & Johns, 1999, p. 78).

The purpose of this lesson is to help students organize material they read about Nobel-winning authors from the Spanish-speaking world. This has always been a troublesome unit for the students, with a great deal of information to organize.... The cluster revolves around country of origin. Each "sunflower petal" is an author, with room for facts about each. I then provided a summary area for those who needed a different visual approach. In previous years, I did not use a graphic organizer for this reading. I felt that using the "sunflower" would help students better organize and remember the information.... I found this to be a very successful exercise for most students, although some felt it was pretty "grade-school," and they would prefer to take notes in a more traditional format.

Summary

Many of the partners who participated in the Spring, 1999, Orange County Content Area Literacy project expressed a desire to continue to communicate with one another to gather evidence of effective strategies for content area classrooms. To help achieve this goal, e-mail and school addresses of educators who participated in the project are posted on a web developed as part of the 1998-99 Tri-County Reading Preservice Grants (Imperial, San Diego, and Orange Counties): www.icoe.org/reading (*Resources/Content Area Literacy*). Educators who collect evidence from their content classrooms are invited to contact teachers listed on the web site

References

Alvermann, D.E., and Phelps, S.F. (1994). *Content reading and literacy: Succeeding in today's diverse classrooms.* Boston: Allyn and Bacon.

Alvermann, D.E., and Swafford, J. (1989). Do content area strategies have a research base? *Journal of Reading,* 32, pp. 388-394.

Armento, Nash, Salter, and Wixson. (1991). *Across the centuries.* NY: Houghton Mifflin Company.

Atwell, N. (1987). *In the middle: Writing, reading and learning with adolescents.* Portsmouth, NH: Boynton/Cook.

Austin, M., and Morrison, C. (1963). *The first R: The Harvard report on reading in elementary schools.* NY: Macmillan.

Bean, T.W., Singer, H., and Frazee, C. (1986). The effect of metacognitive instruction in outlining and graphic organizer construction on students' comprehension in a tenth-grade world history class. *Journal of Reading Behavior,* 18, pp. 153-169.

Beers, K., and Samuels, B.G. (1998). *Into focus: Understanding and creating middle school readers.* Norwood, MA: Christopher-Gordon.

Bond, G.L., and Bond, E. (1941). *Developmental reading in high school.* NY: Macmillan.

California Department of Education. (1997). *Standard for the preparation of single subject teacher credential candidates for reading, writing, and related language instruction in English.* Sacramento, CA: Author.

California Department of Education. (1998). *English-language arts content standards for California public schools: Kindergarten through grade twelve.* Sacramento, CA: Author.

California Department of Education. (1999). *English-language arts content standards for California public schools: Kindergarten through grade twelve.* Sacramento, CA: Author.

Chapman, A. (Ed.) (1993). *Making sense: Teaching critical reading across the curriculum.* NY: The College Entrance Examination Board.

Cochran, J. (1993). *Reading in the content areas for junior high and high school.* Boston, MA: Allyn and Bacon.

Combs, M. (1997). *Developing competent readers and writers in the middle grades.* Upper Saddle River, NJ: Merrill.

Conley, M.W. (1986). Teacher's conceptions, decision, and changes during initial classroom lessons containing content area reading strategies. In J.A. Niles and R.V. Lalik (Eds.), *Solving problems in literacy: Learners, teachers, and searchers.* Rochester, NY: National Reading Conference.

Conley, M.W. (1995). *Content reading instruction: A communication approach.* NY: McGraw-Hill.

Duffy, G.G. (Ed.) (1990). *Reading in the middle school* (2nd ed.). Newark DE: IRA.

Dupuis, M.M., Joyce, J. W., Badiali, B. J., and Askov, E. N. (1989). *Teaching reading and writing in the content areas.* Glenview, IL: Scott Foresman.

Early, M.J. (1957). What does research reveal about successful reading programs? In M. A. Gunn, et al. (Eds.), *What we know about high school reading.* Champaign, IL: National Council of Teachers of English.

Estes, T.H., and Piercey, D. (1973). Secondary reading requirements: Report on the states. *Journal of Reading,* 17, pp. 20-24.

Farrell, R.T., and Cirrincione, J.M. (1984). State certification requirements reading for content area teachers. *Journal of Reading,* 28, pp. 152-158.

Gray, W.S. (1925). *Summary of investigations relating to reading* (Supplementary Educational Monograph No. 28). Chicago, IL: University of Chicago Press.

Gray, W.S. (1948). *Reading in the high school and college.* Forty-Seventh Yearbook, Part II, of the National Society for the Study of Education.

Irvine, J. (1998). *Reading and the middle school student.* Boston, MA: Allyn and Bacon.

Lenski, S.D., Wham, M.A., and Johns, J.L. (1999). *Reading & learning strategies for middle & high school students.* Dubuque, IA: Kendall/Hunt.

McKenna, M.C., and Robinson, R.D. (1993). *Teaching through text: A content literacy approach to content area reading.* White Plains, N.Y: Longman.

Moore, D.W., and Stefanich, G.P. (1990). Middle school reading: A historical perspective. In G. G. Duffy (Ed.), *Reading in the middle school* (2nd ed.). Newark, DE: IRA, pp. 3-15.

Olson, C.B. (Ed.) (1997). *Practical ideas for teaching writing as a process at the high school and college levels.* Sacramento, CA: California Department of Education.

Pearce, D.L., and Bader, L.A. (1986). The effect of unit construction upon teachers' use of content area reading and writing strategies. *Journal of Reading,* 30, pp. 130-135.

Readence, J.E., Bean, T.W., and Baldwin, R.S. (1998). *Content area literacy: An integrated approach.* Dubuque, IA: Kendall/Hunt.

Roe, B.D., Stoodt, B.D., and Burns, P.C. (1995). *Secondary school reading instruction: The content areas.* Boston, MA: Houghton Mifflin.

Ryder, R.J., and Graves, M.F. (1994). *Reading and learning in content areas.* NY: Macmillan.

Silver, J.F. (1998). *Real-life reading activities for grades 6-12.* West Nyack NY: The Center for Applied Research in Education.

Tierney, R.J., Readence, J.E., and Dishner, E.K. (1990). *Reading strategies and practices: A compendium.* Boston, MA: Allyn and Bacon.

Vacca, R.T., and Vacca, J.L. (1999). *Content area reading: Literacy and learning across the curriculum.* NY: Longman.

Whipple, G.M. (ed.) (1925). Report on the national committee on reading: *24th yearbook of the National Society for the Study of Education.* Bloomington, IL: Public School Publishing.

REDEFINING LITERACY FOR THE INCLUSIVE CLASSROOM

J. Dixon Hearne and Dawn Hunter

In the ongoing dialectic among literacy experts, researchers, and educators, there remains a strong tendency to define literacy in terms of the *typical student* in the *general classroom*. Indeed, most of the research in whole language and literacy over the past twenty-five years has centered on students in general classroom settings. Literacy has become a national quest—if not obsession. However, when we define literacy as a *common standard*, we invite both elitism and criticism. By this, we mean that "literacy" is a *relative* term. How it applies to teaching and learning could (perhaps should) *vary* according to classroom populations.

Inclusive schooling, for example, brings many new challenges to classroom teachers—as well as to present conceptions of literacy. How then would we apply literacy standards—as defined by the *general* classroom curriculum—to persons whose learning characteristics, modalities, and/or abilities fall outside these parameters, or whose limitations preclude success? How might we reframe "literacy" as a multidimensional model—as a "prism" through which we might view the strengths of students whose backgrounds and/or special needs impact learning? How might literacy be defined and measured (demonstrated) among students who have autistism? How might literacy vary for students with developmental disabilities or learning disabilities? Attention Deficit Disorder? Behavior disorders?

At what point do we stop perseverating on bringing every child in the classroom up to minimum competency standards and/or predetermined literacy standards and begin to explore and define literacy in terms of the individual—rather than the curriculum?

A Definitional Problem

> **literacy** - *n*. the state or quality
> of being literate, ability to read
> and write. (Webster)

When one asks, "What is literacy?", nothing that follows seems to be quite sufficient. This is due in great part to the "fine" distinctions and attributes that we—either individually or collectively—ascribe to the concept. Most persons would probably respond to this question by identifying its attributes and intentions. Because it is a *theoretical* construct, however, it retains an openness to interpretation, in much the same was as, say, the construct "morality." When we hear *morality*, most persons have a sense of what we mean by the word. For centuries, philosophers and theologians have examined and reexamined the concept, struggling to define it—without consensus. It has also remained a perennial topic of discussion and debate among educators and psychologists, who tinker with meanings and tweak the finer points.

Defining *literacy* seems to pose a somewhat similar challenge. Today, we speak of "computer literacy," "art literacy," "cultural literacy," and other "literacies" as if a single word somehow "fits" each. But the meaning of literacy as it applies to *computers* cannot possibly have the same meaning as it does when applied to *culture*. When we invoke Webster's definition (above), it would seem to apply to neither. Elliot Eisner (1992) states it better: "To talk about literacy as if it were a single skill applicable to all forms of text is to underestimate the special demands that different forms of language exact" (p. 3).

How then does a term take on connotations beyond its definition? The answer is, of course, through general usage and acceptance. When most persons hear the term, *computer literacy*, they know what is implied by it—knowledge of computers and computer language. When one hears *cultural literacy*, it implies a level of knowledge and understanding of cultures. It seems we have begun to expand our definition and view of literacy as being something much more than the mere ability to read and write.

Why then, has it retained a narrow definition among many educators? For example, when we pose the statement, "Literacy is…"

to teachers and ask them to brainstorm responses, the result is typically a web resembling the following:

Figure 1. Typical responses from pre-service and in-service teachers, when asked to respond to the cue, "Literacy is…"

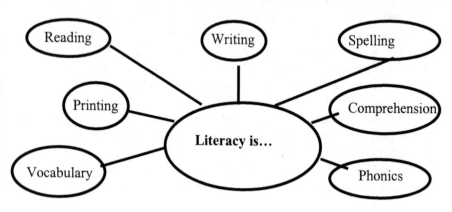

This web is much more *definitive* than *connotative*. It seems to reflect conditioned responses. However, when these same persons are then engaged in broader discussion about the possibility of literacy "forms," there is typically an "aha" experience that somehow allows them to reformulate their conceptions of literacy to include other aspects or dimensions. This *expanded* view of literacy can be seen in Figure 2. Participants are asked probing questions intended to challenge their present conceptions. As each *literacy* is introduced, it creates disequilibrium, the catalyst for change in one's present understanding. For example, the concept of *art literacy* could not be developed merely through reading and writing. It is also dependent upon perceptual (or *viewing*) ability. And because meaning in art is negotiable, it also engages thinking (cognitive ability), intuitive knowledge ("felt knowledge") and emotional intelligence.

Figure 2: Responses from pre-service and in-service educators after engaging in discussion of "literacy forms" yielded this "expanded" view of literacy.

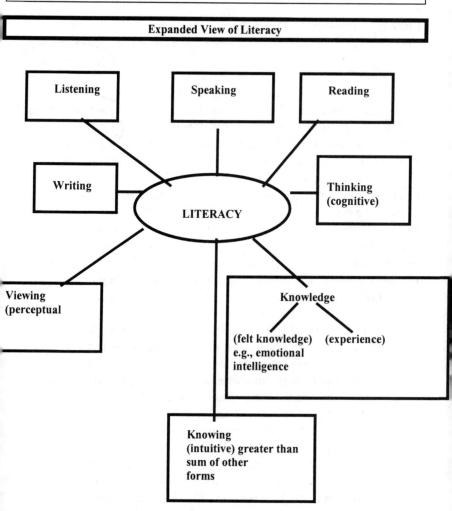

Likewise, *cultural literacy* presents equal challenges to participants' present conceptualizations of *literacy*. How does one come to be literate about a culture without venturing beyond the printed page? What does it truly mean to be culturally literate?

For that matter, when viewed collectively, what does it mean to be *literate*? Can one be literate in one context and not in another? Should literacy be "criterion-referenced?" If so, how might this look? How would it serve special populations?

Literacy Through the One Lens

> *Man by nature seeks to know.*
> Aristotle.

Using Aristotle's dictum, schools would acknowledge that *all* populations within their walls want to *know*—to make meaning of the world around them. They would also acknowledge that individuals construct their *own* worlds and their own meanings to explain them. To presume that individuals with developmental disabilities, learning disabilities, autism, or cerebral palsy construct meanings that are somehow inferior or undesirable would be ludicrous. Their constructions of meaning are relevant to their *own* learning and knowing, and they are as valid as those of their non-disabled peers—simply different. For this reason, the road toward literacy must allow for multiple forms and multiple ways of attaining them. In short, we need to consider the notion of "personal literacy," that is, literacy attainment measured by individually established criteria.

> If education as a process is aimed at expanding and deepening the kinds of meanings that people can have in their lives and if literacy is conceptualized as a process concerned with the construction and communication of meaning, then school programs must, I think, attempt to provide time for the development of multiple forms of literacy. Not to do so is to create a kind of epistemological parochialism that limits what people can experience, and therefore, what they can come to know. Literacy is far more than being able to read or to write. Such conceptions are educationally anemic and short-change children in the long run. The development of human sensibility and the provision of programs that address the several ways in which experience has been represented—propositional, literary, poetic, visual, auditory, choreographic—ought to be fundamental educational aims. Regrettably, many of these

representational forms are marginalized in our programs. We simply do not see far enough (Eisner, 1992, p. 9).

Perhaps the biggest argument for a *criterion-referenced* view of literacy can be found in special education classrooms. Over the past thirty years, schools and society have wrestled with the implications of civil and human rights for America's public schools, and how to best meet the needs of a growing population of "special students". While school age children today receive individual support through the development of individualized education plans (I.E.P's), the majority of their I.E.P's are "deficit-centered." The aim is to bring students closer to the norm—however it is defined. In language arts, for example, the norm is typically viewed as "reading and writing at grade level." Students with learning disabilities, Down Syndrome, autism, and/or other cognitive differences present special challenges for schools. With literacy as both *norm* and a *goal*, these students may be labeled as "at risk." The response of choice has been predominantly reductionistic in nature. The basic curriculum is reduced and segmented into discrete parts, which are then selected for drill-and-practice. The assumption of this approach is that it leads to the eventual mastery of skills, subskills, and knowledge. Therefore, students identified as having reading and learning problems have spent the majority of their school day focusing on their deficits—to the virtual exclusion of their interests, strengths, or talents. While their non-disabled peers are immersed in books and stories and group projects, students with learning problems have been immersed in worksheets and individual tasks.

While differential standards may exist for students with learning difficulties, they are continually compared to their non-disabled peers. For example, some of the nation's school districts have adopted differential graduation standards to address the *problem* of students with disabilities. They might receive a certificate simply stating that they have undergone a curriculum of study—not the *official* curriculum with its requisite standards. Hence, the certificate is a statement of not merely the *level* of attainment but the quality of one's attainment as well. The inherent problem in such a plan is that it does not educate the public or prospective employers as to the personal strengths and abilities of individuals with disabilities. It merely summons to mind their differences and deficits.

In the final analysis, the threshold of understanding and literacy attained by a student with learning disabilities, autism, Down Syndrome or cerebral palsy is not generally regarded as equivalent in value to that attained by non-disabled students. Schools do not typically maintain multiple thresholds of literacy—equally valued.

Toward an Inclusive Multi-dimensional Model

With the foregoing points in mind, we can begin to explore ways of "reframing" literacy to consider "special" populations in our definition and usage. We might begin by considering the populations themselves. The *Education of the Handicapped Act*, Public Law 94-142, was passed in 1975 and amended by P.L. 99-457 in 1986 to ensure that children with disabilities would have a free, appropriate public education available to them which would meet their unique needs. It was again amended in 1990, and the name was changed to the *Individuals with Disabilities Education Act,* or IDEA (Public Law 101-476). IDEA, and its reauthorization in 1997, defines "children with disabilities" as having any of the following:

Autism	Deafness
Deaf-Blindness	Hearing Impairment
Mental Retardation	Multiple Disabilities
Orthopedic Impairment	Other Health Impairment
Serious Emotional Disturbance	Specific Learning Disability
Speech or Language Impairment	Visual Impairment Including Blindness
Traumatic Brain Injury	

Each category falls within one or more of three general classifications of disabilities: *mental, physical* or *sensory.* However, there is no presumption that *all* persons with a specific disability are exactly alike. On the contrary, individuals bring their own unique backgrounds and experiences to bear on literacy development. Likewise, individuals with disabilities are at differing points in their development, despite their grade or classroom placements—just like their non-disabled peers.

When we begin to consider literacy plans for students within these categories, almost immediately we recognize that learners within most of them can be quite successful in the general curriculum with only minor modifications and support. Hence, literacy for these students would be defined by the standards of the general curriculum. For those students whose learning abilities and characteristics preclude success with the general curriculum, literacy takes on a different meaning. Once again, it is not merely a matter of degrees or levels of attainment toward the literacy of the *norm* (defined by age/grade level). Rather, it is—and should be—literacy as defined by personal attainment. How, then, might literacy differ for students with learning disabilities, autism, developmental disabilities, or cerebral palsy (cerebral palsy is included in discussion here simply because of the "processing time" frequently used in arguments for more restrictive placements). At least some ideas are offered here:

How might approaches to literacy development *differ* for each of the following categories?

For students with Developmental Disabilities, educators might begin by:

- identifying students' strengths and working through them to promote learning and literacy—as functional equivalents of attainments by their peers who have no disabilities
- observing situations that produce empathetic responses towards others.
- observing situations that produce laughter—a demonstration of a sense of humor (both a cognitive and emotional response).

For students with Autism, educators might:

- examine (and value) knowledge/understanding conveyed through intricate drawings.
- communicate and/or instruct through head phones.
- study patterns of literacy development over longer blocks/periods of time.
- utilize students' interests in developing curriculum.

For students with Deaf-Blindness, educators might:

- approach literacy development through "oral" channels, e.g., audio tapes, oral instruction and/or discussion, story-telling and student story re-telling, oral exams, etc. if a student has some residual hearing.
- use tactile sign language.
- create and/or use large-print books and materials if students have some residual vision.
- encourage oral reading, dramatic readings, demonstrations and performances.

For students with Cerebral Palsy, educators might:

- make broad use of assistive technology (e.g., laser eye glance) which might allow students' to more fully and accurately demonstrate knowledge and understanding, and to express ideas and feelings.
- observe choices students make during free time—things that might indicate literacy development (e.g., using computers that generate voice output, watching the news rather than *Barney* on TV).

For students with Learning Disabilities, educators might:

- incorporate students' interests and talents in curriculum planning.
- allow students to choose their own ways of demonstrating literacy development (e.g., drawings, paintings, graphics, computer products, oral exams, demonstrations, performances, etc.).
- study broad patterns of attainment across the school year— rather than examining smaller segments or "chunks" of the curriculum (e.g., language arts)—in assessing development.

What constitutes literacy for students with disabilities (in each category) might look fundamentally different from *literacy* as it is used to describe "reading and writing proficiency" for most classroom students—and that's okay. For this reason, we need to rethink our definition.

Figure 3: Implications of four approaches to teaching and learning in the general classroom.

Implications for the General Classroom
Integration

- Multimodal approach - to engage all senses (visual, auditory, kinesthetic, tactile)
- Engage all aspects of communication - listening, speaking, reading, writing, viewing, thinking, drawing, painting, etc.

Experiential Learning

- "Hands on" direct experience approach - concretize learning and concepts
- Inquiry-based projects approach - interactive learning

Multiple Intelligences (MI)

- Engage all intelligences - nurture fuller development of potential and interests
- MI-centered curriculum and authentic assessment

Adaptive Curriculum

- Curriculum designed around all aspects—listening, speaking, reading, writing, viewing, thinking, knowledge, and knowing
- Curriculum adaptations—resources/space to accommodate diverse needs
- Differentiated instruction—to accommodate diverse populations, individual needs.

If literacy describes or *implies* our command of communicating our knowledge, thoughts, ideas, and feelings—using whatever tools that allow us to accomplish this—then we must recognize that there are many tools and that each should be valued equally.

Because a student needs assistive technology to communicate knowledge, it should in no way be viewed as inferior to paper-and-pencil

communication. Stephen Hawking would demonstrate literacy
development in ways fundamentally different from his peers. Literacy
development for Helen Keller differed greatly from that of her peers.
Had she attained only *one* form of communication, it would still have
been a remarkable exemplar of *literacy* development. The young actor
with Down syndrome on the TV show, *Life Goes On* has clearly
demonstrated the "fundamental equivalent" of literacy through his
acting. We simply cannot have a narrow and discriminating definition of
literacy. Nor can we "give up" or exclude any of our children. When we
allow multiple means of demonstrating knowledge and understanding,
we increase opportunity for students with disabilities—and we expand
our understanding and conceptualization of what it means to be *literate*.

The four general instructional approaches described in Figure 3 seem
particularly promising in promoting literacy development among
students with disabilities. The <u>Integration</u> approach, for example,
attempts to engage and integrate as many of the senses as possible during
classroom learning. Whereas most students demonstrate literacy through
oral and written responses, a student with disabilities might need several
modalities (visual, auditory, kinesthetic-tactile) to produce indicators of
literacy development. Another model, <u>Experiential Learning</u> is an
interactive approach aimed at promoting "learning by doing." Engaging
learners in projects, for example, provides many more opportunities for
students to demonstrate learning and literacy attainment than mere
paper-and-pencil tests. The <u>Multiple Intelligences</u> model, advocated by
Howard Gardner and his followers, is another broad-brush approach to
teaching and learning. Because it begins with the presumption that all
persons have multiple intelligences, there is an implicit argument for
identifying and nurturing *all* students' strengths and aptitudes. The
preoccupation of our schools with verbal and logico-mathematical ability
has generally diverted our attention from other aspects or kinds of
intelligence that reside within every child. If music, art, and divergent
thinking were valued more highly than these two intelligences, would we
not have a different group of students labeled *disabled*? Might
individual differences in personal attainment styles be honored *and*
utilized through thoughtful and carefully-planned curriculum and
instruction? The answer to both of these questions is a resounding
"yes." Where the general curriculum does not meet the learning needs of
individuals, however, it is incumbent upon educators to "make the school

fit the child"—rather than the reverse. We must recognize that the curriculum and methods that have already failed learners are typically just as ineffective when they are merely "watered down and stretched out" in special education classrooms (Meltzer & Reid, 1994; Poplin & Cousin, 1996). Teachers open to planning for individual differences and personal attainments might begin by developing an <u>Adaptive Curriculum</u> which allows for: (a) modifications of the general curriculum, (b) adaptations/accommodations (e.g., assistive technology) and/or (c) alternate tasks, materials, products, and forms of instruction and assessment. Moreover, the selection of "learning tools"—to be used in demonstrating learning and literacy attainment—should be a negotiated process with the learners themselves.

Concluding Remarks

Although the schools still operate in a paradigm structure that is deficit driven, students caught up in the physical and pedagogical manifestations of our rhetoric probably care little about definitions and the elusive constructs we build to study their disabilities. They continue to learn things—many things—that are important and useful to them. We see evidence of this both inside and outside the schools. Some of us still shake our heads in awe at the wonderful things our students with disabilities *can* do. Their personal attainments in all areas—including literacy development— must be valued as fundamental equivalents of the learning demonstrated by peers who do not have disabilities.

While educators are presently "re-defining" literacy, we should also be "reframing" it to address populations formerly excluded from discussions—specifically, students with disabilities whose performance is compared to norms set by their peers without disabilities. There are numerous ways to begin to think about what literacy *is* and *is not* in students who have been labeled as having a disability that has interfered with the "typical" learning process (if there is such as thing as "typical").

"Different" does not imply "deficit" or "deficient." As educators we know that often students with disabilities have many skills that are difficult to measure using traditional means of assessment (Hearne & Stone, 1996; Poplin & Cousin, 1996). That is, we simply do not have the skills, training, necessary technology, persistence, creativity, and/or attitudes to accurately assess the "real knowledge, understanding, and skills" that a student may possess. Often, our inability to accurately assess students is then used to describe their *deficits*. That is, we "blame the victims" of our professional ineptness. How different things might be if we approached literacy from a posture of "presumed competence" rather than "assumed deficits."

In conclusion, we invite readers to join us in our research and discussion. We believe we raise important issues worthy of further study. Productive lines of inquiry might include:

- literacy as personal attainment
- criterion-referenced models of literacy
- personal literacy and authentic assessment
- personal literacy across the disciplines
- differential instruction and assessment
- models of instruction for the promotion of personal literacies.
- the role of parents in promoting personal attainment and literacy
- the role of support personnel in promoting personal attainment and literacy.

References

Eisner, E.W. (1992). "Rethinking literacy." In P. Dreyer (Ed.), *Claremont Reading Conference 52nd Yearbook, Reading the world* (pp. 1-16). Claremont, CA: Center for Developmental Studies, Claremont Graduate University.

Hearne, J.D., and Stone, S. (1995). "Multiple intelligences and underachievement: Lessons from students with learning disabilities." *Journal of Learning Disabilities, 28* (7), pp. 439-448.

Meltzer, L., and Reid, D.K. (1994). "New directions in the assessment of students with special needs: The shift toward a constructivist perspective." *The Journal of Special Education, 28*, pp. 338-355.

Poplin, M.S., and Cousin, P.T. (1996). *Alternative views of learning disabilities: Issues for the 21st century*. Austin, TX: Pro-Ed.

LEARNING STRATEGIES OF CHILDREN WHO KNOW CHINESE

Nancy Pine, Huang Ren-song, Huang Ping'An, Zhang Wei-jiang

Introduction

When living within an alphabetic world it is easy to assume that all children learn to read and write by mastering the sound system of their spoken language and associating it in various ways with the symbols of their writing system. Teachers in the West, no matter what their persuasion or teaching methodology, instruct from an underlying assumption that there is a fundamental connection between the sounds of the spoken language and the symbols of their written language. And justifiably so.

The writing system of the Chinese language, however, employs a different foundation of knowledge. Although there is some dispute as to what cognitive mechanisms are triggered while reading Chinese (Cheng, 1992; Perfetti & Tan, 1998), it is clear that Chinese requires some skills that are quite different from English, Spanish and other writing systems that utilize a Latin alphabet. Recognizing and remembering Chinese characters appear to require different strategy configurations.

Studying how Chinese children learn Chinese characters is therefore useful for two reasons. First, by studying what skills are associated with learning to recognize and remember characters, we can learn what skills and strategies children from Chinese speaking backgrounds are likely to bring to English literacy learning. Depending on how teachers treat them, these skills and strategies can become either strengths to build from or barriers that impede English learning.

Secondly, Chinese and U.S. children appear to develop some learning behaviors that are quite distinctive to their literacy communities (Pine, 1992, 1993; Regan, et al., 1995; Stephenson, 1994; Tao & Zuo, 1997). By uncovering the learning strengths of one linguistic community we can learn about untapped areas for potential development in the other. Since teachers often struggle against multiple odds to do the very best for their students, learning about the literacy foundations of their students as well as their untapped potential can provide innovative ways to enhance English language literacy instruction.

We will first describe beginning Chinese lessons in China and what teachers stress as they teach children to read and write Chinese. We then describe the results of a study that investigated what children say about how they recognize and remember Chinese characters.

Description of a First Grade Chinese Lesson[1]

To the Western observer, used to seeing children sitting at groups of moveable desks and alternating between working independently and collaboratively, the Chinese classroom is markedly different. The 100 plus first grade classes we have observed or have had described to us each contain about 50 six-year-old students who sit in rows of fixed seating. During Chinese lessons, the teachers instruct from the front of the room, aided by a blackboard, colored chalk, small slate-like boards with characters written on them, and poster reproductions of textbook illustrations. The teachers deliver energetic lessons, have very well developed "hand writing" and continuously involve the students through questioning and practicing characters in a variety of ways. From a Western perspective, Chinese lessons in first grade are fast-paced, energetic and noisy.

A few essential differences between Chinese and the Latin alphabetic system are essential to point out before continuing.[2] In order to be literate enough to read a newspaper by the end of sixth grade a child must learn approximately 2500 characters. Although some repetition occurs, especially when simple characters appear as components of more complex characters, the learning task for Chinese is far greater than that required by an alphabetic system. English beginning readers must learn 26 letters; Chinese beginning readers must memorize

---

[1] Chinese instruction is not broken into reading and writing. Rather the two are taught as one process.

[2] This paper discusses characters currently used in the People's Republic of China, excluding Hong Kong. Since the founding of the PRC characters have been simplified to promote general literacy (Yin & Rohsenow, 1994). Hong Kong and Taiwan continue to use the earlier, more complex characters.

hundreds of tightly constructed characters. A character is comprised of multiple strokes—sometimes as many as 30—which have a proper order and method of writing. It has balance and geometrical beauty of itself, and is situated within a visualized square space (Regan, Stephenson, & Pine, in press). In other words, when literate Chinese envision a character, they envision black lines within a white space rather than just black lines, and when they write a character they envision a white square intersected by crossed lines into which the character is placed. Finally, except for the simplest (and first learned), characters are comprised of components. Sometimes they have a component on the left and another on the right (see Figure 1). Sometimes one up, one down. Sometimes a character has three characters embedded within it, and so forth. The skills Chinese children develop in order to become literate are therefore quite different at some points than those required of English or Spanish literacy.

Figure 1. Character structures; writing square for beginners.

Characters with Different Arrangements of Components

Left/Right   Top/Bottom   Inside/Outside

绿   露   圈

Writing Square for First Grade

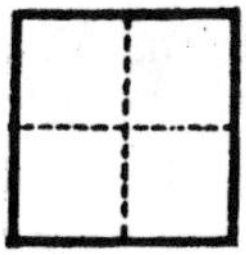

It should also be pointed out that at the very beginning of first grade (which is the first year of elementary school) children learn Pin Yin, a system of Chinese sounds written in the Latin alphabet, with (for the mainland Chinese language, Putonghua) four tones for each syllable. Children learn this phonetic system quickly—within the beginning four to six weeks of first grade—and it is employed as an early decoding aid. The two systems (Pin Yin and characters) work side by side during the first grade. As children increase their character memory bank, Pin Yin then drops away, and in upper elementary grades it is only used to introduce new characters.

During lessons that the authors have observed, teachers use a variety of methods while the children have the textbooks in front of them. The teachers follow the textbooks carefully while being innovative in how they involve their students in various ways that are thought to embed characters in children's memories. They ask questions of individuals or the group and have students read aloud, practice characters aloud, state what a given character or passage means, and play verbal games. The children are also asked to finger-write characters in the air while either reciting their names or the stroke names (of which there are 23) aloud.

Overview of First Semester, First Grade Chinese Lessons

The national textbook for the first semester of first grade introduces 160 characters. The text moves quickly into teaching Pin Yin, both the sounds and the related symbols which are Latin letters. The teachers' manual suggests spending six-and-a-half weeks on teaching the children Pin Yin and then another two-and-a-half weeks connecting the Pin Yin to characters and concepts. In other words, a little over half of the semester is used to introduce Pin Yin and to teach how the Pin Yin system works side by side with characters. The rest of the semester focuses on learning characters, with Pin Yin as a tool. Both Pin Yin and character teaching utilize pictures as prompts. In the third month of first grade, the teachers begin teaching characters and sentences with visual aids and paragraph comprehension. The story topics and progression of lessons are listed in Figure 2.

Figure 2. Table of contents of first semester, first grade Chinese textbook (People's Education Publishing House, 1993a). Translated by Zhang, W-J.

It should be noted also that children at this stage are often learning standard Chinese as many Chinese children speak a different dialect at home. These "dialects" are often less alike than Spanish, Portuguese or Italian, but they share a common writing system. This is a very difficult concept for Westerners to grasp, but an essential one to struggle with.

The textbook also has extra drills and texts to learn, and homework at this age, in our experience, is comprised of writing characters— usually 5 to 10 times each—plus other exercises such as writing a daily journal or reading aloud simple stories.

What Chinese Teachers Stress[3]

First semester instructions for Chinese teachers stress that children should master Pin Yin, master and understand 160 characters, learn to listen to and speak Standard Chinese, and read a text aloud and understand it. The 23 consonants, 24 vowels (including tones) and 16 syllable combinations are to be learned quickly so that children will "be able to use Pin Yin to learn characters, correct pronunciation, read Pin Yin text and children's readings, and learn to speak standard Chinese" (People's Education Publishing House, 1993b, p. 2). Teachers are then to teach children the basic method of recognizing and then learning to write a character, including perfection of strokes and their sequence. They are also to teach the meaning of characters through pictures and phrases, and how to analyze and memorize character shapes.

When the teachers first introduce a character they have the children look at it carefully as a whole and then inspect its details. They next introduce the small units within it. For example, one of the characters introduced in the third month of first grade is (妈 , mā). It includes two components, one on the left, one on the right. The one on the left (女 , nǚ) was introduced as part of another character (好 , hǎo) during the previous drill. The one on the right (马 , mǎ) was introduced three lessons before while teaching children to combine Pin Yin with characters. Therefore, the teacher at this point will have the children notice two separate parts and call their attention to where they have seen them before.

Instruction then proceeds to how to write the character, including focus on various units, but always within the context of the whole, balanced character. The teacher demonstrates on the blackboard with care and emphasizes how each stroke is made, in what order it is written and its proper place within the character. Correct stroke writing and

---

[3] Drawn from observations and teacher and parent descriptions and observations of over 100 first grade classrooms in a variety of cities in Eastern and Central China.

stroke sequence are viewed by teachers as essential to learning characters. Children are instructed to write the separate units in the air while saying the stroke names. This is done aloud with great enthusiasm. The children then are asked to write the whole character on worksheets that have gridlines (see Figure 1) so that they can create balanced, well-proportioned characters.

The newly learned characters are then read within the context of a verse or story. The character example above (妈), for instance, is part of a two-line sentence related to a picture. The teacher often reads the story or verse aloud, has the children carefully discuss it, and then the children practice reading it aloud. Finally, there are follow-up exercises and homework that includes such activities as copying characters and reading stories correctly.

What Children Say about How They Remember and Recognize Characters

Having spent many years probing how Chinese children learn to write characters and how different their processes seem to be from how children decode words in the United States, we designed a research project to probe Chinese children's perceptions of how to learn and remember characters.

We assumed that the children's views would, in part, mirror what and how their teachers taught them, but that it would also mirror the influence of the greater literacy community as well as their individual learning styles (Pine, 1992, 1993; Regan, et al., 1995; also see literacy biographies in Perry & Su, 1998). An initial set of child interviews in a friendly, relaxed environment of one of our apartments in China indicated that this approach could yield rich data.

Several pilot projects taught us how to pique children's willingness to talk about characters. We found that children talked the most when a character they knew had a mistake in it and when they were asked to teach characters to a younger child. Therefore, the final study consisted of two tasks—finding and talking about mistakes in incorrectly written characters that had been taken from their grade level textbooks and pretending to teach a younger child how to write two characters. We will discuss the first task in this paper.

We presented each child individually with four grade-level characters, one at a time. Each character was one they should already have been taught and each was written with a mistake in it (Figure 3). We introduced children to this activity by using characters from their previous school year. First grade children began with kindergarten characters and so on. Once the children seemed comfortable with this little game of finding and talking about the mistake and how they remembered to write the character correctly, we proceeded to their grade level set, presenting one character card at a time. In a few instances, when the children were unable to identify any of their own grade level characters, we used the characters from an earlier grade in order to encourage them to talk about characters they knew.

The characters were selected by those on our research team knowledgeable about young children's developmental processes in general and about what is taught in the first three years of elementary school—first, second, and third grades. Four characters were selected from the list at the end of the textbook for each grade level.

The Research Setting. The research was conducted in two widely separated cities. The interviewers, native Chinese speakers familiar with the school communities, were selected for their experience with research, their ability to work with children, and their ability to communicate in English. Both were fluent standard Chinese speakers and also understood the primary "dialect" of the children. The English-only researcher was present during all of the pilot and final interviews, which were tape-recorded and translated to English and double-checked by Chinese.

One working-class community school was selected in each city and 15 children randomly selected for interviews in each school—five from each of the first, second, and third grades. The children at each grade level in each school had quite varied knowledge about recognizing characters. Following are small sections of two typical interviews. Each one is from a first grade child. The character cards referred to in the interviews are shown in Figure 3.

Figure 3. Samples of card pairs used for children's interviews, incorrect and correct characters, by grade level.

Set #	Incorrect Character	Correct Character	Pin Yin & English
K.1	电	电	diàn [electricity]
K.2	球	球	qiú [ball]
1.2	燕	燕	yàn [swallow]
1.3	出	出	chū [exit]
2.2	闵	闷	mēn [stuffy]
2.4	裤	裤	kù [trousers]
3.2	鞠	鞠	jū [bow]
3.4	躺	躺	tǎng [lie down]
All grades	唱	唱	chàng [sing]

Child 2x; yàn, swallow [a type of bird]

Interviewer: [showing child a character with a mistake] Do
you know this one?

2x: This is.....

I: What?

2x: (It's) <u>yàn</u> [swallow].

I: Yes, the character for swallow. Is it right or wrong?

2x: It's wrong.

I: Why is it wrong?

2x: The part below should be four dots, but not a
horizontal bar?

I: Can you write it down?

2x: [writes character correctly]

I: Then how do you know that it should be four dots
instead of a bar?

2x: Because we have learned this character.

I: You have learned it before. Then how do you remember
that it should be four dots but not a bar?

2x: I remember all that I have learned.

Child 2z; <u>chàng</u>, to sing:

Interviewer: [showing child the incorrect <u>chàng</u> card]
What's this character?

2s: It isn't a character.

I: It is wrong, isn't it? You write down a correct one.

2s: [Writing it correctly]

I: Hmm. What is it?

2s: It's <u>chàng</u> [sing].

I: <u>Chàng</u>. Hmmm. How do you remember it?

2s: It's a character of shape and sound. The left part is <u>kǒu</u>
[a component which means "mouth"]. It shows the
meaning. We use our mouth to sing, so it's <u>kǒu</u> [mouth].
The right part is <u>chāng</u>[4] [another character] and it gives the
sound. So it's <u>chàng</u> (sing).

---

[4] <u>Chang</u> is a different character from <u>chàng</u>, but with a somewhat similar sound, though a different
tone. The shapes and meanings of <u>chang</u> and <u>chàng</u> are different.

The Children's Responses

Ten categories of talking about and remembering characters have emerged from the children's responses. They are listed in Figure 4. The categories appear to reflect the nature of Chinese character structure and shape and are, one could conjecture, quite different from how Western children talk about reading and remembering words.

Structural analysis. By far the most widely used categories by the 30 children (*a*, *c* and *g* in Figure 4) are related to structural analysis of whole characters and their smaller units. Interviews with the children encouraged open-ended responses at each grade level, and the children chose to use a variety of structural terms to talk about most characters. For example, referring to the character yàn [swallow], the following interchange took place between the interviewer and a first grader:

> I: Is it right or not?
> 5x: No.
> I: How do you know that?
> 5x: Because the end part of it shouldn't be this horizontal bar but four dots.

In another example, talking about diàn [electricity] a first grade student said,
> 1x: This stroke should be pointed out [of the character]...The stroke should go beyond this horizontal line.

Students frequently divided characters into their constituent parts and then described them in relation to other characters or character parts. The following response by a second grader describing yàn [swallow] is typical.

> I: ...Then how do you remember it?
> 6z: I divide it into several parts. The bottom part is four points; the middle part is a kǒu [mouth, 口] and a separated běi [north, 北]; the upper part is a cǎo [a component meaning "grass" 艹] and a dash. *[Hand motions accompany all 3 parts-- upper, middle, lower.]*

The child first identified the whole character and then explicitly separated it into parts that she related to other characters. Notice the specificity that is used and the ability to analyze the character structure.

Figure 4. Coding categories derived from children's interviews. (Categories of ways children say they recognize and remember characters.)

a.	Child associates the character with another character or a part of another character. For example, the child associates the various small units of the character with other characters or small units.
b.	Child uses stroke order and/or stroke names.
c.	Child uses structural analysis of characters or parts of characters. For example, the child describes what is wrong with the incorrect character by referring to specific strokes or to the function of different parts of the shapes.
d.	Child uses the relationship of shape to meaning. For example, the child describes the character <u>kou</u> [mouth] as having the shape of a mouth.
e.	Child uses kinesthetic means to remember or talk about character; writing appears to activate knowledge. For example, the child finger writes in the air while talking about the character.
f.	Child uses a brief story or narrative to explain or remember a character or part of a character.
g.	Child separates character into explicit parts.
h.	Child states that without a given stroke or element "it isn't a character any longer."
i.	Child "knows it," but reasons given are very general, saying, for example, "I know it because we have learned this character."
i.	Child "hasn't learned it" because, for example, "The teacher hasn't taught us."
j.	Child refers to the appearance of the character, in general, by saying something like, "It's a character because it's nice looking."

Other categories used by the children, though less frequently, included reference to and naming of specific strokes within a given character. This was used by first graders, but was almost never used by second and third graders. Also younger children who were not able to talk about a character as specifically as the above second grader, often stated that it was not a character. Although they could not give details, they already had embedded in their memory an image of "what *is* a character."

Children habitually used their fingers to write characters on their laps or moved their pencils above the paper to work out what a character should look like. This is a strategy that appears to be used by adults as well (Regan & Zhang, 1997).

<u>Linking Shape and Semantics</u>. The strategy of linking character shape directly to meaning was almost never used by the children. This is an interesting development since in our experience most Westerners assume that characters pictorially represent an object or idea. Almost no children talked about character/object shape similarities as a means for remembering or recognizing a character.

Stories, however, were used by a number of children to describe how they remembered a few particular characters. As one interviewer put it, "Connections made between a character and the thing it represents, though not logical or reasonable, may serve as a prompt to learn that character when one is young." These stories tended to be associated with a few specific characters and were used by many of the children. Possibly they were taught by the teachers or passed along from one child to the next, a bit like the English saying, "When two vowels go walking, the first one does the talking." An example of one of these is associated with the character <u>men</u> [stuffy]. A child from one city responded:

> I: How do you know this is an extra piě [diagonal stroke]?
> 8x: Because inside a ... door... In one's heart, he feels depressed. That... that's why we can't put a piě here.
> I: { It should be a ...
> 8x: { It should be a <u>xīn</u> [heart] inside the door.
> I: Should be a <u>xīn</u>?
> 8x: Yes.

A child from the second city responded similarly:

> I:...How do you remember it then?
> 14z: <u>Mēn</u> [stuffy] is a character of shape and sound. <u>Mén</u> [door] has the similar sound as the character "stuffy" and the heart means that you feel bored in your heart.

This story, it is important to note, relates to the two characters embedded within the character for mēn [stuffy]. It does not directly relate to a picture of the idea.

Implications for Western Teachers

To Westerners some very specific characteristics jump out of the Chinese children's strategies. First is the very clear distinction children made between recognizing characters and learning to write them. In relation to the character qiú [ball], one first grader said:

> 3x: We haven't learned this character.
> I: You haven't?
> 3x: I only can recognize this character.

They seemed to have an imprint of the correct character in their memories. They seemed to have no idea of how to describe its complex structure; they could, however, write it correctly.

Another characteristic is the strong focus on structural components and structural analysis. Almost all of the children chose to talk about several different characters by referring to structural components and how they were linked to the whole character as well as to other characters. They visually segmented the characters.

Linked to this is the "unusual" (from a Western perspective) detailed noticing employed by young Chinese children. In the following typical example, this first grader already demonstrates having a detailed, internalized reference for what is and is not a character.

> I: How do you know that it should be four dots but not this bar?
> 5x: Er...If it is this bar, it isn't a character any longer.

The young children talked about the mistakes with considerable specificity. This specific noticing may not all be taught in school, but in part may be embedded in cultural behaviors and nuances picked up long before school (see, for example, Perry & Su, 1998 and Pine 1992, 1997). The fact remains, however, that by mid-first grade, children have acquired a very specific type of knowledge and way of learning that tends to include the ability to notice highly detailed, small nuances of character structure. This appears to be a very different learning strategy from those used by Western beginning readers.

Also quite foreign to Westerners are the use of stroke order and stroke name which take on great significance to first graders as they begin learning Chinese and appear to become embedded in their memory bank and fingers by the end of first grade. These kinesthetic patterns are strong enough so that when several children were stumped by the incorrect characters, they were still able to write them correctly. Although this latter behavior may be similar to an English writer who is trying to remember how to spell a word, the finger writing or pencil-above-paper writing are not usually seen in the West, but were commonplace among these 30 children.

Conclusion

What are the implications for Western teachers of the learning exhibited by these Chinese children? What strategies would they bring to English literacy if they were suddenly transported to the United States? They appear to have learned to envision and reproduce highly complex characters that have quite different characteristics from the English alphabet. Although children who know Chinese may not understand how to approach English words phonetically, they carry with them into U.S. classrooms a highly developed knowledge base which can be used as a foundation for learning. They appear to have well-developed analytical skills to segment and interpret detailed, complex shapes that carry visual information and semantic value. These skills might provide an entree into visually decoding or constructing words and quickly perceiving the visual similarities among root words. The children might need considerable help to decode English phonetically, however, and to have this skill introduced explicitly, with the understanding that it might be a completely foreign concept to them. The challenge for the teacher is to notice what strategies the children employ and build from them, using them as a strength.

The children's abilities to notice detail and to hold complex shapes in memory and analyze them suggest potential areas for learning that we may not have tapped in the West. Although we are in no way suggesting that Western schools should imitate Chinese schooling, it is helpful to know what children in other cultures have learned to do in the normal course of literacy development. The children discussed in this paper provide a glimmer of the potential that lies within all children.

References

Cheng, C.M. (1992). "Lexical access in Chinese: Evidence from automatic activation of phonological information." In H.C. Chen and O.J.L. Tzeng (Eds.), *Language processing in Chinese.* Amsterdam: Elsevier, pp. 67-91.

People's Education Publishing House. (1993a). *Chinese textbook (primary school, grade one, book one).* People's Education Publishing House, The People's Republic of China.

People's Education Publishing House. (1993b). *Teacher book for book one, Chinese textbook for primary school, grade one.* People's Education Publishing House, The People's Republic of China.

Perry, K., and Su, X-J (Eds.). (1998). *Culture, literacy and learning English: Voices from the Chinese classroom.* Portsmouth, NH: Heinemann.

Pine, N. (1992). "Early traces of literate behavior: Graphical knowledge demonstrated by three-year-olds in the United States and China." In R.M. Brend (Ed.), *The Eighteenth LACUS Forum 1991.* Lake Bluff, IL: Linguistic Association of Canada and the United States.

Pine, N. (1993). *A comparison of two cultures' complex graphical knowledge prerequisite to literacy.* Unpublished doctoral dissertation, Claremont Graduate School, Claremont, CA.

Pine, N. (1997). "Looking and noticing as culturally specific behavior." In A.K. Melby (Ed.), *The Twenty-third LACUS Forum 1996.* Provo, Utah: Linguistic Association of Canada and the United States.

Regan, J., Stephenson, J., and Pine, N. (in press). "Attention to microspace: Plotting the connections of a cultural theme." In D.G. Lockwood, P.H. Fries, and J.E. Copeland (Eds.), *Functional approaches to language, culture and cognition* (Amsterdam studies in theory and history of linguistic science, Series IV). Amsterdam: John Benjamins.

Regan, J., and Zhang W-J. (1997). "'Edge of the eye' phenomenon." In A.K. Melby (Ed.), *The Twenty-third LACUS Forum 1996.* Provo, UT: Linguistic Association of Canada and the United States.

Regan, J., Hao K-Q., Huang P'A., Zhang W-J., and Yang C-Q. (1995). "To learn three thousand 'letters': Early literacy in China." In P.H. Dreyer (Ed.), *Toward multiple perspectives on literacy, Claremont Reading Conference 59th Yearbook.* Claremont, CA: Institute for Developmental Studies, Claremont Graduate School.

Stephenson, J. (1994). "On the copying ability of young Chinese and American children." In V. Makkai (Ed.), *The Twelfth LACUS Forum.* Ann Arbor, MI: Linguistic Association of Canada and the United States.

Tao, L., and Zuo, L. (1997). "Oral reading practice in China's elementary schools: A brief discussion of its unique roots in language, culture, and society." *The Reading Teacher, 50,* pp. 654-665.

Yin, B-Y., and Rohsenow, J.S. (1994). *Modern Chinese characters.* Beijing, China: Sinolingua.

The research reported in this paper has been supported by a Professional Development Grant from Mount St. Mary's College and by visiting scholar support from the Center for Educational Studies, Claremont Graduate University.

NOTES ON CONTRIBUTORS

CAROLYN ANGUS is associate director of the George G. Stone Center for Children's Books of Claremont Graduate University. She is a frequent presenter of workshops for teachers, librarians, and parents. Her areas of special interest are children's literature and elementary science.

JEAN M. CASEY is currently on the faculty of California State University, Long Beach, California. Dr. Casey holds a Ph.D. from the University of Southern California and has conducted 14 years of research on early literacy and how technology can make early reading and writing successful. Her areas of expertise include: Early Literacy: The Empowerment of Technology, TeacherNet: Supporting teachers on-line, and Reading Acquisition: K-8, RICA, technology integration.

PATRICK DIAS is Professor Emeritus at McGill University in Montreal, Canada, where he served on the faculty in the Department of Education for more than twenty-five years. Educated in Karachi, Pakistan and Montreal, Canada, Dias is widely known for his work in the area of school curriculum, writing, poetry, and reading. Among his publications are *Making Sense of Poetry: Patterns in the Process* (1988), *Writing for Ourselves/Writing for Others* (1992), *Transitions: Writing in Academic and Workplace Settings* (in press), and *Worlds Apart: Acting and Writing in Academic and Workplace Contexts* (in press).

JANET GHIO is currently chair of the English Department at Lincoln High School in Stockton, California where she has taught for twenty-six years. She has provided staff development as a district mentor teacher, member of the California Literature Project, and as a consultant for the Center for Language in Learning.

J. DIXON HEARNE is co-chair of the Elementary Education program at Chapman University. Research interests and publications have focused on topics in literacy, learning disabilities, and elementary and secondary education.

DAWN HUNTER is assistant dean and associate professor in special education at Chapman University. Research interests and publications have focused on topics in special education and public policy.

JANET KIERSTEAD, Ph.D., Adjunct Professor, Claremont Graduate University, and former classroom teacher, is a nationally recognized leader in the field of curriculum integration and interdisciplinary teaming. She has shared her expertise with thousands of teachers and administrators within California, throughout the United States, and in Canada. She is currently contributing to the design of a reform effort for UNESCO to bring interdisciplinary, project-based learning to underdeveloped nations in Africa, Latin America and Asia. As a consultant to the California Department of Education, Dr. Kierstead designed and lead the highly successful, multi-year curriculum integration efforts for state-funded High School Partnership Academies and for Tech Prep Interdisciplinary Teams, using her Action-Based Project approach. As a member of the Middle Grades Task Force she contributed substantially to Caught in the Middle. Her Action-Based approach is featured in CDE's video, *Integrating the Curriculum through Interdisciplinary Teaming*--as well as in training modules for the California School Leadership Academy.

LEONA MANKE is a professor at Albertson College of Idaho in Caldwell, where she is a language arts specialist and chair of the department. Leona majored in Spanish at the University of Oregon, served in the Peace Corps in Paraguay, and earned an M.A. (1972) and Ph.D. (1985) from Claremont Graduate School. She has taught in bilingual classrooms in California and in community college English composition classrooms in Washington. Currently Leona is writing a book on the use of technology in the literacy classroom.

PETE C. MENJARES is currently Chair of the Department of Education and an associate professor of Education at Biola University in La Mirada. Dr. Menjares has taught courses in secondary reading and educational psychology at Biola for the last six years where he also supervises secondary student teachers in English and Social Science. He received his Ph.D. in Education from the University of Southern California with a specialization in Language, Literacy, and Learning.

LINDA MCCORKEL CLINARD, Ph.D., is an instructor in elementary and secondary reading assessment and methods at the University of California, in Irvine. She received her Ph.D. at the University of Michigan in Ann Arbor, and her M.S. in reading education at the Indiana University in Bloomington. Her recent publications include "What Mentoring Does for Mentors: A Cross-Cultural Perspective," in *European Journal of Teacher Education*, Vol. 21, No. 1, 1998, co-authored with Dr. Tamar Ariav, Beit Berl College, Israel; and *Family Time Reading Fun*, published by Creative Teaching Press in 1997.

GRETA NAGEL is an associate professor at California State University, Long Beach, California. She teaches courses in literacy and coordinates several alternative certification programs. In 1992, Greta received her Ph.D. in multicultural curriculum and instruction from Claremont Graduate University and San Diego State University. In addition to teaching in Anaheim and Placentia, she taught in Chicago and Oakland. She has served as a public school principal and as a Chapter 1 reading specialist. Greta is the author of *The Tao of Teaching* (1994, 1998, 1999) and *The Tao of Parenting* (1998).

NANCY PINE, HUANG REN-SONG, HUANG PING'AN, ZHANG WEI-JIANG are members of a research group that have explored a number of cross-cultural and inter-cultural behaviors related to literacy development. The principal investigator for the studies reported here is Nancy Pine, Director of Elementary Education and Associate Professor at Mount St. Mary's College in Los Angeles. She has conducted research in China and the United States for the past 10 years, beginning with her dissertation which studied young children's preliterate knowledge in China and the U.S. Huang Ren-song is Professor Emeritus of Preschool Education at Nanjing Normal University. She has conducted extensive research and written widely about young children's education in China, and she has vast experience comparing Early Childhood Education in China and the United States. Huang Ping'An is Dean of the English Department and Associate Professor at Xi'an Jiaotong [Communications] University in Xi'an, the ancient capital of China. Zhang Wei-Jiang is Dean of the English Department and Associate Professor at Wei'nan Teachers' College, adjoining the site of the ancient terra cotta army excavations in the heart of China. He has worked extensively on research related to the Pettus collection at the

Claremont Graduate University and both he and Huang Ping'An have been associated for several years with the China/U.S. research groups convened at the Claremont Graduate University by John Regan.

MARY POPLIN, Ph.D., received her graduate degrees from the University of Texas. Since then her work has centered on issues of classroom instruction as it relates to various learning theories (from behaviorism to constructivism, feminine, multicultural and critical pedagogies), cultural diversity, school transformation, student and teacher growth, and spirituality and education. With a special emphasis on issues of cultural diversity, Poplin directed the teacher education program the Claremont Graduate University for ten years, from 1985-1995. She developed and directs the Institute for Education in Transformation which is committed to seeking better ways for diverse students and teachers to grow within the context of schools and classrooms. She is the author of many publications in the areas of diversity, values, and learning theory in regular, special, and multicultural education. Using participatory research methods, Mary is the primary author of the popular national report on schooling, *Voices from the Inside: A Report on Schooling from Inside the Classroom*, which has sold 50,000 copies.

In addition to her university work, Mary volunteered to teach morning ESL class for a semester in a local high school, and, most recently, volunteered with Mother Teresa and the Missionaries of Charity in Calcutta in a home for children during the spring of 1996. She is most interested in understanding and promoting an education for all children and adults that leads them to fulfill their special purposes in life--to become the best person they can become.

MARSHA THICKSTEN, Ph.D., is Assistant Professor of Education at the Chapman University Academic Center in Ontario, California, where she acts as coordinator for elementary teacher education.

GAIL L. THOMPSON, Ph.D., is an assistant professor of Reading/Literacy at California State University, San Bernardino. She is the director of a literacy program for third graders who are reading below grade level. She taught secondary public school for 14 years.

LIL THOMPSON has been a speaker at the Claremont Reading Conferences for over 26 years and always brings a special energy about teaching and a love for young children which inspires and informs everyone who has contact with her. Before her retirement she was headmistress of a children's school in England, and she now resides in Wolverhampton, West Midlands, England.

CHARLOTTE VAN RYSWYK is the library/media aide at Vista del Valle Elementary School in Claremont, California. A graduate of Carlton College and the University of Wisconsin at Madison, she is also a talented musician who teaches violin and uses music extensively in her work with children at her library.

KATHRYN Z. WEED, Ph.D, is an associate professor in education at California State University San Bernardino. She was a Fulbright Senior Lecturer at the Ecole Normale Supérieure in Dakar, Senegal in 1997-1998. Presently, she is residing in Hermosillo, Sonora, Mexico where she is continuing her research on language and literacy learning in children.

JANET WONG received the 1999 Stone Center for Children's Books Recognition of Merit Award for *Good Luck Gold and Other Poems* and *A suitcase of Seaweed and Other Poems*; and the 1994 Southern California Society of Children's Book Writers and Illustrators award in poetry for *Good Luck Gold and Other Poems*. She has also written *The Trip Back Home* about her return to Korea at age five. Ms. Wong holds a B.A. degree in History from UCLA and a J.D. degree from Yale Law School. She was a practicing attorney in Southern California for several years before beginning her writing career.